HOMES OF THE GREAT

Original photographs by
CLAUDE ARTHAUD

assisted by the Studio
RICHARD ET BLIN

assistant photographer
JACQUES VAINSTAIN

A Selection of International Book Society.
A division of Time-Life Books.
Distributed by New York Graphic Society Ltd,
Greenwich, Connecticut.

HOMES OF THE GREAT

Conceived and written by
CLAUDE ARTHAUD

Translated from the French by
PETER BURGESS

ARTHAUD

Acknowledgments

I should like to express my thanks to the many people who have kindly assisted in the compiling of this book:

Monsieur Malraux, French Cultural Affairs Minister,
the Prefect of the Seine,
the Curator of the Odense Museum,
the Curator of the Vittoriale Museum and the Mondadori publishers in Milan,
the Curator of the Library of Decorative Arts, Paris,
the Curator of the National Library, Paris,
the Curator of the Balzac Museum, Paris,
the Curator of the Saché Museum,
the Curator of the National Library, Vienna,
the Curator of the Buffon Museum, Montbard,
the Director of the National Trust, London,
the Curator of the Cervantes Museum, Valladolid,
the Curator of Vallée-aux-Loups,
the Curator of the Convent of Valdemosa,
the Curator of the Goethe Museum, Frankfurt,
the Director of the Vega-Inclán Foundation, Madrid,
the Curator of the Metropolitan Museum of Art, New York,
the Curator of the National Gallery of Arts, Washington,
the Curator of the Prado Museum, Madrid,
the Curator of the Santa Cruz Museum, Toledo,
the Curator of the Strasbourg Museum,
the Curator of the Mozart Museum, Salzburg,
the Curator of the Hogarth Museum, London,
the Curator of the Sir John Soane Museum, London,
the Curator of the Victor Hugo Hauteville House Museum,
the Curator of the Royal Library, Windsor,
the Curator of Les Charmettes,
the Curator of the Staatsgemäldesammlungen Museum, Munich,
Monsieur A. Gaston, architect of Les Bâtiments de France, Blois,
the Curator of Coppet Castle,
the Curators of the National Portrait Gallery, London; the National Museum, Stockholm; the Art and History Museum, Geneva; the Louvre Museum, Paris,

I should also like to thank all those people who have kindly given me free access to their homes:

the Comtesse d'Andlau at Coppet Castle,
the Comtesse J. de Chabannes at La Brède Castle, who showed me her own residence and that of her ancestor Montesquieu,
Madame Lambert at Ferney Castle,
the Comte de la Tour du Pin at Combourg,
the Comte Eric de la Varende, who so willingly brought to life the past at Chamblac Castle for us,
Mrs. Maxwell-Scott,
the Comte R. de Noblet d'Anglure, who pro-

vided us with much useful information on his grandfather Alphonse de Lamartine at Saint-Point,
the Comtesse J. de Pange,
Monsieur Lucien Psichari at La Béchellerie Castle,
Monsieur Saint-Bris at Clos-Lucé Castle,

Mademoiselle Marie-Louise Stevens, who allowed publication of little-known letters written by Alfred and Arthur Stevens, concerning Charles Baudelaire.

Finally, I am especially grateful to Monsieur Daniel Apert who gave his valuable advice in the literary documentation of this book.

Introduction

The houses in this book have remained largely unchanged with the passing of the years, due to the fame of their one-time owners. They are very special houses, often quite simple ones, often hidden or little-known, selected as homes by people with outstanding destinies.

Their imagination and way of living transformed these places and they marked them with their character. These walls saw more romances and witnessed more sorrows than most, for the simple reason that creative beings cannot conform to accepted behaviour. Here genius was freed and great work produced in most favourable surroundings. Things belong most to those who enjoy them most, and if this is true, then there are certainly some houses that belong forever to admirers who have gazed on them. The present proprietor can never seem anything else but an intruder to the small minority of devotees, who will recognize each other after a brief word or two when certain houses which they alone know are referred to in their presence. Among each other these people have the same reserve and susceptibilities as collectors of *objets d'art* or paintings. They tend to be laconic when they like something, but become talkative when they are indifferent toward the house that is mentioned. They differ from real proprietors because they never make excuses for the faults they see in homes they admire. They love them for themselves, and re-live moments of their past history in the mind; yet, they would not attempt to bring the houses to life again, for fear they might produce some feature in contradiction with the past. But no man can put the clock back with impunity. If he struggles against the passing of time, he will end up sooner or later apart from the rest of society, which suspects that he is unfaithful to his own epoch. The devotee who does not possess an ancestral home by birth feels removed, just like the proprietor, as a result of his taste for the past. He is, however, unwilling to accept the great sacrifices that go with loyalty to a single dwelling. If he had one of the famous homes he yearns for he would not be satisfied with it, but would need to go off and look for more. He is not of a settled nature and each week, each month, each year he needs new discoveries to satisfy his curiosity and standards. Like the stamp collector, he sometimes prefers the modest discovery of a unique variety to a finer residence that has duplicates. He lies in wait for the small ads in the newspapers, but his eyes come to rest only on the sections dealing with old houses, castles and estates. When he thinks he is on the track of a new type of house, he will go and see it, even though it may be hundreds of miles away. Once on the spot, he waits anxiously as the place is opened up for him. With the door ajar before him, he waits as the agent opens the shutters. Through the damp air the sun reveals the eighteenth-century woodwork he has never seen before, or the set of naïve paintings done three centuries earlier and still in the original panels. It is at this moment that he catches the distinct mood of this hitherto unknown house. The odds and ends of furniture, the upholstery of an armchair, the overloaded trimmings lead him on to further discoveries. He is stimulated by the chance of entering into a world he has never personally belonged to, but which for a few moments in time he actually possesses as his very own.

There is no doubt that he is a divided soul when he looks on these forgotten homes that have been shut up for years. If he actually buys the property, he himself may dominate the past, slowly stifling it with his own presence. He would be unable to resist correcting a few things here and there, converting the building. He would feel obliged to repair what is falling into ruin, only to realize that the house has lost its very power to evoke the past for him, and that never again will his heart be clutched with the same emotion as on the first day. The desire to live in some of these houses is like forcing them to die with us. The enthusiast eventually resigns himself. His taste for dead things may be suspect. A strong interest in death is contained in his love for some ruined Rhineland castle or an old Venetian palace whose strength is sapped by the water in the gondola shed underneath. These ancient walls enable us to converse with the dead. All aesthetic disciplines bring suffering; in this case, the beholder finds more pleasure in looking at the house just once, than caring for it during a whole lifetime.

Some families in the past had several old homes and they would visit them as the seasons came and went. This was true of palaces and patrician homes in the Ukraine, Sicily, Castile, Scotland, Bavaria, the Black Forest and, later on, the French villas on the Channel coast or around Bordeaux. In summer they sprang to life, but with the coming of harsher weather they were forsaken for town houses in Rome, Madrid, London, Saint Petersburg, Munich or the Faubourg Saint-Germain in Paris. In spring and autumn the owners would stay in other houses again, homes given over to the delights of hunting or of making love. There were houses in the woods, follies, temples of love in the Bavarian forests, cottages from which people went hawking, hunting or shooting. Their existence was really only a pretext for personal rebirth. People had as many lives as they had homes. The strangeness one felt at staying in these places for only a short while is experienced by the enthusiast of modern times who stays in no single place but is always moving from one to another.

By loving an old home you draw it away from the owner. You also share his taste, his feelings and get to know his character. If the owner had an artistic gift as well, you can even penetrate into his work.

The buildings where an artist lived and created are no less revealing than his paintings or a study of his mind's development. An example is George Sand's house in Nohant. This is a house with a double history: as a family residence and as an author's home. Sand wrote most of her books there and lived out most of her love affairs. It was the meeting place of intellectual Paris in the 1830's, and in summer it was occupied by such figures as Delacroix, Turgenev, Liszt, Balzac and Gautier. They would always be sure of finding a seat at table and a room ready for them.

Nohant reflects the maternal and passionate temperament of an emancipated woman of the age; the feminine and conformist intimacy of the nineteenth century drawing room is echoed in the first floor room which Chopin's mistress, in a state of fury after their last quarrel, turned into a mineralogy museum; the stones, collected one by one, symbolically erased every memory of their common past.

At Balzac's house in Paris we can see huge gilt picture frames and red materials which he said were the colour of the dress worn by Madame Hanska on the day they first met. These show us something of the author's character. The house reveals his nostalgia for the interiors in the Faubourg Saint-Germain inhabited by the erstwhile nobility, as well as his regret at not being born "de Balzac", and his disappointment at being passed over by his mother in favour of a half-brother, the illegitimate son of Monsieur de Margonne.

Similarly, Sir Walter Scott's castle with its armour, skeletons and historical

9

objects tells us as much as his books do of the author's personality and his conviction that the age of chivalry must be passed on to Scottish posterity.

Certain of these homes are particularly revealing of the gifted occupants' love life or their peculiarities. Others were the starting point for a vocation. We have for example Les Charmettes where Rousseau lived with Madame de Warens at the age of sixteen; in this residence, Rousseau felt drawn to the search for solitude and the simple life. The books *Emile* and *Rêveries d'un promeneur solitaire* were born at Les Charmettes. Another example is the Frankfurt family residence of Goethe, whose taste for brothels and later for aristocratic *salons* so sharply contrasts with Beethoven's way of life. These inclinations were certainly not unconnected with the childhood he experienced under a father who deliberately collected Flemish and Italian paintings, and allotted a precise cultural function to every room, in a house where comfort was coupled with narrow-mindedness. Other homes yet were created by fecund personalities whom one art alone could not satisfy. Anatole France and Victor Hugo both dreamed of being "decorators" of genius. Hugo became one at Hauteville House. Out of a fisherman's dwelling in Guernsey, the exiled author successfully produced an eastern-style palace bedecked with mirrors, Chinese curios, cut Aubusson tapestries, carved woodwork and personal escutcheons. Of all the homes he possessed, this was the one he liked most since it totally reflected his personality, and because he could converse with the dead by table-tipping in the deep of the night.

There remain those homes that were unloved by their occupants. They were ignored or rejected by owners who felt they had no place in them. Such a residence is Tolstoi's estate of Yasnaya Polyana which he shared with his mujiks. The property was the arena for a continual struggle between Tolstoi and his wife, and she won in the end over Tolstoi's ideas. He fled during the night, at the advanced age of eighty, because he finally could stand it no longer. That house for Tolstoi symbolized all that slavery of the mind could be.

The smaller facets of genius were given free play within these walls, and the development of style might almost be scientifically studied from the houses.

Homes of the past, in their original state, show that the occupants of the eighteenth century were not exclusively concerned with Louis-Quinze or Louis-Seize furniture, but also frequently kept items they already had. We can see also that the nineteenth century was not solely an age that rejected the past; the period of divided upholstery, and of Empire, Victorian and Biedermeier furniture, was not as sectarian in the matter of style as were later times. It was the "history of art" trend of this century that gave rise to the liking for "purism" and the belief that a Louis-Quinze room could be right only if it was exclusively Louis-Quinze.

Although Lamartine and Chateaubriand came under the spell of their times and changed their ancient walls into 1830 Gothic, nevertheless the Louis-Quinze and Louis-Seize furniture stayed in their houses and the eighteenth century paintings, medallions and miniatures remained on the walls.

So it is that the homes of artists shed light on the lives of the famous people they became, for they retain the imprint of their human existence. Some of the contents were there and have remained, others have been brought in afterwards and underline the taste of a generation. This book is an attempt to demonstrate the blending of personal taste with that of an age as a whole.

Andersen

in Odense

It is scarcely possible to imagine Andersen living within four walls. He was more like someone in a bottle trying to get at the light outside. In fact, for sixty-one years he wandered throughout Europe, from city to city and lodging to lodging, writing of heroes who moved from cottage to castle.

Yet once upon a time, Hans Christian Andersen had a home which, as a lonely sensitive adult, he describes as follows : "In 1805, a young couple who loved each other tenderly lived in a modest room in Odense. He was a cobbler hardly twenty-two years old, wonderfully skilled and with a poet's soul. She was a little older, a woman of simple ideas and a big heart. Past master in his trade, the man even made his own cobbler's workbench. He fashioned his nuptial bed from a catafalque that had borne the coffin of one of the Counts of Trampe ; the shreds of black cloth around it recalled its original purpose. In this bed, on April 2, 1805, arrived a sturdy baby—me. Hans Christian Andersen took over from the remains of the count.

"At first, my father stayed with my mother and read scraps of Holberg to her, while I cried lustily. He apparently protested at this intrusion into his reading sessions and scolded me, half in anger, half smiling : 'Are you going to sleep, or listen properly ?' But I continued to bawl forth.

"On the day of my christening I was no better at the church. My mother did not forget for a long time the comment of the pastor : 'This child cries like a squawling cat.' My godfather Gomard, a poor French expatriate, consoled him by saying : 'The more the child cries now, the better he'll sing later.'

"My childhood home consisted of a single room, packed with tradesman's tools, the bed and the benchcot where I slept. But on the walls were some pictures, and some lovely cups and cut glasses stood on the sideboard next to the window. Near the chair where father worked, there was a shelf full of books and songs. In the tiny kitchen over the food cupboard shone some pewter plates. This small room seemed large and opulent to me, and the door with its panelling decorated with country scenes was as precious to me then as a whole gallery of paintings today.

"A small staircase led from the kitchen to the loft. In the guttering between our house and the neighbour's, we had a box where spring onions and parsley grew. This was my mother's entire garden, and in *The Snow Queen* it continues eternally to grow."

This house, so graphically described, is today the Andersen Museum. In it, he dreamed until the age of fourteen of the theatre and poetry, while he dressed up little dolls. Only his mother had any faith in his future as a poet, and one day in 1819 he left the house to try his luck in Copenhagen. He was to become a chorister, and later won a royal scholarship to complete his education.

Andersen emerged as a critic but was mocked by colleagues. Later, at the age of forty-two, Europe lauded his talent, but in Denmark, people continued to nag him for his spelling mistakes. There was just one other Dane who recognized him as a brother : Kierkegaard.

It was also in Copenhagen that he found the loves of his life : Riborg Voigt, Louise Collin and Jenny Lind. All three escapades ended sadly. Was it perhaps because he was loath to replace his childhood in Odense, where happiness seemed everywhere, like the wood-fire smell described in his fairy-tale chimney pieces, by another more demanding way of life ? Indeed this nostalgia affected even his visit to Goethe's house in Frankfurt which impressed him less than the fact that "the mother of the powerful Rothschilds piously remained in her humble cottage in the street of Jews, where she had borne her sons and brought them up".

The underwater palaces of stones and pearls that Andersen conjured up makes us quite sad because from down there the Little Mermaid dreams of a warm world of human beings and love. The royal balls glittering in the light of a beggar's matches, are only the visions of an innocent soul dying of hunger. It seems that, in Andersen's world, wealth and power are but illusions born of poverty and frustrations. Yet, the atmosphere of the Snow Queen's kitchen is filled with life because Hans Christian is dreaming of his mother's kitchen at Odense.

Possibly the most interesting souvenir to be seen in this house are the examples of paper cut-outs that he was doing even at the age of sixty-two. These designs seem to vibrate with the breath of childhood, for they were inspired by the imagination of his father. Near the close of his life, Andersen cut out, for children and friends, the same windmill his father created for him, "a windmill whose sail made the miller dance". Also, Hans Christian produced more complicated designs, like the manlike theatre in which a head laughs and the heart is pierced with a window, or the tree whose branches are in the shape of angels.

Finally, after years of wandering, Andersen, in 1866, acquired an apartment and decided to fill it with the furniture from Odense. To his friend Jonas Cotlen he wrote with foreboding : "I am going to have a home now ; yes, a bed, my own bed. The idea appals me. The furniture, the bed and the rocking chair, not to mention the books and pictures, all overwhelm me. If I went to a hotel I would have the impression that I had wings, that I were free. But now I have a home that costs me twenty-five risdales a month."

The fairy tale writer Andersen died in this apartment, on a small bed shielded by a screen decorated like a scrapbook, which Countess Wanda Danneskiold had given him : on it were the faces of history's people of genius from Napoleon to Goethe, from Madame de Staël to Walter Scott. He had admired them and envied them but never had he imagined himself as figuring on the screen.

1. The window of Andersen's childhood home looks out on a cobbled street of Odense. It was here that he heard and loved tales by Shakespeare and Sir Walter Scott. This modest home was to remain in his memory and pervade his works.

2. *An oil-painting depicts Andersen reading his fairy tales to the children of his friend Mrs. Baumann.*

3-4. *In October 1866, Andersen rented a room in Copenhagen. This room (at right) has now been recreated in Odense. He wrote his friend Jonas Cotlen: "Now I shall have a home, yes, a bed, my own bed. It terrifies me! Furniture, bed, rocking chair, books and paintings overwhelm me. If I went to a hotel I would still feel I had wings. But now I have a home that costs me twenty-five risdales a month!" In this room, which so oppressed him, he cut out windmills and paper figures (above) at the age of sixty just as he had in his childhood.*

6

6. *Frustrated joy: this drawing was found among Andersen's papers.*

◁ 5. *Andersen created this charming theatre out of paper. As a child he so loved the atmosphere in theatres that he made friends with a programme vendor in Odense so he could get in each evening for nothing.*

7. *Andersen drew this self-portrait with a cat-like wife to amuse the son of the Roy Theatre choirmaster Ludwig Zink.*

▽

5

7

Andersen

8. *Andersen's cutouts, such as the one below, could well illustrate his fairy tales. But when he promised the fantasy images of his dreams to the women in his life, they thought him mad and his love life met with failure. Children and princes were his only friends.*

8

8. *Andersen's cutouts, such as the one below, could well illustrate his fairy tales. But when he promised the fantasy images of his dreams to the women in his life, they thought him mad and his love life met with failure. Children and princes were his only friends.*

9

9. *Riborg Voigt, his first love.*

10

10. *Louise Collin.*

11

11. *Jenny Lind, "the Swedish nightingale".*

D'Annunzio

from the Capponcina villa to Vittoriale

Italy preserves two homes of Gabriele d'Annunzio. One is in memory of his poetic and lyrical work, now somewhat fallen into oblivion. The other is in homage to the patriot who for a short while gave Italy the port of Fiume.

D'Annunzio was forty-five when in 1908 he took up residence at the Capponcina villa on the Settignano hill in Tuscany. From the age of seventeen he had known fame as a poet, rich and beloved by women. One such was Eleanora Duse, who played in his dramas, and on occasions allowed them to infiltrate into her life. Another was the celebrated Russian dancer Ida Rubinstein whose wealth subsidized *The Martyrdom of Saint Sebastian* and *The Pisanella*, plays in which she took a role.

But Gabriele d'Annunzio looked on women in the same manner that he gazed on the rare and valuable objects he loved to collect around him. In *The Child of Pleasure* he describes himself as feeling "jealousy, envy and a supreme egotistical and tyrannical intolerance". Such was his nature, and it sometimes led him to wish almost the destruction of a woman he had sought and possessed, so that she could henceforth belong to no one else. Nobody else must drink from the cup he had used. The memory of his presence should be enough to fill a whole life. His mistresses must remain forever faithful despite his infidelity. Such was his proud idea.

He disliked the publication or divulging of beauty's secrets. There is no doubt that if he had owned the Discobolus of Myron, the Doryphorus of Polycletus or the Aphrodite of Cnidos, his first thoughts would have been to lock the masterpiece up inaccessibly and keep the enjoyment of it for himself, for fear that the pleasure it gave others should reduce his own.

D'Annunzio had the words *Solitudo, Silentium, Clausum* engraved on the door of the Capponcina villa, but in reality he lived there in an atmosphere of passion. Maurice Barrès detected that "the little hard-eyed Italian" hid, in 1910, a man at his wit's end, hard up for money and a "harsh conqueror foraging with jabs of his beak". In 1923, just after the First World War, Barrès realized that "this tough little soldier" was not merely a businessman and a fop, but a mystic.

D'Annunzio began by living sumptuously at Capponcina. But, as he wrote in *The Triumph of Death*, "insatiable desire enthuses into the headiness of destruction".

This destruction simply took the form of bailiffs in 1911 appearing on the scene.

But the master of this Moorish-style villa fought to save his dream. "My dogs have been reduced to seven in number and my horses to three. I submit with good grace to the numbers of the Pleiades and the Charities," he wrote to his publisher. "I have lost seven kilos and regained my youth as well, so that I can work twenty-two hours running at the same oak table."

21

12. The adventurous d'Annunzio knew love, fame, military conquest. A volunteer in the First World War, he was hurt in the right eye and lost his sight for months.

The publisher, inspired no doubt by one of the Charities, replied : "I rejoice at your good news and at the reduction in your horses and dogs, although they seem to me three and seven times too many."

Despite economies, the furniture at the Capponcina villa, valued at one million lire, had to be placed with the Banco di Roma, and the poet's publisher each half-year paid in his royalties.

D'Annunzio around this period was worried by superstition. Madame de Thèbes warned him that he would die a violent death on July 17, 1909. D'Annunzio refused to leave his study and determined to complete his entire work before the fateful day. He sent the lot to his publisher, nine volumes for publication after his death. A tile happened to fall from his roof, tearing the top of his automobile. He found it so ridiculous to have avoided such a death so narrowly that he decided to seize the initiative with regards to his own death, and vowed it must be a glorious one. He galloped off on one of his horses and merely succeeded in working it up into a fury. Right up until midnight he waited in his study for a death that never came.

The nine volumes he sent to his publisher saved the villa from creditors for a short while, but d'Annunzio's fight for Capponcina ended soon with the failure of *Phaedra*. Everything was seized and sold, even to the "child of pleasure's" shirts. How costly it had become to live like Tristan ! D'Annunzio left for France in 1910 to live in a small house at Arcachon.

His other home, still to be viewed in Italy, bears witness to another side of his personality and another period of his life, which in fact ended there in 1938. This is the Vittoriale hermitage on the shores of Lake Garda. It was given to him by the government at the same time he was awarded the title Prince of Montenevoso, after Nitti's troops had chased the poet out of Fiume. Today the soldier rather than the man of letters is recalled at this residence.

In the Vittoriale garden, d'Annunzio anchored the ship on which he brought back the bodies of his comrades fallen at Fiume. They repose beneath stone arches. The aged poet on holidays had gun salutes fired from the bridge of the ghostly vessel. Julien Green describes this weird structure : "It is a marble warship, with only the bow a true part of the ship, advancing out into the lake and halted in its voyage by cyprus trees around it. But this huge ship in the trees does not lack a mysterious probability, just like the copper bed which the surrealists once put in the rushes of a marsh. We took a lot of time to see over it, climb up the stairs, look round the porticos and rotundas. So that is what the poet had in mind when he was writing ; his secret, his interior vision thus emerges into the sunlight. The automobile in which he entered Fiume is kept as a relic ; it looks like something Charlie Chaplin might have used in an early movie, and has on the door some fantastic kind of heraldry, which evokes the idea of a cardinal's arms, perhaps the city's arms.

"You can also see the airplane which looks like an affair of hair pins and hat boxes, in which he vaunted himself over the skies of Vienna. His plane, *Nel Cielo di Vienna*, contained the proclamations he threw out over the Austrian capital in 1917 and 1918. But even so this folly has a certain grandeur about it. He dared to be the character he took himself to be."

D'Annunzio's period as an Italian patriot is located in time between the possession of these two fine homes ; between the Capponcina which he lost through excessive luxury and the Vittoriale which he won through services to Italy. The First World War changed d'Annunzio's destiny. He had been one of the keenest champions of Italian entry into the war on the side of the Allies. He wrote in August 1914 : "To make war against Austria will for me be the most beautiful, the most joyous opportunity to return to my country."

Italy entered the war in 1915, and the poet returned to his homeland on May 4 of the same year with the words : "Long live the just war." He sought a job in the air force, but the Italian government refused to risk the life of so famous an author. He wrote : "I am not an old-fashioned author in a cap and slippers. It is perhaps easier to keep back the wind than me. I am a soldier. You want to safeguard my precious life, you look on me as a museum piece, good to keep in packing and sacking. Well, I don't care about my life—just for the pleasure of contradicting you and not caring. I beseech you, my great and dear friend, arrange for the odious refusal to be withdrawn."

The refusal was withdrawn. D'Annunzio for several months carried out difficult missions in the air. On January 16, 1916, his plane made a forced landing; he was hurt over the eyes, a slight wound that was badly looked after and led to the loss of his right eye. The other one was only just saved after months of complete blindness. At the time of Douaumont, Barrès tried to comfort him, but d'Annunzio replied: "Do not worry about my eyes, my brother, but save the world's beauty for eyes that are to come." With him, gesture was everything. Once recovered, he resumed his aerial missions, but was unable to carry on. He finished the war as an infantryman. Later people were to compare the ideal of the hero, a little pompous, with the notion of the militant. But both merged in a certain self-renonciation.

At the end of the war, d'Annunzio was awarded five silver military medals, a gold medal, three war crosses, a wound insignia, a Savoy cross and the *Légion d'Honneur*. He was promoted three times for war service.

But this was not enough for him. The peace terms did not give Fiume back to Italy. He took Fiume himself on September 12, 1919, with a small contingent of 287 men. On the eve of the event he wrote: "My dear comrade, the dice are thrown. Tomorrow I shall take Fiume by force of arms. May God and Italy help me! I rise from my bed with a temperature, but the task cannot be delayed. Once again the spirit will dominate contemptible flesh."

A general tried to arrest him the next day. He told him: "General, if that is the case, you have two targets: my gold medal and my medal for my injuries. Tell the men to fire." So d'Annunzio took Fiume. Shortly afterwards, Barrès wrote that he was one of those people who "exhaled an animated power like Peter the Hermit, Gambetta and Clemenceau". He saw in d'Annunzio "a person who acts by his individuality and not like an expert, not with a speciality".

We should not smile too much at the ruin of the Vittoriale hermitage or the other remains that lie on the red and gold dining room tables: the saints and gods of many religions, and in the study the antique mouldings, romantic busts, Indonesian cloths, old books, humanist bric-a-brac of 1900. Nor at the twist of mind that made him have marked on the low door to his study the enigmatic words: "Mind your head", nor at the First World War museum entered through a triumphal archway, nor the chapels dedicated to Napoleon and Saint Francis of Assisi nor the very beautiful objects lying with the junk. D'Annunzio furnished his home as he filled his life. He accumulated as many souvenirs as possible, just as he collected as many exalted moments as possible, in love and in heroism.

Outside of Good and Bad, he was avid for all sensations: apart from the Beautiful and the Ugly, he dedicated Vittoriale to the knowledge of all possible forms of worship.

The trait that specially characterized d'Annunzio was a kind of search for "spasms". He would have liked to have lived several lives at the same time, and in the same way he wanted to have several homes in the same one at Vittoriale. In an aura of mystery he eked out his life of a fallen prince, surrounded by mistresses dressed up as Franciscan nuns.

Like Wilde or Byron, he was a Renaissance figure who cared most of all about aesthetics. Life had to be a poem for him.

He was husband to a Roman duchess, seducer of a Sicilian princess, dramatic author for the love of the greatest actress of the age, dissipator of a fortune, an exile kept by a rich Russian dancer, a soldier and hero respected by troops and veterans. D'Annunzio gave Mussolini's Fascists their cry: "*Eia Eia Alalà*", together with the ancient Roman right-arm salute.

Vittoriale was offered to him by a régime

that flattered and feared him. He died in 1938, carefully publicizing himself until the end.

An eye-witness told Julien Green : "His body lay in a music room surrounded by Michelangelo-like statues whose shadows fell on the poet's remains. Within a few hours they took the body into another room, this time in a baroque décor with red curtaining. A little later, he was moved to another place, watched over by a golden Venus de Milo. So he continued play-acting until death."

Of this witness to the end of European romanticism, spoilt by Italian exageration and rhetoric, there remain over and above the noise, worldly scandals and political successes, a few poetic pages and verses that are more than formal successes. He is always on the borderline of disaster, into which he slips on occasions, for he is one of those people whom ridicule cannot kill. His thoughts are often deliberately obscure and morbid. Sensuality, melancholy and a feeling for nature prevent him slipping into oblivion :

"Fresche le mie parole ne la sera
ti sien come il fruscio che fan le foglie
del gelso ne la man di chi le coglie
silenzioso..."

(May the freshness of my words in the evening
Be for you as the rustling of leaves
On the mulberry tree in the hand of he who picks in silence...

May the softness of my words in the evening
Be for you like the hissing of the rain, tepid and fugitive...)

"Tepida e fuggitiva..."

13

15. The cluttered study at Vittoriale reveals the somewhat pompous humanistic side of his nature, as opposed to his military character.

17. D'Annunzio was a celebrated poet at the early age of seventeen.

18. A later picture shows him at an age when political adventures counted more than aesthetic ideals.

19. D'Annunzio is seen here with his ▷ great friend, Benito Mussolini. The poet had written "Il Duce" on the eve of his victory: "My dear friend, the die is cast. Tomorrow morning, I shall take Fiume by force of arms. May God and Italy help me: I rise from my bed with a fever!"

16. D'Annunzio anchored the ship in which he brought back the bodies of comrades who fell at Fiume, under the trees of Vittoriale.

21. "La Duse," the famed actress was passionately loved by the poet.

21

20. D'Annunzio had the tastes and bearing of a Renaissance prince.

20

22

22. Ida Rubinstein became the successor to "La Duse" in d'Annunzio's heart.

23. D'Annunzio is seen here with two of his dogs. Almost ruined at this time by his extravagant tastes, he tried to arouse the sympathy of his publisher, Emilio Treves. "My dogs," he wrote, "now number only seven, my horses, three. I believe I work twenty-two hours at a stretch at the same oak table." But Treves replied shortly: "I am glad to learn of your good news and of the reduction in your horses and dogs, although they still seem to me three and seven times too many."

23

J.-S. Bach

at Eisenach

Born in March 1675, Johann Sebastian Bach spent his earliest years at Eisenach. Orphaned at ten, his oldest brother Johann Christoph took him in at Ohrdruf and continued his musical education for a period of five years.

We are all too familiar with Bach as an aged man in a wig. We might however have a glimpse of him first as a child at Eisenach where in the center of a somewhat bare room there still stands his charming cradle. Things have been kept much as they were at the time and it is rather surprising to see that the childhood of this genius was in what appears to be an ordinary bourgeois home.

This Thuringian family were musicians, just as they might have been millers or joiners, and none of the rooms truly reflects the presence of a genius. There were thirty-three members in the family between Bach's grandfather Veit Bach and himself. The old man who died in 1619 was in fact a miller and baker with a penchant for zither-playing. No fewer than twenty-seven members of the family were singers, organists or musicians of the city or the court. The renown of the family was to continue well into the nineteenth century. Johann Sebastian Bach's father Johann Ambrosius was proud of their combined abilities, and his uncle Johann Christoph even more so. It was he who first evoked Bach's interest in the organ. The two brothers were musicians at Eisenach town hall although Johann Christoph stood out as the leader of the "tribe" owing to his reputation as a composer.

Bach's father and uncle disagreed over the upbringing of the children. His uncle wanted them to undertake a university course along with their musical training, but his father held that, at fourteen years of age, the children should give up school and become apprentice musicians. This was a custom not only in the Bach family but in many local families.

Thuringia has traditionally been a cradle of German music. After the age of minstrels came the choir of students and trades-people and the child Bach naturally belonged to a local choir. Perhaps it was this Eisenach experience which directed his interest toward church music.

Music was of major importance to Eisenach folk, and Bach's house was quite near a library well stocked with original manuscripts by foreign composers. Some of these had never even been played, and he used to consult them and copy them out for the pleasure of it. In this way at a young age, between his father's music lessons, he searched through the unknown treasures of that library out of curiosity, thus acquiring a notion of musical styles abroad. It was a pastime that preoccupied him throughout his early years.

Childhood was, in his case, an entirely natural process in contrast to Mozart, who when he was losing his baby teeth had already reveal-

33

24. *Johann Sebastian Bach became organist on 14 August 1703 at the new church in Armstadt, competing against several candidates who played on this two-keyboard organ. His first religious cantata ("Denn du wirst meine Seele lassen") was heard in the church on Easter Sunday 1704.*

ed himself as a precocious genius and was known in the courts of all Europe. Bach just lived out his ordinary family life. The family gave him full liberty to find his own feet. He did not have to suffer in adult life the humility of being cast off by princes who had praised him as a child as did Mozart. The Bach family had neither the inclination nor the time to make an idol out of young Johann Sebastian. He was spared the hollow joys of posing in court costume for his portrait in front of a clavichord, which Mozart had to undergo.

Mozart used to tell the story of how he slipped on the floor at the Austrian court of the future Queen Marie-Antoinette who picked him up and whom he offered to marry when he grew up. Bach had neither the taste nor the occasion to engage in such gay repartee. The two children were to become adult composers with a totally different turn of mind, although they both reached glorious heights. In Mozart's music there is a superficial approach which he imbibed from European courts. He was unable to throw off the influence of a childhood spent trying to please a demanding aristocracy. With Bach on the other hand, religious beginnings remained engraved on his character; at Eisenach he began life with less of a flying start, and the instruction he gave himself was aimed more at pleasing himself than anyone else.

At an age when Bach was singing in a choir at Eisenach to help pay for his keep in the family, the brilliant Mozart was receiving jewels from an adoring aristocracy, and at one moment he resorted to hanging two watches on his belt so that people would give him money instead of more timepieces. We can clearly see the influences of these differing experiences in the works the two men produced: Bach is the genius of the cantatas, the *Passion* and the *Mass in B*, whereas Mozart produced *Eine Kleine Nachtmusik*. Their works could hardly have been more different, one writing masses for monasteries, the other music for royalty.

Bach's austere life is devoid of anecdotes and limited to a family existence run on patriarchal lines. The grandeur of his work was to emerge later when the romantics led by Men-delssohn were to "discover" him with delight, but the people of his age hardly realized his genius. Frederick II regarded him as merely a virtuoso who could be used to try out all the harpsichords in the palace and he was gene-rally considered a "difficult" musician. It was the nineteenth century that recognized him as the inimitable genius we enjoy today.

The romantics adopted him as their own at once. The music of Bach gave comfort, in its serenity, to the mystical "children of the century". Artists in the nineteenth century were inclined to blend pagan and divine love, and in Bach they found their spiritual father and at the same time the man who contrasted most with the eighteenth century materialistic mood. Death, man's eternal companion, was ever-present in the minds of such people as Chopin, Musset, Beethoven, Byron and Schiller. Bach also sang of death in his works, and it was this theme more than any other in his music that attracted them. The idea of death present in nineteenth-century thought was undoubtedly but one aspect of the century's subjectivity. It may have been a matter of style inspired by social and religious attitudes. The image of death produced by Bach is probably not exactly what the romantics had in mind; they instinctively felt an affinity with him since, behind his cold very classical musical technique, he concealed such vast passionate themes. Bach's music might be described as a perpetual yearning for God's presence. This desire for the Absolute and the Infinite matches in with the spirit of the early nineteenth-century writers, and in this sense we may call Bach a romantic.

However this great musician's entire life was directed toward research and not toward the outpouring of sentiment. From his early days at Eisenach he never ceased to study and analyse the music of his foreign contemporaries, and, in a contrapuntal manner so to speak, he had the underlying support of life in a large family, over which he ruled in patriarchal manner. He had two wives and twenty children. He let only a year to go by after his first wife died before taking to himself another. Nearly every year a child was born and another died.

On top of that he adopted several of his pupils.

Bach also loved teaching, for it was one of the ways in which he expressed his love of humanity. He ended his career as master of Leipzig. He wanted around him a world that was as carnal and lively as his music was serene and his research abstract. The life of a tribal chief counterbalanced the mathematics of his music, and away from the work desk he enjoyed life, was a big eater and hearty drinker, and prolific producer of children.

He was also, in his capacity as master of the chapel, quite able to forget his children and responsibilities. He could go off leaving the key under the mat, as it were, when he learned of a musical system he had never heard of so far. He would walk for weeks to hear and learn about such music, with the sole desire to assimilate the thought of a musician hitherto unknown to him.

The Eisenach genius was well able to dispense with passionate love in his creative effort, in contrast to Chopin and Beethoven who often used it as a stimulus for their work. Bach somehow erected watertight partitions between his personal life and his music, and the former was always to be subservient to his creative side. His constant idea was that the security of his family provided the soundest basis for the fulfilment of his work. His life's pattern was carefully staked out for the benefit of the creative urge.

In Bach's time, musicians had to work either for a court or for a church, and in due course he had posts in a prince's orchestra and in a big chapel. Freedom of expression did not always fit in with responsibilities but he constantly sought it despite the restriction.

Although quite prepared to accept the daily routine arising from official duties, he would not hesitate to abandon his duties if he had to travel in order to enrich his musical experience. He moved from court to church and back again as the demands of freedom dictated. He was criticized for this, but he was never one who sought specially to please. He was a proud composer and he had his own "tribe".

The orphan Bach left his Eisenach home

at the age of ten and his brother's place at Ohrdruf at fifteen. His first job was at Saint Michael's Church in Lüneburg. He was often paid in kind—wood, wine, candles or fish—but he liked it because he met Thomas de La Selle, former pupil of Lully, who introduced him to contemporary French music and in particular that of Couperin. It so happened that Prince Georg Wilhelm of Brunswick-Lüneburg, whose wife was French, dreamed of turning his palace into a second Versailles. Bach wrote to him in French, referring to French musicians. This exchange of letters indicated that his musical culture was already equal to the demands of this court which also offered him freedom of expression.

In 1703, when he was eighteen years old, we find him titular organist at Neue Kirche in Arnstadt. This otherwise calm fellow became so demanding toward his choristers that they decided to beat him up. On one occasion he struck a chorister with a sword, but this would not have jeopardized his position if only he had not been absent so often.

One morning he announced that he was going away for a few weeks to hear the organist Buxtehude at Lübeck. He arranged for a stand-in and walked the whole 300 miles returning four months later. The church authorities grew concerned at the sudden change in musical style he adopted. To their ears his music had a "foreign tone" after this Lübeck visit, and he even played secular music on the organ for his cousin. Such liberties were hardly expected to satisfy his employers and he was soon asked to leave, having in the meantime married Maria Barbara on October 17, 1707. Johann Sebastian had wanted to marry one of Buxtehude's daughters but the old man was keen to get his girls married in the right age order and offered Bach one that was seven years his senior. Johann Sebastian left forthwith and never dared return, although Buxtehude would have left Bach his professional post when he died.

He and his first wife were to have four children who lived. He was often absent for long periods and returned home one day to learn that Maria Barbara had died some time ago. Within a year he had married Anna Magdalena Wilcken, who produced thirteen children, nine of whom died. The two marriages provided a total of eight live children, enough to form a family orchestra.

While employed at the court of Weimar, the Duke of Weimar had a new organ built for him in the Schloss Kirche. An orchestra and several choirs were made available to him, and Bach wrote one cantata a month for them to perform. Abou this time, Dresden authorities had the idea of a harpsichord competition between Bach and the French musician Louis Marchand. This "duel" failed to take place since Marchand disappeared during the night before Bach arrived.

Shortly after this incident, Bach came into contact with the twenty-three-year-old widowed Prince of Anhalt-Coethen, a music-lover. He implored Bach to come to his court. The composer asked permission of the Prince of Weimar who turned the idea down, and put Bach in prison for a month. On emerging from captivity, Bach tore up his contract, and moved on to Prince of Coethen where he stayed six years.

He lived on strikingly good terms with his new employer who allowed him to buy whatever instruments he needed, and supported Bach's enthusiasm with his own. The new patron was a passionate lover of Bach's music and caused a scandal by paying him as much as the highest dignitaries of the court received. But unfortunately the Prince of Coethen subsequently married a princess who diverted her husband's attention from his love of music. Bach preferred to resign than to suffer such "desertion". He had written for the prince some of his gayest works, obviously composed to mark their friendship : the suites for orchestra, the *Brandenburg Concertos*, the first part of the *Well-Tempered Clavichord*, and cantatas—a total of fifty works in the two years. In exchange for the prince's patronage and his erstwhile friendship, destroyed by a woman, Bach took up the post of master at Leipzig, a badly-paid job.

Leipzig was to be the final phase of Bach's musical life following his periods at Arnstadt, Mülhausen, Weimar and Coethen. He spent twenty-five years there, ruling over a load of scamps who slept three in a bed in rooms with no windows. His task was to teach music to children who were quite often actively opposed to the idea.

He was fully aware of the burden he was taking on when he applied for the post, yet he competed to get it. He knew that his employers, local officials, would give him no mercy, so why did he so want this position rather than another ? The explanation can only be that, for some time, he had felt the desire to return to purely religious music, to go back again to the source of his inspiration.

Thus it was that the gay secular works composed for the Prince of Coethen were now followed by the *Mass in B* and the *Saint Matthew Passion*, which he wrote for Saint Thomas's Church in Leipzig—and for his God. But once again he crossed swords with those who employed him. The passionate mood of his religious works shocked the Lutherans of Leipzig. But even more disturbing was his belief that matters of dogma were open to debate. Deeply religious, and a Lutheran, he accepted the idea that different ways of thought and different values could co-exist. Such liberal notions caused his own fellow-worshippers to reject him.

Bach's life had an underlying sense of unity about it. His lack of any religious sectarianism was allied with his need to create, spread and develop himself in his family life. Bach put little trust in intelligence as such, believing more in the secret voice of nature than in those fancies of the mind met with in certain kinds of love. He believed in man's thirst for God whatever form this took in individuals, rather than in a single religion. The bourgeois citizens of Leipzig did not understand him any more than had those of Arnstadt when he made use of the style of a foreign master, Buxtehude. In Leipzig, Bach was fully himself and utterly dissimilar to the circle he lived in.

His universality disappointed the people around him, for it suited neither their religious principles nor their musical chauvinism. From his childhood onwards he never ceased to discover and appreciate new musical values, which he frequently adopted. He "de-composed" and "re-composed" for his own pleasure the work of Heinrich Schütz, great master of German religious music. He copied and transposed the concertos of Vivaldi, studied Scarlatti, Couperin and Lully. Bach overlooked nothing. Leipzig society attacked him but, fortunately, left him enough time to write 200 cantatas, despite the increasingly restrictive demands the Saint Thomas authorities imposed on him, as they claimed their revenge for his individualism and the liberties he took with their religious codes.

Once, as she listened to the *Saint Matthew Passion*, a lady of Leipzig exclaimed : "May God protect us. It's a comic opera." He was bitterly attacked for composing the *Mass in B minor* for the coronation of Augustus III in Poland—because it was a Catholic work. The King himself was able to counter-attack by appointing Bach as *Hofkapellmeister* of the Saxe court in Leipzig.

Eventually, Bach did contemplate leaving Leipzig, where his music was considered too modern and revolutionary. Frederick II interviewed Bach in Berlin but the meeting ended in mutual disappointment. Upon meeting the composer the king exclaimed : "Ah! At last we have old Bach within our walls", and he ordered his musicians to stop playing at once. While Bach was there, Frederick played the flute and suggested several themes for the composer's fugues. He made use of one in his *Musical Offering*, dedicated to the monarch. Sadly, this royal encounter led to nothing. Frederick failed to detect the genius in Bach, but merely saw in him the same kind of virtuoso he was himself. And neither did Bach see in the king the man who was to launch the German romantic movement. Historic meetings of this kind are often disappointing : they start off with fine ambitions and finish up frequently as a mere acquaintanceship that peters out into mutual disappointment.

So Johann Sebastian returned to Leipzig and his local bigwigs, one of whom pronounced at his funeral : "He was perhaps a good composer, but he was certainly a bad master."

The master adopted several of his pupils and looked after them in true partiarchal manner. It is somewhat surprising to learn that he was regarded at the time as a bad master, although this attitude may have been a reaction to his individualistic ways.

The joys of life and the dramas of death came and went around Johann Sebastian Bach without a trace of them being recorded in the titles of his work. Yet the events of his life were quietly absorbed into his music, colouring it without being officially acknowleged. The works he composed during his stay at Coethen have a gaiety and lightness which can be explained only by the enthusiasm which the prince evoked in the composer he so admired, whilst the religious compositions of his life's last years reflected his decision to seek inspiration in his faith, its true source. One might compare Bach's life with a fugue that constantly interprets the same theme in differing ways. Bach composed when some of his children were crawling on all fours and others were already married. Two wives succeeded in maintaining some permanency in the home, whose members were to live in a good many different towns. Events were constantly renewing the course of his life, but everything seemed to possess a certain continuity, and he himself desired it so.

On his arrival back in Leipzig after his interview with Frederick II, he completed the great work, the *Art of Fugue*, which is a spiritual as well as a musical exercise. It may not be Bach's most-loved composition but it is the one that most interests those who venerate him ; they find in it the will of the composer to forsake the easier paths of life and music. It was "pure" music, and Bach's sole form of sectarianism ; and even that was only partial, since during the period he also created much freer work. The highly mathematical *Art of Fugue* might possibly be a subject for parody by means of a computer, but at the time Bach saw it as a discipline he must impose on himself, just as monks in their nocturnal offices desire to fulfil a religious discipline. Such constraint enabled Bach to produce "cleaner" work.

When Bach died in 1750 at the age of sixty-five, an indifferent world saw in him only a good musician. It was a hundred years before people took any interest in him again. His "rehabilitation" was gradual and took place over several decades, while the later posthumous recognition of Vivaldi and Albinoni was quite rapid. They probably benefited from the taste the public acquired for Bach's music.

In 1829 Mendelssohn "discovered" the *Saint Matthew Passion* and twenty years later a Bach Society was formed in England. The full Passion was not yet publicly performed, and in France it was only partially produced. Alexis Dupont in Paris sang for the first time an aria from the *Passion* in 1840. Then Habeneck, a violinist, played an *andante* from a Bach concerto.

More importantly, Gounod brought fame on himself by transcribing a Bach prelude for piano, organ and violin and adding words by Lamartine. "These few works did more for Gounod's fame than everything he had written so far," Camille Saint-Saëns later observed.

At the close of the nineteenth century the French Société des Concerts du Conservatoire organized performances of the *Fifth Brandenberg Concerto* (1889) and the *Mass in B* (1891). In the 1920's Marcel Dupré finally made the great organ works of Bach fully known in France, and this marks the true musical resurrection of Bach. Wanda Landowska in 1933 introduced to Paris her harpsichord version of the Goldberg Variations. It is interesting that Bach came into popularity with the *Art Nouveau* period, acting as an artistic foil to the sensitive Beethoven, Wagner and Debussy. In his *Journal* in 1917, Gide wrote : "Beethoven's pathos affects me today much less than does the contemplative adoration of Bach." Debussy who contrasts so much with Bach, wrote of him : "The beauty of the *andante* in his *Concerto for Violin* is so immense that, quite sincerely,

one does not know where to go or what attitude to adopt in order to hear it with fitting dignity." (1913.) Everyone to his own Bach. Stravinsky allowed himself to be influenced in the first movement of his *Dumbarton Oaks Concerto*, which was subsequent to the *Rite of Spring*. This appreciation amounts to a neo-classical assertion following the earlier romantic expressionism of Fauré and Debussy.

Perhaps the composers Bach influenced most of all are those who appeared after the Second World War : Alban Berg, Webern and Schoenberg.

Today, Bach represents a "non-committed" art form. If he lived in our age, he would certainly have wanted to absorb into his own music the research work done by the exponents of *musique concrète*. His own research was never merely academic ; if he copied out the concertos of Vivaldi and the music of Corelli and was inspired by them, this was because he appreciated the effect their richness could have on the northern German baroque style of a Buxtehude and his school. The baroque phenomenon was a consequence of the Renaissance, translated in musical terms into "the exaltation of the monodic chant accompanied by spectacular instrumental development." Bach's role was to give its style an equilibrium. So it was, for exemple, that this *Actus Tragicus*, written at the age of twenty-two when musical baroque frequently slipped into rococo, is noteworthy for its clean instrumental lines.

Although he assimilated the musical trends of his age, Bach indisputably produced a style of his own, in a range of achievements that is infinitely varied. He was a Lutheran who wrote Catholic music, a court musician who preferred the mastership of a school, a collector of theological works disputed by local Huguenots.

Bach possessed a boundless spirit concealed behind an existence that was banality itself.

Next page:
26. *Bach's cradle is the center of this room at Eisenach where he was born.*

25. *This harpsichord on which* ▷ *Johann Sebastian played is now in a room at Eisenach containing Bach's instruments.*

28. Bach went to Lübeck to concerts, such as the one depicted here, in order to hear Buxtehude who had a major influence on his work. He would have liked to stay longer and he asked for the hand of his prettiest daughter. Buxtehude offered him his eldest and ugliest girl, according to the custom, but Bach left, never to return.

29. The youthful Bach by an unknown artist.

30. Bach as a young man. Music-lovers today regard him variously as a baroque, classical, pre-romantic and pre-polytonal composer.

31. The composer at the close of his life. He was a choirmaster and devoted himself to religious compositions.

32. "Old father Bach" was considered however as a very mediocre choirmaster.

◁ 27. Bach played this piano for Frederick II in the drawing room of the sovereign's castle at Potsdam.

Balzac

from Passy to Saché Castle

Only two of Balzac's many homes remain today roughly as he left them. These are the house at 47 Rue Raynouard, formerly Rue Basse, in Paris and the Château de Saché where he paid many visits.

The Paris house in the Passy district has retained all of its romantic charm with its green shutters and benches, its neo-Gothic garden chairs, privet hedges, lilac trees, sunflowers and tall thin trees. A grape vine leads straight up the central pathway to the house, where stand two sphinx statues. Built on one level, this is the house where Balzac wrote the last part of *La Comédie Humaine,* nourishing his dream of marriage with a certain great Russian lady and his visions of castles. Nothing at that moment gave Balzac the slightest notion that one day he would have 200 serfs and become the master of Wierzshow by marrying Madame Hanska. He had rented this house from a local butcher's wife, as a hideaway, after having been forced to leave a property called Les Jardies because his debts prevented him from making the necessary payments on it.

His new home was in a former orangery, part of a group of eighteenth-century buildings, split up at the time of the Revolution and rented out as apartments. Honoré de Balzac found in it a safe harbour where he could write without fear of creditors. Among other advantages it had two exits.

To visit the theatre or call on his publisher at the Palais Royal, all he had to do was take the coach from Versailles which passed the end of his garden and in fifteen minutes he was in central Paris. Even so, the general atmosphere of Passy at the time was quite rural, and he could relax in peace and calm—as befitted a journalist of those days who lived by his pen.

Although heavily in debt, he had not hesitated to buy art treasures and eighteenth-century furniture when he took the house. It was a passion with him. Several pieces, he liked to tell, came from the Château de Versailles. The publisher Solar has left behind an account of a meeting he had with Balzac, which includes the sole description we have of the house at this period. Solar called on Balzac to ask him for the manuscript of a novel, first using the secret password, "I should like to see Madame..." (Balzac had taken the precaution of renting the house under the name of his governess to side-track his creditors). Even so, Solar recounts he had difficulty in persuading the maid to let him in. Finally inside, he entered the author's study. The lilac-filled garden shed faint light on it. The walls held pictures without frames and frames without pictures. In the middle was the same table that stands there today, bearing a single book—a French dictionary.

"Balzac", Solar wrote, "enveloped in a large once-white monk robe, was lovingly wiping a Sèvres china cup." This was part of

45

33. "Balzac à la canne" was sculpted by Daumier in 1835, the year he wrote "Le Père Goriot." He was thirty-six and had already been in love with a countess, Madame de Berny, a duchess, Madame d'Abrantès, and a marquise, Madame de Castries.

his collection, which he immediatly showed to Solar, saying that he bought the cup, "a Watteau *chef-d'œuvre*", in Germany, and the saucer in Paris. He estimed that the pair, brought together with such good luck, was worth at least 2,000 francs. He then showed his visitor a *Judgement of Pâris* by Giorgione, for which a gallery had offered him 12,000 francs which he had refused—naturally! Moreover his paintings and other valuables were certainly worth 400,000 francs. Among these was a portrait of a woman by Palma the Elder, the "King" of the Palmas, and the portrait of Madame Greuze, by the inimitable Greuze. His first sketch of her, it was a valuable work for the artist never again succeeded in reproducing her features as perfectly. The *Portrait of a Knight of Malta*, Balzac told Solar, cost him much more money, time and diplomacy than he would have needed to conquer the kingdom of Italy. If that painting was not by Raphaël, then Raphaël was not the world's best painter, he declared; nothing less than a million francs for that, or he would give it away! Next masterpiece was an item of furniture in ebony encrusted with mother-of-pearl that had belonged to Marie de Médicis. Two Cellini statuettes followed plus a third, all worth their weight in gold, and two Chinese vases...

The publisher, keen to get the novel out of Balzac, observed that he really needed the Louvre to house all these wonderful things, to which Balzac calmy replied : "I am building it up, yes, building it up!"

Clearly, as his comments show, Solar was not taken in by this particular Balzac comedy. "I called on him to obtain material. He had calculated, quite rightly in general though not in my particular case : 'If I show this dealer that I am a millionaire, he will not bargain with me, because one does not bargain with those who do not need to sell.' This time it was he who was doing the bargaining and the roles were reversed. I was left with the role of artist; I esteemed him highly and accepted the first figure he put forward. The deal was concluded and I left with some curiously corrected manuscripts, topped by *La Dernière Incar-*

nation de Vautrin, which is one of Balzac's greatest masterpieces."

As an interesting side-light, it is surprising to know that this man of genius spent hours in the Rue Vieille-du-Temple tracking a small tradesman of the Marais district, so that he could get an idea of his habits and include him the same evening in his next chapter of *La Comédie Humaine;* yet he needed, in order to maintain his own self-esteem as well as that of others, to purchase signed objects, paintings by the great masters, and old furniture of royal or imperial origin. He himself reveals that at the entrance to the house in Rue Raynouard, he set up a bust of Napoleon on a stand with the words : "I shall be Napoleon of the pen !" He declared this at twenty years of age, and by dint of perseverance, succeeded in making Madame de Berny believe it; at the time, she must have been very much in love with him to accept the idea.

When he was thirty years old he still believed this, even when all was going wrong and debts piled up higher than ever. He wrote to Madame Hanska that he was sure to end up meeting an excentric Englishman who would take an interest in him, just as there had been people interested in Napoleon. The benefactor would certainly say : "Here you are, Monsieur de Balzac, this ought to settle your debts and enable you to write in peace."

Balzac's moods at Passy ranged from high excitement to utter despair. He was a writing Napoleon one day and a penniless beggar the next. At the same time, he packed the house with pieces of furniture that ruined him, with the idea of satisfying the tastes of Madame Hanska and himself one day in the future. He would lay bare to her the state of his finances and of his mind. He did this with such ardour that it is almost surprising she took so long to marry him after her own husband died. He wrote to her from Passy : "My secret life consoles me for everything. You would shudder if I told you of all my anguish. Like Napoleon on the field of battle, I forget it by keeping to my little work table. Well, I am alive, I am at peace. This little table will one day belong

46

to my darling, my Eva, my wife. I have had it for ten years and it has witnessed all my hardships, wiped all my tears, seen all my projects and heard all my thoughts. My arm has almost worn it out as it moves across it while I write."

By 1844 the whole of the furniture had been sold, except for this little table which miraculously remained in Passy.

He told her (June 28, 1844) that he had draped the drawing room in purple velvet because "the first day we met your dress was purple; you do not know that and I have never mentioned nor written about it to you, but since that day my little drawing room has been purple." Actually the room was red, and it still is today.

He added: "I have always liked purple. I still have a Persian carpet in that colour and a table covered with a purple cloth and twisted cording in purple which are sacred to me."

On one wall in a large gold frame was a portrait of Madame Hanska standing out "like a star" from this "rich" background.

It is certain that Balzac was often very conscious of his similarity to the young provincial in *Les Illusions perdues*, blinded by the luxury of grand houses, by ancestral portraits in their gold frames, eighteenth-century furniture and hangings with heavy cords such as are found in the large Parisian homes where he had never lived. At the Rue Raynouard house he tried to recreate the atmosphere he liked to find in the homes of the women he desired. Most of them came from aristocratic families of the *ancien régime* or the Empire, whereas he was from the nineteenth-century bourgeois class that owed its very existence to the Revolution but was dissatisfield with its lot, and dreamed of acquiring more through the intermediary of high-born women from the mysterious past.

He would probably have felt his inferiority less had he been born in Paris. As a provincial, he had discovered simultaneously the big capital, its *salons* and its intrigues. He would recognize a given psychological situation between certain people in a *salon* and

forthwith reproduce it in his work together with the décor of the room. People he met provided the characters for his novels; as to the décor in which they played out their roles, he reproduced that at the Passy house. But unfortunately while his genius brought back to life these activities in his novels, the artisans who decorated his home could not always reproduce the right effect. Draperies copied from the private residence of Madame de Castries, when hung in Passy, were in less sure taste than his manner of recounting his unfortunate love affair with that lady in *La Duchesse de Langeais*.

His taste for the grandiose, even though we may not care for it ourselves, gives as true a picture of Balzac as do his own novels. It is likely that he did not fool himself with his ostentatious display of wealth, as in his encounter with the publisher recorded above. On other occasions, he spoke of the treasures only in reference to the debt they caused, forcing him to wear out an already exhausted mind. Like his father, he went through phases of elation and dejection all his life.

At Passy the true Balzac is to be found; the period when he had four rooms, a bed, a table and a few items of castle furniture.

Today all the furniture has disappeared except the famous writing table. His goods were seized on several occasions and he took to Avenue Fortunée when he moved, only what his creditors left him! He moved in on his arrival from Russia and in due course died there, everything being sold by auctions subsequently. Thus it is that we have at Passy only a few items owned by the author. In the bedroom he occupied for seven years, are some cartoons his contemporaries did of him, a portrait of Benjamin Roubaud whom Champfleury described as "the living image of Balzac", portraits of his friends the Duchess of Abrantès, George Sand, Eugène Sue, Théophile Gautier, Gavarni, Henri Monnier. And also some small statuettes in terracotta by Pierre Ripert of *La Comédie Humaine* characters, the like of which are not seen today.

In the drawing room there are engravings of people who counted in his life and whom he loved, in particular a portrait of Madame de Berny, his first love. Of her he wrote : "Although married, she has been like a god for me. She has been a mother, friend, family, companion and adviser. She has made the writer, consoled the young man, created taste, wept like a sister, laughter has descended every day as a beneficial sleep to give repose to suffering... Without her, it is certain, I would be dead." When they loved each other, she was forty years of age and he was only twenty.

But the important thing to note is that she was the god-daughter of Marie-Antoinette ! It was the *ancien régime* he chiefly loved in her. He was a mere bourgeois, flattered by this love affair. She gave him more than she received in return, and he had to admit that she had been his only true love. It was for her that he wrote these last words in *La Duchesse de Langeais* : "Only the last love of a woman can satisfy the first love of a man."

The Passy house contains memories of Madame Hanska to this day. There are a few miniatures and a portrait of Julie Carraud who wrote to Balzac : "Love me for a year and I will love you a lifetime." He replied : "You are my public, you are a few *elite* souls whom I wish to please." She was a friend of his sister and he gave her only friendship.

The room of his governess is now simply a museum, but the tiny corridor between rooms still contains a display of dolls Balzac used as an *aide-mémoire* for *La Comédie Humaine*. Further on are two volumes of the complete works of Molière and La Fontaine, one of the first sets, which were to lead him into his first debts. With them is a letter embodying the remark : "I am thirty and have 150,000 francs in debts. Belgium has the one million francs I earned." This was a reference to the publishing of false editions of these works in Belgium in 1838.

From the garden in Passy it is possible today to see through the windows of his study casting red and yellow patches on the table he promised to Eva. On it, he was to write *La Rabouilleuse, Une Ténébreuse Affaire, Catherine de Médicis, Les Mémoires de deux jeunes mariés, Albert Savarus, Splendeurs et Misères des courtisanes, La Cousine Bette* and *Le Cousin Pons*.

Another part of Balzac's world is the eighteenth-century Castle of Saché on the Loire owned by Monsieur de Margonne, which Balzac would almost certainly have liked to possess. He had his eye, too, on the near-by residence of La Grenadière, which is the title of a novel whose opening pages give an admirable description of the Val-de-Loire. He also coveted Moncontour Castle at Vouvray. These last two castles were used as a stage for certain scenes in *La Femme de trente ans*.

At Saché he felt at home. A room was ready for him at all times, papered in blue with autumn leaves, and containing a bed without a canopy fitted into a flowered cretonne alcove. It was there that he wrote on his knees *Le Lys dans la Vallée*, heedless of the bell that rang out meal times. Still to be seen is the yellow leather-covered Louis-Seize bergère easy chair, a rose opaline desk lamp, a paper guillotine brought from Rue Visconti, a coffee jug bought on the Quai de Conti, a crucifix and a small inkwell. In this room he thought up *Louis Lambert, La Recherche de l'Absolu, Le Père Goriot* and probably *Eugénie Grandet*—writing all night and sleeping throughout the day.

In *Le Lys*, Balzac leaves us a description of what he saw from the window, in particular the trees and the river. It was a very peaceful contryside that enabled him to write in peace.

Monsieur de Margonne who let him come to the castle as a child and young writer, welcomed him as his own son. He was a country aristocrat, who had, for many years, been the lover of Balzac's mother ; they produced a son who was Honoré's half-brother. This boy was the pride and joy of his mother but a cause of hurt for Honoré since his mother preferred him. Honoré was exactly like his father : ruddy, short, stocky, a realist, gay, sure of himself and his destiny, full of common sense and mad ideas, loud-speaking yet with a sensitive heart rather than fine manners.

By a strange providence, de Margonne adored Honoré whose lively mind amused him. He took more of an interest in Balzac than in his own son. The half-brother did badly at his childhood studies, had bad health, did nothing with his life and was the despair of his father, and also of Balzac's father who gave him his own surname.

A decidedly provincial atmosphere pervaded this ivy-covered castle. The first-floor drawing room where Balzac played as a child remains Restoration although de Margonne took up residence there during the Consulate period. Still to be seen are the contemporary wallpapers, the drapery with its optical illusions, held back by lion-head devices, the fruit-tree wood armchairs with red plush upholstery, sofas with flowered material and vases containing wild flowers and wild oats.

Later de Margonne was to invite Balzac to read his new novels to the gentry. These readings were veritable stage performances of *La Comédie Humaine*. According to an eye-witness, Balzac would get heated, gesticulate, jump up and stride around the room speaking from memory even though the manuscript was in his hands. Lighting was specially placed on various tables around the room so that he could give a glance at the manuscript from time to time.

The hall of the castle is sixteenth-century and is right next to the romantic drawing room. On the whitewashed walls are two portraits : Madame de Balzac, *née* Laure Sallambier, and her husband. The visitor naturally makes comparisons with the features of their son. Madame de Balzac has a Boucher type of face, mild, pleasant and very eighteenth-century. The author's father, like the Balzac himself, has a head shaped like a cane knob. One wonders if Balzac inherited anything at all from his mother ; possibly his immoderate liking for the aristocracy, which led her to burst into the life of Monsieur de Margonne, just as Honoré entered the life of the Duchess of Abrantès, Madame de Berny, Madame de Castries and Madame Hanska.

Balzac, despite his immense output and his marriage to a very rich woman, returned from Russia to die at Avenue Fortunée in Paris, in a house he was still paying for. It was finally acquired after his death by Countess Hanska.

This Avenue Fortunée house where Balzac spent his final moments has disappeared, but Victor Hugo has left us an unforgettable account of it : "On 18 August, 1850, my wife came back from a call on Madame de Balzac, to tell me that Monsieur de Balzac was dying. I rushed round. He had suffered for eighteen months from heart trouble. After the Revolution in February he had gone to Russia and got married. A few days before his departure I saw him on the boulevard and he was already suffering and breathing heavily. In May, 1850, he was back in France married, rich and dying. On arrival he already had swollen legs and four doctors examined him. One of them told me on July 6 he had not six months to live." It was the same complaint as Frédéric Soulié had.

Hugo continued : "I had my uncle Général Louis Hugo, to dinner on August 18. As soon as we got up from the meal, I left in a *fiacre* which took me to 14 Avenue Fortunée in the Beaujon district, where Balzac lived. He had purchased what remained of Monsieur de Beaujon's hotel plus a few low buildings that happened to have escaped demolition, and had fitted out these remains magnificently to make himself a charming little place with a porch to the Avenue Fortunée. The garden consisted of a long narrow courtyard where the paving stones were broken up here and there with grass patches.

"I rang the bell," writes Hugo. "It was a moonlit night with some clouds. The street was deserted, and nobody came to answer. I rang again and the door opened. A servant appeared before me with a candle. She said : 'What do you wish Sir ?,' crying the while. I gave her my name and she bade me enter the drawing room on the ground floor, where I saw on a bracket opposite the chimney piece, the colossal bust of Balzac in marble by David. A candle burned on the rich oval table in the centre of the room with its six gold statuettes in the best of taste in place of the usual legs.

"Another woman came, also weeping. She said : 'He is dying. Madame has returned home and the doctors have given him up since yesterday. He has a sore on his left leg and it has got gangrene. The doctors don't know what they are doing. They said that Monsieur's dropsy was a buffy dropsy, an infiltration, that's what they said, that the skin and flesh was like lard and they couldn't prick it.

" 'Well, last month when going to bed, Monsieur banged himself on a piece of furniture, and the skin broke and all the water he had inside him poured out. The doctors said 'Well, fancy that!' and they were surprised and since then they have pricked him. They said : 'Let's imitate nature.' But then there was an abcess on his leg and Monsieur Roux operated. The appliance was taken off yesterday and the sore, instead of running, was all red dry and afire. So they said : "He's finished' and they never came back. We went to get four or five other doctors but to no avail. They all said : 'There is nothing to be done.' Last night was a bad night and today at nine o'clock Monsieur couldn't speak any more. Madame went to get a priest who gave him extreme unction, and Monsieur gave a sign that he understood. An hour later he shook hands with his sister, Madame de Surville. Since eleven o'clock he has been rattling and sees nothing. He won't get through the night. If you wish, Monsieur, I can go and fetch Monsieur de Surville who is still up.'

"The woman left me and I waited a few moments. The candle hardly gave any light to the splendid drawing room furniture and the magnificent Porbus and Holbein paintings on the walls. The marble bust stood out vaguely in the shadow like the ghost of the man who was dying. The odour of a body filled the house.

"Monsieur de Surville came in and confirmed everything the servant told me and I asked to see Monsieur de Balzac. We crossed a corridor, went up a staircase laid with a red carpet and cluttered with *objets d'arts*, vases, statues, paintings and credence tables bearing enamel objects, then along another corridor and I saw an open door. I heard a high sinister rattle, and I was in Balzac's room."

Hugo went on : "In the centre of the room was a bed of mahogany with, from top to bottom, a whole series of cross pieces and belts giving hint of an appliance for moving the patient. In this bed lay Balzac, his head on a stack of pillows and red damask cushions taken from the sofa in the room. His face was purple, almost black, tilted to the right, unshaven, hair grey and short. He had a fixed stare. I first saw him in profile and he looked like the emperor.

"An old woman, the nurse, and a servant stood upright beside the bed, and a candle burned behind on a table, another on a chest of drawers next to the door. A silver vase stood on the night table. The man and woman were silent and with a kind of terror listened to the dying man's noisy rattle.

"The bedside candle near the chimney brightly illuminated the portrait of a man who was young, red-faced and smiling. An unbearable smell rose from the bed and I raised the covers taking Balzac's hand which was covered in sweat. I pressed it. He did not reply to the pressure.

"This was the same bedroom where I had come to see him a month earlier. Then, he had been gay, full of spirits and in no doubt that he would get well, showing off his swelling with a laugh. We had discussed and argued politics at length, he reproaching me for my demagogy, he being a legitimist. He said to me : 'How could you so serenely give up your title of Peer of France, the next best to king of France ?'

"He also said : 'I have the house of Monsieur de Beaujon, except for the garden, but with the balcony facing the church on the corner. On the stairs I have a doorway into the church. A turn of the key and I'm at Mass. I think more of that balcony than the garden.'

"When I left him he showed me to that stairway, walking with effort, and pointed out the door shouting out to his wife : 'Be sure you show all my paintings to Hugo.'

"The nurse declared : 'He'll die at daybreak.' I went down again taking with me an image of that livid face. As I crossed the drawing room, I saw again the immobile bust, inscrutable, haughty and vaguely radiating, and I compared death with immortality."

34. At this home in Rue Basse, Balzac could work in peace. His house had two exits, one opening on the garden, so that he could easily outwit his creditors.

35 to 39. *Contemporary figures showing characters in his work "La Comédie humaine".*
Théophile Gautier wrote: "Although it seems odd to say it in this nineteenth century, Balzac was a clairvoyant. His gifts as an observer, his perspicacity as a physiologist and his writing genius do not suffice to explain the infinite variety of the two thousand or three thousand types playing a more or less major role in "La Comédie humaine". He did not copy them but lived them, wore their clothes, took on their mannerisms...

36

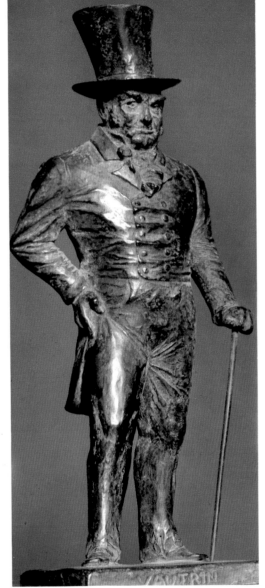

35

37

38

39

40. *It was on this table in his house in Passy that Balzac wrote "La Comédie" humaine. He drew his characters from life, wandering all day in the streets, sometimes following someone whom he had seen as a type for this great work. In the evening, he would return to Rue Basse to record the details of his character's behaviour.*

41. *The Castle of Saché was also a home to Balzac. In 1831, he wrote to a friend: "I live under the severest of despotisms—that which one imposes on oneself. I have come here to seek refuge in a castle as in a monastery."*

42. *The* salon *at Saché remains as it was in Balzac's day, with its Restoration draperies and its light-toned furniture. It is a very rare example of the French romantic style. It was on the flowered settee that Monsieur de Margonne bounced little Honoré on his knees. Later in this same* salon, *the youthful Balzac read his first works to the gentry from local castles.*

42

46

46. *Balzac at twenty years.* △   47. *Balzac at thirty years.* ▽

44. *At twenty years of age Balzac fell in love with Laure de Berny who was forty-three. After her death in 1831, love for him became the quest for the unttainable. While thinking of her he wrote in "La Duchesse de Langeais": "Only the last love of a woman can crown the first love of a man."*

47

45. *Evelyn Hanska, Countess of Wierzschownia, wrote to him her first letter as an admirer on February 28, 1832. He met her in 1833 in her garden at Neuchâtel, but it was ten years before Count Hanski died and another seven before Balzac could persuade the countess, who was horrified by his debts, to wed him in the Ukraine on March 14, 1850.*

48. *Balzac on his deathbed.*

◁ 43. *In this bedroom at the Castle of Saché, Balzac wrote "Louis Lambert", "Séraphita" and "Le Lys dans la vallée".*

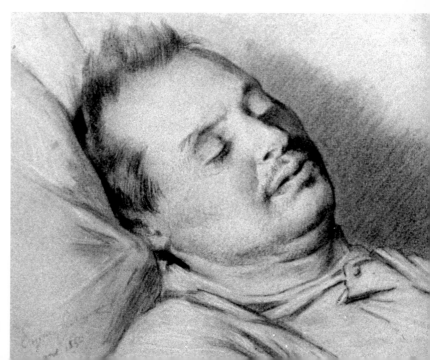

48

Baudelaire

from the Hôtel Lauzun to the Hôtel du Grand Miroir

Once a private home, the Hotel Lauzun at 17 Quai d'Anjou, Paris, is the splendid achievement of Louis Le Vau. Its architectural style reflects the seventeenth century's love of power and grandeur. It was there that, two centuries later, Charles Baudelaire was to write *Les Fleurs du mal*.

When Baudelaire went to live there in 1843, he is believed by Asselineau to have occupied a three-room attic overlooking the Seine. The proprietor, Baron Pichon, allowed him to use one of his very fine panelled drawing rooms, with windows looking out onto the Quai d'Anjou. Gautier turned it into the "Haschischins Club" which was frequented by several writers and painters including Daumier, Constantin Guys and Manet—all young men like Baudelaire, who was but twenty-four at the time. Baudelaire also met Balzac in this gracious *salon*, with its woodwork set off with dull gold and with paintings of nymphs by some pupil of Le Sueur or Poussin. On the marble mantle stood a golden elephant bearing a battle tower and incorporating a clock dial. The armchairs and sofas were in old-fashioned style. There was much talk of the effects of hashish. Baudelaire tells us how Balzac used to listen and ask questions with attention and an amusing vivacity. As a result people supposed that he must be interested until his reactions proved otherwise.

"He was given" says Baudelaire, "some hashish and he examined it, sniffed it and gave it back without touching it. The struggle between his almost childish curiosity and his repugnance to surrender showed on his expressive face in a striking way. The love of dignity won through."

A strange meeting it was in this residence which Lauzun had bought from a wealthy tavern-keeper's son in the seventeenth century—the two greatest poets of the nineteenth century consulting on something that is for ever topical: the faculty of dreaming. This was Baudelaire's happy phase. Though little published as yet, he was already well-known by his elders and a familiar figure in editorial rooms and studios. Soon Gautier was to take umbrage at this and the two men heartily detested each other from then on. We know now that Gautier, to whom *Les Fleurs du mal* is dedicated, did not bother to go to Baudelaire's funeral and that his absence was regarded as scandalous. On the other hand, Baudelaire did write that Gautier was "just a stringer together of words". The young dilettante cared little for the views of professional men of letters, and hated writing as a "trade". During his Hôtel de Pimodan days, poetry was for him only a means of perfecting the dandy he wanted to be. It was an aspect of his elegance, like copying the blue frock-coat with silver buttons that Goethe had, or taking as his mistress "that strange deity, brown as the night" whom he invited to bathe

59

in the Seine, before the horrified eyes of Baron Pichon.

His philosophy then was that of a rich young man about town. He had just returned from a visit to Mauritius, arranged by his family to make him meditate, and had also received his share of his father's inheritance, which was enough to enable him to play the dandy. According to his ideal "the idle rich man, even if *blasé*, should have no other occupation than the pursuit of happiness; he who is raised in luxury... has no other profession but elegance..."

But his way of enjoying this "high life" was decidedly rowdy and Baron Pichon could not cope with it. One day he asked his tenant to make less noise "in this respectable building".

Baudelaire replied: "I do in my own home only what all respectable people do in theirs."

Pichon replied: "But we can hear furniture being moved, people hitting the floor and shouts at all hours of the day, and night."

"I can assure you, Sir, that nothing extraordinary is going on. I chop my wood in the *salon*, and drag my mistress around by her hair like everybody else..."

The celebrated photographer Nadar wrote of him: "Monsieur Baudelaire wore pink gloves and walked in jerks as do little wooden actors, seeming to choose the precise spot for each step, as if he was walking between eggs."

His apartment at the Quai d'Anjou, rented at 350 francs a year, comprised two rooms and a toilet. The main room served as a bedroom and study. The walls and ceiling had red and black wallpaper on them and the room possessed only one window whose glass was only partly cleaned "so as to reveal only the sky". Between the bed alcove and the chimney was a portrait of the poet by E. Deroy and above the divan, which was perpetually loaded with books, was a copy of Delacroix's *Femmes d'Alger*.

Baudelaire's stay in this apartment left its mark on his whole life. In order to furnish the place he contracted debts. He was not content to furnish the rooms once, but would seek out antique dealers, select his treasures, move the new acquisitions in and the old things out. His family alarmed at his behaviour, put him under the supervision of a lawyer and he suffered from this humiliation forever after. In order to cast off the insult and to prove his genius to the family, he made a bid to become a member of the Académie and to obtain the *Légion d'Honneur*. But he was forced to give up this approach, and use his literary gifts as means of making a living. His profits were always abysmally low. Twenty years later he and Catulle Mendès calculated that with his poems, translations and articles he had earned 1.70 francs a day on average.

On top of his debts and the bother of the legal business, he had another worry in the form of a venereal disease that never really cleared up. This was too much for the dilettante who had rented an apartment at the Hôtel de Pimodan because he could live only in the midst of beauty, fine things, calm and pleasure. One day in 1845 despair overcame him and he tried to kill himself with a knife. He had earlier written that suicide was "the only sacrament in the religion of the dandy".

After this incident, he spent a while at the Hôtel de la Place de Paris, in the Place Vendôme, where his mother was living with his stepfather, Général Aupic, military governor of Paris.

When Baudelaire moved out from the two-room apartment he loved so much, he had completed the main poems in the first edition of *Les Fleurs du mal*. In 1848, the discovery of Poe led him to new inspiration, but his works thereafter never possessed such intensity as the poems composed at the Quai d'Anjou. Baudelaire the dandy was dead, at least a certain kind of dandy. Some believe that the new man with his tight mouth, sack-like overblouse and large shoes was another kind of dandy, and it was said he slept on public benches. In fact, it is known he rented a room in a modest hotel in the Rue des Mathurins-Saint-Jacques (now Rue du Sommerard). There he stayed for the rest of his days, a prey to what he termed "the great malady of horror of the domicile".

60

He would wander around, going along one street and then another, as chance led him. If he saw a cat meditating on a window ledge, "in the noble attitude of the great sphinxes stretched out in the depths of solitude", he would stroke it and magnetize it, so to speak, with his look.

To his mother in 1852 he wrote : "Sometimes I leave my place so I can write, and I go to the library or reading room, or to a wineseller's or a café, like today."

He would read his verses to his friends in a café in the Rue Saint-André-des-Arts or the Rue Dauphine.

Later, under Napoleon III, when he "looked less like a poet of bitter pleasures than like a priest of Saint-Sulpice", according to one person who caught sight of him, he went to the Madrid or the Café Dagneaux, the Café Riche or Café de Robespierre near the Italian Theatre. There he would sit alone, drinking a beer or smoking a pipe. He would smoke away without saying a word all evening. In *Mon cœur mis à nu* he wrote the phrase : "Feeling of solitude from my childhood up. Feeling of a destiny forever solitary." Neither love nor art could cure him of this feeling which struck him after his mother's second marriage to Général Aupic.

At all times his appearance astonished those who met him. Their observations, taken in sequence, read like the pictures in a film of his life at various stages :

1840-41 (19-20 years of age) : "Not one crease in his extraordinary clothes. A black suit, always the same one, at any hour or season ; a long waistcoat buttoned high up, ruffled cuffs, his trousers corkscrewing onto shoes of irreproachable lustre", (Charles Cousin).

"Thin, an open neck, a very long waistcoat, a light cane with a golden knob in his hand ; a supple tread, almost rythmic... His face a little yellow, and with a light beard", (Ernest Prarond).

1843 : "Medium height, entirely in black, except for the bull blood cravat, clothing unusually free from the body, with very small flares cut on the bias. Linen very white. In his pink gloved hand he carried a hat, superfluous by reason of the overabundance of pitch-black curled hair that fell onto his shoulders", (Nadar).

1844-45 (aged 23-24) : "Hair cut very close and beautifully black with ends falling over a forehead of striking whiteness ; his eyes the colour of Spanish tobacco, and a look that was perhaps too insistent, very white teeth, silky moustache, black blouse, nut-coloured trousers, white stockings and shiny shoes, the whole being meticulously clean," (Gautier).

1848 : "His hair practically shaved off, lip sly and sensual. A haunting worry about his hands seemed to claim him during the meal. He did not gesticulate at all while speaking and cleaned his nails. He wore a wide waistless blouse. Nothing to indicate the concern over dress which the legend of his youth recounted", (Charles Bataille, in *Le Charivari*, 1867).

1852 (aged 31) : "His suit was of heavy material ; a madras handkerchief held together the neck of his shirt which was in a cloth so heavy that it seemed natural-coloured... His blouse was like a sack, hair cut very short, clean-shaven, smiling but little", (Maxime Du Camp).

1857 (aged 36, having supper at the Café Riche) : "With no cravat and the neck bare, head shaved, dressed up as if for the guillotine... Small hands carefully looked after like a woman's and with it all, a maniac's head, a sharp voice like steel and his diction aiming at the decorated precision of a Saint-Just", (Goncourt).

1867 (year of his death, aged 46) : "The collar of his greatcoat was invariably turned up. Two eyes you could never forget, like drops of coffee. Lips tight and bitter, evil looking, and hair silver before its time... A face that was hairless, clerically shaven", (Nadar).

"His face had worn thin and become as if spiritualized ; his eyes seemed bigger. He had fine, silky, long hair, thinning out and nearly all white. An almost priestly look", (Gautier).

Baudelaire moved from hotel to hotel with "horror of the domicile" until he finished up in 1864 during a Belgian lecture tour, at the

Hôtel du Grand Miroir in Brussels. Also there were his friend the art critic Arthur Stevens, his publisher Poulet-Malassis (also known as the Perching Parrot) and his mother. The publisher had been ruined by the condemnation of *Les Fleurs du mal* and had just done six months in prison.

On the second floor of a steep narrow staircase, with steps in varnished yellow, Baudelaire's room was furnished in mediocre style. It contained a bed in artificial mahogany with a green eiderdown, a wardrobe, a chest of drawers, a threadbare sofa and a table against the wall. It was in this room that he would have his last experience of an abyss before him and would reel about and clutch in support at the furniture. We know that this must have been a frequent experience for he made eighteen separate references to it in *Les Fleurs du mal*. One of them reads : "Pascal had his abyss moving about with him..."

Baudelaire gave five lectures : one on Delacroix, one on Théophile Gautier and three on stimulants. In his thin, biting, high-pitched voice he spoke seated at a table in the middle of a platform. His smooth, pale face looked out over a white cravat. He was forty-three and had a crown of white hair. He spoke to almost empty halls that emptied even further as he spoke. He would thank those who remained, three times, and then go back to his hotel.

The trials of Baudelaire as an orator were to last more than two years. At the end of March 1866 he lost the power of speech, and therewith the lectures came to an end. He uttered only one more word : "crénom" (shortened form of "sacré nom de Dieu") which alarmed the nursing nuns at the Institut Saint-Jean et Sainte-Elisabeth where Arthur Stevens had him taken pending arrival of his mother. The correspondence of the Stevens brothers, Arthur, Alfred and Joseph, gives us an insight into Baudelaire's final homes : a clinic and a cemetery.

On April 1, 1866, Arthur Stevens wrote : "I have just taken poor Baudelaire into a hospice (not a hospital). He is lost. I have looked after him and watched him like a mother. I

had to write to his family, get a nun, send messages, find doctors, be present at the operations, find out where to take him and not leave him for a single minute."

In July, 1866, his mother took him back to Paris. After his departure from the Institut Saint-Jean, the nuns had an exorcist in to clean up his room. He would have liked to have known that !

At forty-six, his features were hollow, his hair white, and his paralysis had given him the look of an old man. On August 31, 1867, he died in a clinic at Chaillot.

The burial was on September 3. It was attended by about 100 people who accompanied the body to the Saint-Honoré Chapel, Place d'Eylau, opposite the Hippodrome. Under a cloudy sky, some went as far as Montparnasse cemetery. A peal of thunder broke out as the cortège entered.

Joseph Stevens, present at the internment, gave his impressions to his brother Alfred on the poet's arrival at his last resting place. The letter is missing to posterity but Alfred's reply included the passage : "The incident you relate to me, and the entry of Baudelaire's body into the cemetery, with his coffin battered by the wind and covered in leaves falling down from the trees, have deeply affected me. Like you, I see great poetry in it and I am certain that Baudelaire would not have desired a better arrival at death's door. How like him ; this burial suited a poet, and it was not like anyone else's. From that point of view, Baudelaire would have been satisfied."

We can perhaps take from *Mon cœur mis à nu* this proud epitaph : "I have cultivated my hysteria with enjoyment and terror." The marble stone on the ground where Baudelaire now lies with his mother and step-father, Général Aupic, is dedicated to the glory of the General ! : "Former ambassador, member of the Nord Département General Council, Grand Officer of the Imperial Order, of the *Légion d'Honneur*, decorated with several foreign orders." If Charles Baudelaire could read that "poetry", he would perhaps regret having written : "France has a horror of poetry."

50. The balcony of the Lauzun Hôtel, 17, Quai d'Anjou, Paris, looks out on the Seine River. It was in this old private house that Baudelaire wrote the first poems in "Les Fleurs du mal".

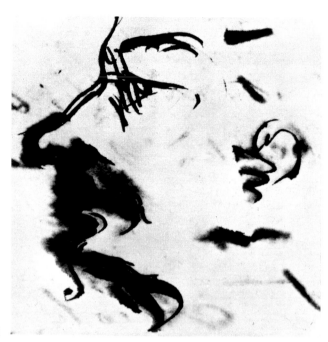

51. Baudelaire, as drawn by himself.

52. Jeanne Duval, "the strange goddess, brown as the night".

53. Théophile Gautier, as seen by his neighbour, Baudelaire.

54. Inner courtyard of the Lauzun Hotel, reflects the ▷ graceful architecture of the seventeenth century.

55. "In July, Baudelaire's mother, who took over from Ancelle at his bedside, brought him back to Paris. 'He got out at the Gare du Nord', wrote Asselineau, 'assisted by Arthur Stevens, supported at his left arm and carrying his stick hooked in a coat button'. One can imagine the crowd keeping clear of this lurching man, like passengers on a South Sea liner used to do at the spectacle of the albatross, but nobody laughed." ("Baudelaire" by Antoine Blondin, Réalités, September 1861.)

57

55

◁ *Through Arthur Stevens, art critic and collector and friend of Baudelaire, we know something of the last period in the poet's life. Baudelaire wrote about him to the minister of fine arts that "his intro-* duction to the collectors would be facilitated through a person whose profession and contacts enabled him to bring out the value that few people see". Arthur Stevens even acted as his secretary (Claude Pichois).

56

△ 56. Baudelaire at his life's end.

◁ 58. Poulet-Malassis published "Les Fleurs du mal". A verdict condemning the book led him to ruin and prison for debt.

58

59. It was in this elegant panelled room, in the Lauzun Hotel, that Gautier started the "Club des Haschischins". This drug-taking fraternity included Baudelaire, Daumier, Constantin Guys and Manet who were all young men with him.

◁ 57. The Hôtel du Grand Miroir, Brussels, where Arthur Stevens lived. He also took rooms for Baudelaire and his publisher Poulet-Malassis.

60. On Beethoven's desk at Moedning is a portrait of
Marie Pachler Koschak who inspired him in his later years.

Beethoven

at Gneixendorf

Ludwig van Beethoven lived in Vienna for thirty years, in no fewer than thirty-five homes. In other words, he spent his time moving about everywhere and never became attached to any one residence.

It was fifty miles from Vienna, however, that he spent the most moving and pathetic hours of his life, in his brother Johann's house at Gneixendorf.

Beethoven and his nephew Karl, his adopted son, arrived there on September 30, 1826. Johann van Beethoven had gone to fetch them in Vienna and handed them over to his wife. A dramatic situation that had been developing for more than ten years between uncle and nephew had just resulted in a suicide attempt by the young man.

Beethoven went to collect Karl from the hospital, and after returning to his uncle's house, Karl decided he would join the army. "Where can I go with him until he leaves?" Beethoven wrote. "I could take him to Stutterterheim's place but he would have to have his hair cut before leaving." A rather strange preoccupation over this nineteen-year-old boy on the part of the choleric genius, then aged fifty-six.

Karl had been preparing for exams at the Polytechnic Institute before the suicide attempt. He could no longer stand his uncle who made him go around with him everywhere to make sure he did not frequent the cafés, or see his mother or meet a friend of whom he was jeal-ous. On July 31, Karl went to the ruins of Rauhenstein near Baden and fired two bullets at his head. One missed but the other entered his skull. A carter found him on a rock and took him bleeding to his mother, who informed Beethoven. It was at this time that Johann invited them both to come to Gneixendorf.

At first Ludwig would not go to Johann's house. Johann in a second invitation signed himself "Johann van Beethoven, real estate owner" to which the composer replied "Ludwig van Beethoven, brain owner." Finally, he relent-ed and in the country house at Gneixendorf, Karl and Ludwig seemed to regain a certain confidence in life.

The passionate music of Beethoven evokes dreams in many women. But those he loved turned him away while those who gave them-selves to him failed to give him any satisfac-tion. Historians who have turned him into a romantic lover have embroidered the facts to suit themselves. Stress has been laid on his despair as a lover. His platonic attachments have been emphasized. But in reality the details of his love life are too little known for any defi-nite conclusions to be drawn. Beethoven spoke only indirectly of the women he loved. The supposed portraits of Teresa von Brunswick and the letter "To the immortal beloved" (thought to mean the singer Amalia Sebald) found in a drawer after his death have led to major impor-tance being attributed to these women. Who were they really ? Biographers are not even sure they have been correctly identified. On the other hand, through Beethoven's "conversation books" (he was deaf at an early age) we are learning more all the time of his nephew's importance in his life.

This relationship began on November 22, 1815, when a court judgment gave Ludwig van Beethoven sole guardianship of Karl, who was then nine years of age.

On his death bed, in a weird piece of bargaining, the elder Karl van Beethoven had granted Ludwig this tutelage in exchange for the anulment of a debt he could not pay back. Later his written will modified this agreement. Although he had assured Ludwig he would be the sole tutor of his son, he gave the mother back her rights by means of the will. So Beethoven went to court to confirm his rights. In order to win the case, Beethoven did not hesitate to call his sister-in-law a prostitute and therefore unfit to raise the boy.

Young Karl was definitively given over to Ludwig under the court ruling. But the uncle could never make the child forget his mother, unworthy though she might be, nor the dreadful rows during and after the case.

For Beethoven, Karl apparently replaced all other love. According to friends, even when he lodged the claim to his tutelage, Beethoven had already lost all interest in women and given up any idea of marriage. He had gone through eventful love affairs : some people have subsequently wanted to picture him as some kind of angel, although in fact he spent all his time in the company of women, some of whose names are known to us. A friend wrote : " At Vienna, at least as long as I lived there, Beethoven was always having some love affair. During this time he made conquests that would have been very difficult, if not impossible, for men like Adonis." Beethoven loved often, but "never more than seven months," as he himself said.

Beethoven's love for Amalia Sebald, the young singer he met at Töplitz, "the immortal beloved", has led certain romantic historians to give us an idealistic view of the composer. Ludwig wrote to her on one occasion :

"My angel, my all, my 'me'. Just a few words today and with a pencil only—yours. My lodgings will not be fixed until tomorrow ; what a wretched long time for such things ! But why this deep sorrow when necessity speaks ? Can our love exist otherwise than through sacrifices, through the need to avoid demanding everything ? Can you do other than be wholly mine and I wholly yours ? Oh, God. Contemplate beautiful nature and set your soul at rest over what should be. Love demands all and rightly so. So it is with me toward you, you to me. But you forget so lightly that you must live for me and I for you ; if we were wholly united, you would feel this suffering as little as I do...

"No doubt we shall see each other again soon. So today I can relate to you only some observations that I have made about my life over the last few days. If our hearts were always close one to the other, I would not tell you. My heart is too full to be able to tell you anything. Ah, there are times when I find words are still nothing; cheer up, stay faithful to me, my only treasure, my all, as I am to you. As to the rest, the gods will decide what should be and what should become of us."

"Your faithful LUDWIG."

Another time he wrote :

"In bed my thoughts hurry already toward you, my immortal beloved. Sometimes they are joyful, then once again sad, awaiting for destiny to answer us. Live, I cannot, because whether entirely with you or completely apart, I have resolved to wander far, until the day when I can fly into your arms and can say I am completely in my homeland. Then, near you, I can plunge my soul with you into the kingdom of the spirits. Yes, alas, it must be. You will recover much better, the more you know my faithfulness toward you. Never will any other possess my heart, never, never. Oh God, why must I be apart from what I love so, even though my life in Vienna is a wretched one. Your love has made of me the happiest and the most miserable of men. At my age now, I require a certain steadiness. Can a regular life exist with our relationship ?... Only by a calm contemplation of our being can we arrive at our object, to live together. Be calm, love me, today, yesterday. What aspiration bathed in tears, with you, you, you, my life, my all! Adieu. Oh, continue to love me. I never repudiate a faithful heart. From your loving L. Eternally to you, eternally to me, eternally to us."

Another beloved was his pupil Giuletta Guicciardi. It was for her he composed the *Moonlight Sonata*. He loved her and asked her to marry him. She preferred someone else.

Beethoven was a demanding and tyrannical personality. He revealed this to Amalia Sebald. With his brothers he was authoritarian. He intervened to oblige Johann at the age of thirty-five to break off a relationship; he even went so far as to denounce him to the bishop and civic authorities, who then told his mistress to quit the town within a short time limit. A row followed among the brothers, but Johann married his mistress before the time limit was up and Ludwig returned to Vienna to finish his eighth symphony. He got on no better with his other brother, Karl. Ludwig was very disorganized and lived in fear that someone would steal his manuscripts. He gave them to Karl to look after and then called him a thief.

The disorder in which he lived struck everyone who called on him. His room was "strewn with papers and clothes everywhere, a few trunks; there were empty walls, no chairs to sit on apart from the rickety one in front of the Walter piano (one of the best available at that time)," as one of his pupils wrote in 1800.

In the course of his constant moving, he lost his musical scores, and claimed his friends or his servants had them. He moved practically every year.

Another account tells us that owing to his sloppy dressing habits, the appearance of Beethoven in the street caused considerable surprise. "He gesticulated... spoke loudly. The persons he was with had to write things down in a 'conversation book'." Urchins used to shout after him. For this reason his nephew Karl detested going out with him.

Fear of dying of consumption like his mother obsessed him. When he coughed, he spat into a handkerchief to see if he was coughing blood, a habit which was embarrassing to those who were with him. In fact he did have consumption and several times spat blood.

Ludwig van Beethoven was sometimes called "the Spaniard" because of his dark skin. He was small, with an ugly red face marked with smallpox. His brown hair was stringy. He spoke in dialect using vulgar expressions. After he became deaf he completely disregarded others, walking straight ahead in the street in his carelessly buttoned, worn-cut coats. His hands were very strong, the young Karl Czerny noticed, covered with hair, and his fingers very flat, especially at the ends. From adolescence, he had poor vision which he corrected with highly concave lenses. Bettina Brentano commented that people had to be very careful not to upset him.

The adopted son Karl had to bear the whole weight of his character. Relations between them were not made any easier by the fact that Beethoven had to be spoken to in writing. He was strict with his beloved nephew and severe even about small faults. He moved him from schools because he had bad reports. Above all, he could not bear to let Karl see his mother, and his jealousy went as far as moral torture. Karl has often been accused of lacking gratitude. But Karl had an extremely difficult life, caught up between a mother who wanted him to go back and live with her but who no longer had the legal right to have him back, and a foster father who would not even allow him to receive a new hat as a present from her. Several times, Karl mentioned suicide as the only way out of this situation. Beethoven took away Karl's two pistols when he learned of this, but the boy pawned his watch to get some more. When he did finally attempt to kill himself, the hospital managed to extract the bullet. During convalescence, Karl applied to become an army cadet, not wishing to live with his uncle any longer. Beethoven, on first learning of the suicide bid, was seized with fury at the disgrace of it. At the time, suicide attempts were punishable by a term of prison. But Beethoven himself had contemplated suicide in 1797 when he first started becoming deaf at the age of twenty-five and at the outset of his career. Karl evidently did not have the spiritual bounce of his foster father.

Beethoven had unconsciously pushed Karl into the act of attempted suicide. The boy had become gradually alone because of Beethoven's overwhelming affection. One Sunday when Karl failed to visit him, the composer wrote: "Must I therefore experience monstrous ingratitude? No. If the relationship between us is to be broken off, let it be. But you will be hated by all those who hear about such ingratitude..."

When his initial anger died down, Beethoven was overcome by despondency. He had grown incapable of living without Karl. Most of all he was afraid he would go back to his mother when he left hospital. "He hates me," he said. His friend Holz told him: "It is not hate he feels toward you but a totally different sentiment." But Beethoven had lost Karl and he knew it.

The period of the adoption lasted from 1815 to 1827 and corresponded in time with the third phase of Beethoven's musical life. During these twelve years he produced several of his greatest works, the mature ones: the *Ninth Symphony in D minor* opus 125 (1823), and the *Quartets* (1824 to 1827). He planned a tenth symphony, hoping to find at Gneixendorf the time and spiritual calm needed to compose it. He found there only the cares of a frustrated father.

Even so it was in that house that he wrote his last quartets. In the *lento* of the sixteenth quartet, which he called "soft song of repose and peace", one can read *"Muss es sein?"* "Must it be?" and the reply: "Yes, it must." His friend Maurice Schesinger had a letter from him which clarifies the sense of this reply: "You can tell by the 'Yes, it must' that I am an unhappy man. It was hard for me to write that because I was thinking of something else much greater. I wrote only that, because I promised it to you and had need of money; it came to me with difficulty..." All these expla-

nations leave plenty of mysteries. What did Beethoven mean? He was referring to the final quartet, dated October 30, 1826, at Gneixendorf. Would he have preferred to write the tenth symphony? Was he tired of living with his brother? Was he tormented over Karl's return? The final *allegro* of this *sixteenth quartet* is very gay, but sometimes works do not accord with life itself.

At Gneixendorf, Beethoven complains about everything. Two weeks after he got there, the following appeared in his "conversation book": "You see I am now at Gneixendorf. This word sounds a little like a breaking axle. The air is good. As to the rest, one ought to recite the *Memento mori*..." And again: "No decent beef and we even have to eat goose. May heaven help my hunger."

Beethoven's life in Vienna, however, could hardly have been much better in its daily round than that at Gneixendorf. This man of such liberal ideas could not bear any servants for long. The least mistake was a pretext for dismissal, or even accusations of theft. At Gneixendorf, the fact of living with the family and realizing that these were his last days with Karl exasperated the niggardly and highly-sensitive genius, and he became difficult to live with. His stay in this fine residence lasted only one autumn from the gathering of the grapes to the bad weather. He could have been happy there. The house is full of charms with its romantic wallpapers, its light-wood Biedermeier-style furniture, lace curtains, huge lamps, windows crowded with flowers, pottery and flowery carpets. Ludwig, however, was wrestling all the time with his music and quibbling with the servants who looked after his room. An eye-witness Dr Lorenz wrote: "At first the cook used to make Beethoven's bed. One day he started waving his hands, beating time with his foot and singing and humming. This made the cook laugh, and Beethoven suddenly spun round, chasing her from the room without further ado. Another servant, Michael, wanted to run after her, but Beethoven held him back, gave him three twenty-kreutzer pieces, told him there was nothing to fear and that he would make his bed every day and clean his room."

He continued : "Beethoven rose daily at half past six and at half-past seven breakfast was served. Afterwards Beethoven would go for a walk in the country. He strode about the fields, shouted, waved his hands, walked slowly, then very fast, then suddenly stopped and wrote something in a note book. At noon he came back for lunch and stayed until three o'clock. Then he went out again into the fields until nightfall. He would write up to ten o'clock and then go to bed. Sometimes he played the piano in the drawing room."

Nobody but Michael was allowed in his room. When Michael found any money on the floor, he had to give explanations to Beethoven who asked him where he got it. He also asked him what had been said at table that he had not been able to hear. One day Michael lost some money the lady of the house gave him to buy some fish. He was sacked. But Beethoven reimbursed the missing money and insisted that Frau van Beethoven took back Michael. He said he wanted to take him back to Vienna as his servant. In fact, he took back a new woman cook instead of Michael.

In this way, domestic cares overshadowed an otherwise tranquil life at Gneixendorf. As at Nohant, where kitchen dramas drove a wedge between Chopin and George Sand, so at Gneixendorf they brought to an end the cordiality of the early days. Beethoven became subject to increasing peculiar moods. His deafness, the life of the recluse, and his hereditary traits did nothing to help matters.

Was heredity the cause of his instability? The death of his father, it was said, amounted merely to "a loss of tax on drink". His was a Flemish family that took up residence in Bonn in 1732, and contained musicians and drunkards in equal numbers. Beethoven the father, a candle seller, married a German, "a quiet woman but given to the bottle" who died in a tuberculosis sanatorium. Their son Ludwig was only ten when his grandfather died in 1773.

Beethoven's father had been born in 1740 and was master of a chapel ; when his wife died he started drinking. Ludwig, the oldest son, had to bring up his brothers. Beethoven's father, before becoming an alcoholic, had detected his son's gifts before he was even three years old. When he was eight, his father showed him off with the idea of turning him into a precocious genius like Mozart, whose image haunted him. Sometimes late at night he came back home drunk with Ludwig's music teacher and the two men made him get up and play the piano for several hours on end. The boy wept but the hard masters kept him at it.

This unhappy childhood and the hereditary factor doubtless led to the deafness of Beethoven and to his violent character causing him to become excited and petty. Added to which at the University in 1769 he met the extraordinary person of Euloge Schneider, who became guide to his thoughts. This unfrocked monk, seething with revolutionary ideas, was later to be a public prosecutor but would himself be denounced by Saint-Just for his behaviour and guillotined in 1794.

Liberal-minded and tyrannical at the same time, Beethoven cared nothing for the friendship and assistance of the Viennese aristocracy which admired him. He reproached Goethe for being a poet for princes. Despite his generous feelings, Beethoven could never be the liberal-minded father he dreamed of being to Karl. All he did was lead him to attempted suicide.

Beethoven's friend Schindler collected 400 "conversation books" of the composer, but burned more than half of them. What did he wish to hide ? Possibly some details that tarnished the image of the great man. In the nineteenth century it was unthinkable that a great figure should be subject to little foibles. That would have destroyed the legend of him ; diminished his genius in some way, so much was art linked to morals in those days. That Beethoven when at Gneixendorf stopped Karl playing piano duets with his aunt is no surprise to us. Ludwig could not bear that between Karl and him there should intervene either Karl's mother or Johann's wife. This desire to be the sole dominating influence and purveyor of tenderness for Karl led him to start negotiating with Johann, with the idea that he should cut his wife off

73

with nothing and give his inheritance over to Karl. This development in the nature of Beethoven may be explained by the many disappointments in his life. The outcome was that if Karl resisted him, he simply wanted to crush him.

The Gneixendorf "conversation books" show only Karl's remarks to Beethoven:

"Why did you make such a fuss today? Could you not let me go now? I need to relax and will come back later."

"I just want to go to my room."

"I am not going out, but I want to be alone a bit. Will you let me now go to my room?"

Life became impossible in this house where jealousy and love destroyed everything. Johann ended up by sending away Ludwig and Karl. Beethoven said: "But where shall I go with him?" In the end they left in a milk cart for Vienna on December 7, 1826, in the pouring rain. When they completed the fifty-mile journey, Ludwig had to go to bed with double pneumonia, and Karl stayed to look after him. He was a hard patient and his death was the denouement of the psychological dramas of Gneixendorf. Without this forced departure Beethoven would certainly have lived longer.

In the days following their return to Vienna, Karl said to Beethoven (through the "conversation book"): "Must I for the thousandth time protest that I shall never abandon you? Do not so many ties of affection and gratitude make me attached to you? Do not perpetually listen to ordinary people just because they seem to be right."

Beethoven apparently rallied from the pneumonia, and he was thought to be on the road to recovery. But a pleurisy complication set in, coupled with jaundice, and his body became swollen with oedema.

On January 2, Karl joined his regiment at Iglau. On January 3, 1827, Beethoven made him his full legal heir and instructed his new tutor Breuning to look after him. Henceforth he seems not to have worried about his nephew, and he composed no more music. He fought illness all the time as it gained headway daily. Karl did not write often. Did he know about his foster father's real condition?

Thus the house at Gneixendorf was but the décor to the final tragic act of the adoption story. The composer died on March 27, 1827, with a few friends at his side. At the moment of death a storm broke out and a streak of light flashed across the room. Beethoven's reaction was to throw his fist into the air, after which he collapsed and died, while the thunder growled on.

Some 20,000 people attended his funeral. The hearse was drawn by four horses. Musicians, one of whom was Schubert, bore torches. But Karl was not there.

Next pages:
62. Beethoven composed the "Kreutzer Sonata" on this piano in Bonn. On the wall is a portrait of the Elector of Cologne.

63. It was in this room at Gneixendorf near Vienna, in his brother's home, that he wrote his last works, the final quartets.

61. Beethoven used to spend summer ▷ in the country, here at Moedning where his "Missa Solemnis" was written.

64. *This drawing room in Johann van Beethoven's Gneixendorf house was the background to the final scenes between Beethoven and his adopted nephew Karl. They were played out in front of servants and family and the two were forced to return to Vienna. Beethoven caught cold during the journey and died shortly afterwards.*

65

65. *Josephine von Brunswick, Beethoven's pupil in spring 1799, became Countess Deym in the summer. She is believed to have been "the immortal beloved".*

67

66. *Beethoven as a young man.*

69. *Theresa Malfatti, Beethoven new love, also declined to wed hir He wrote: "Poor Beethoven! The is no outside love for you; it is yo who must create everything insid yourself; you will find friends on in an idealized world."*

◁ 67. *Theresa von Brunswick, Josephine's sister, also loved Beethoven and said that one evening in spring 1806 he asked her to wed him.*

70

70. *Karl van Beethoven, the composer's nephew, was adopted by Beethoven in 1815 when his brother died. Loving him despotically, he brought sorrow on himself and the boy. Karl tried to kill himself to escape the tirades of his foster father. Beethoven never got over this.*

71. *Beethoven's death mask. He died almost in solitude, but outside his door a large crowd awaited news. Karl was not there.*

68. *Giulietta Guicciardi, for whom Beethoven wrote the "Moonlight Sonata", would not marry him.*

68

69

71

Buffon

at Montbard

It is to the Paris Jardin des Plantes (botanical gardens) and to Montbard in Burgundy that we must go to find Buffon. In Paris, he was on the king's property, but at Montbard he was in his own home. In Paris, he created, for Louis XV, some fine botanical gardens, and selected the rarest and least known animal and vegetable species in the cause of science and the court.

Buffon was a member of the Science Academy from 1739 onward and keeper of the royal gardens. While in Louis XV's service he had the idea of writing a large scale work called *Histoire naturelle générale et particulière*, which he began in 1744. At Montbard he was to respect in his own private grounds what he had already accomplished for the king. He razed to the ground a medieval fortress located on a hill dominating the countryside. In its place, he laid out a park for which forty feet of special earth were delivered and planted 500 trees. Buffon then added a zoo and aviary containing several thousand species, and sat down to write *Les Mammifères*, *Les Quadrupèdes* and *Les Oiseaux*.

One might ask how this taste for the vegetable and animal kingdoms was acquired by the son of a councillor in the Dijon local parliament. The answer lies in his friendship with his college friend the Duke of Kingston in England, made through his acquaintanceship with the duke's natural history teacher.

From 1730 onward, Buffon and Kingston travelled together in France, Italy, England and Switzerland. Buffon was a mathematics scholar and licenciate in law, and probably studied medicine in Touraine. He was a member of the Paris Science Academy and was noticed after writing a treatise on the truth of Archimede's mirrors using the sun's heat. The king also noted that he had translated English natural science works; in 1735, he translated Hales's work on plant statistics and in 1740, he translated Newton on calculus. He checked certain theories on plant nutrition and wood hardness in the grounds at Montbard.

His appointment at the royal Jardin in Paris was a big opportunity for him, since Louis XV used to receive rare specimens from all over the world, which Buffon could now examine. He could also work with a team of young scientists which he formed. Together they collected material for the future museum at the Jardin.

Buffon it must be said was helped considerably from the outset by the naturalist Daubenton, who aided him in his first research programmes and stayed with him until around 1753. He also had help at Montbard from Guéneau de Montbéliard and the Abbé Bexon who also specialized in bird description. They were influenced profoundly by Buffon, even writing like him, having adopted his style without even realizing it.

83

72. *In the house, at the entrance to the grounds of the former Montbard Castle, Buffon wrote his " Histoire Naturelle". Rousseau later visited it in pilgrimage and, falling to his knees, wept on the steps.*

It is impossible, in fact, on reading the work of Buffon, to distinguish between what he wrote and what his colleagues penned. From 1744 onward Buffon decided to live eight months in the year at Montbard, like a recluse. He would work from five a.m. to the evening, and his output appeared regularly and in great quantity. The tomes were highly successful in the bookshops. His *Histoire naturelle* became a best-seller and was ahead of *La Nouvelle Héloïse* and *L'Encyclopédie*.

Many high ranking people in the eighteenth century possessed rooms containing curiosities, mostly minerals and fossils. Such collections already existed in the seventeenth century, but it was in Louis XV's time that most of them were brought together. Often they were housed in a room, panelled with wood specially to show off their properties better; furniture and display cabinets had grooved designs, and some had shell designs as did the panelling. These rooms were veritable boudoirs where the host could chat with his guests. One wonders whether it was Buffon who started this vogue for the beauty of nature or whether it already flourished and in fact aided his rise to fame.

At the early age of twenty-six, he was already known, lauded and flattered. No doors were closed to him and Paris society clamoured for his company. Yet he had very little to say for himself, according to accounts, and was no conversationalist. He concentrated his analytical mind on research and not on the art of repartee. He was a serious worker who was in fact rather boring in the company of others. He went to live at Montbard because he felt at ease there; he just wrote and did not need to be brilliant. He was to spend some forty years there in a state of solitude, spending only four months in the year in Paris.

However while in the capital he did not scorn to appear in public. He was seen at the *salon* of Madame Necker, who obliged him to talk with her daughter Germaine, the future Madame de Staël, so as to advance her all-round education. But when he returned to Montbard, he was always very glad to be quiet again.

Even so, he was careful to be polite. He wrote to Madame Necker: "Madame and respected friend: I have arrived safely at Montbard. But since great regrets give rise to deep meditation, I ask myself why I have left of my own free will everything I love the most, you whom I adore, my son whom I cherish. On examining the motive behind my action, I recognize that it is a principle which you value that has always governed me; I mean, good order in one's behaviour, and the desire to finish work that I have started and have promised to the public. Because here I am completely on my own, with no other company than my books, which is very insipid company, especially on the first days.

"You might imagine that it is the love of glory that draws me to the desert and places the pen in my hand; but I vow to you that I felt the more sorrow at leaving you since glory can never give me pleasure. It is solely the love of good order that determined my move. I am glad to let you know what I feel in my heart and request of you a few sentiments of tenderness and friendship in return..."

This passion for order caused Buffon, after destroying the old castle and laying out a plant research ground on its ruins, to build a small stone house as his work study. There, he spent twelve hours a day on his manuscripts. From his window he could see the Armançon, a long river that glittered in the calm of a valleyed countryside. The Paris coach went by on the main road, but only twice a month.

In this study there is only a desk, a few chairs upholstered in black leather and a great stone chimney piece. His friend Martinet painted as many pictures he liked of the birds he was studying. These are water colours as fresh in tone and as precise as are Buffon's descriptions. They embody style, accuracy and feeling. He painted birds as Redouté later painted roses.

This silent "bird-cage" sprang to life in the descriptions penned by Buffon... "The finch is a very lively bird; it is always to be seen in motion; this, coupled with its gay song, has doubtless given rise to the proverbial phrase 'gay as a finch'. It starts to sing at a very early hour in spring, and several days before the nightingale...

"There is no single bird that the nightingale does not efface by the complete unity of its diverse talents and the prodigious variety of its chirping, to the extent that the song of each one of these birds, considered in its whole range, is merely a verse of that produced by the nightingale. The nightingale is always pleasing and never repeats itself, at least never slavishly : if it sings a passage again, that passage is invariably animated by some new accent, embellished by new grace notes. It succeeds in every style, it produces every expression, and seizes all features. It is the coryphaeus of spring..."

These birds set in their frames are fixed in their hundreds on the stairwell at the Buffon family residence, situated in the centre of Montbard. Some are also found in his study. Today it is like being in a fairyland to look at these birds, one by one, in this small house in the grounds, with nothing else on the walls. Through the open window one can see trees and a valley that stretches as far as the horizon.

The walls become all pink with the evening sun at the close of the day. Buffon was familiar with the autumn evenings when the sun suddenly flames before dying, and he perched his little house just on the bluff over the valley so as to have no shadow between himself and the sun-drenched plain.

So he lived the simple well-ordered life of a gentleman, harnessed to his project, the *Histoire naturelle*, which Voltaire described as "not as natural as all that". This shaft was to cause bad feeling between them for a few years, but due to Buffon's conciliatory nature, they eventually made up. He was reconciled with Voltaire as with the great figures of this world including the king, by giving presents of bound volumes of his work. He also decided to keep away from the Encyclopedists, when they lost favour at the royal court ; besides, he no longer shared their views. Such flexibility enabled him to become friends again with Voltaire. He wrote to him that he preferred his *Henriade* to the *Iliade* and sent him the *Histoire naturelle*.

This was enough to make Voltaire open his arms to him.

They had argued over some fossils. Voltaire wrote of his theories : "In the Hesse mountains they found a stone that seemed to carry the mark of a turbot and, in the Alps, a petrified pike : it was thus concluded that the sea had reached the mountains. It was more natural to think that these fish, taken there by a traveller, deteriorated and were thrown away, to become petrified in the course of time. But this idea was too simple and too irregular."

Buffon's vexed comment was : "Since I do not read any of Voltaire's stupidities, I have known only through friends of the base things he has been saying about me... He is irritated because Niedham has lent me his microscopes and because I said he was a good observer. That is his particular motive which, coupled with his underlying general motive—pretention to universality and jealousy against any celebrity—turns his bile bitter. It is simmering with age such that he seems to have formulated the project of burying all his contemporaries."

It was Buffon even so who made the first move to clear away the misunderstanding between them. Voltaire, enchanted by the fulsome praise by Buffon over his *Henriade*, said : "I knew well that I could not remain angry with Monsieur Buffon for a matter of a few cockle-shells."

We know the loving care Buffon bestowed on fossils and plants, but we know only a little of his attentions to women. His life seemed so well organized that one might imagine there was only place for the plant nursery and the pen.

But fortunately we still possess the diary of a curious personality called Hérault de Séchelles who managed at his own request to get himself accepted by Buffon. He watched the way he studied the least movement of his animals. We know, through his notes, that Buffon had a dressing gown coloured red with white stripes, that he was very careful with his appearance, wore lace cuffs and blouses and lived with a governess of forty years of age.

This lady was called Mademoiselle Blesseau. She was a peasant from Montbard itself and virtually ruled over Buffon. Another personality was Father Ignace Bougot who called himself Buffon's Capuchin monk and flattered him, which was not unpleasant to him.

We also know from his notes that "Monsieur Buffon despite a sedentary life in the study and a great assiduousness has carried on his work to a most advanced age without feeling any illness. He had a system of his own for keeping well; he claimed that the cold was the main cause of practically all illnesses... One can with some justification reproach him with taking his precautions too far, to the point that he had a Shunammite woman to keep him warm in his old age. But the regular purety of his ways seem to show that this derived uniquely from his system."

He went on : "He was fundamentally good, a constant friend of humanity, and one cannot suppose that he acted in that way with the horrible idea that youth should draw unto itself the morbidic miasmas of the old man : but he thought, in company with several doctors, that the natural warmth of a young person in good health can prolong the days of an old man by maintaining the equilibrium of his moods..."

This was quite an assessment of Woman's Role. Buffon remained eighteenth century in his approach to life. He was a materialist without prejudices nor with any great vices. He lived well, liked reality and had little time for sentiment.

Lamartine snarled at him : "He is too majestic, too monotonous, too ostentatious and above all too insensitive. Buffon describes but never feels anything." This is the reproach of a romantic thinker, but Darwin later gave Buffon the praise he deserved : "He was the first man in modern times who dealt with the question of species from a basically scientific point of view." Théophile Gautier pointed to the place he had won in French literature : "I am surprised to find in the precepts of style used by Monsieur de Buffon, my very own theories on art."

It was in fact Buffon who wrote : "Style is the man", a notion so clear cut and simple that the opposite is just as true : "Man is style". This indeed can be seen in the writings of Chateaubriand or Dumas in *La Tour de Nesle* which was to introduce a new theatrical style. The critic Thibaudet said : "We need to modify Buffon's definition."

Whatever comments have been made, the style of Buffon remains a first class example of clarity and elegance—a "lace cuff" style. He was victim however of parody and repetition, as happens to all the great classicists. But if we clean out his phrases they acquire a new movement, for example : "The greatest conquest that man has ever achieved is that over the proud and fiery animal that shares with him the fatigues of war and the glory of combat : as intrepid as his master, the horse..."

In our time, many famous European families still boast the original editions of Buffon's work, or perhaps those that were produced in the nineteenth century with numerous colour plates. These volumes have remained fresh through the chance of oblivion. They have been abandoned on the shelves of ancient castles and country houses ; and they are so different from the volumes in our modern libraries. But sometimes, through curiosity about some exotic animal, one is drawn to open up one of the innumerable tomes of the *Histoire naturelle*, only to find that a chapter ten pages long is devoted to the behaviour of a single bird or mammal. The species still has the same tricks, the same ways and gestures as the one you possess or have seen. Buffon noted everything, even the stories that travellers of the age told him about the species well before the French Revolution.

73. Stairway at Buffon's private house in the village of Montbard.

74. *Monsieur de Buffon (left),
author of the famed "Histoire
Naturelle" which Voltaire said
was "not so very natural".*

75. *These falcons were painted... ▷
were painted for Buffon by
his friend Martinet and were
published in one of Buffon's
volumes.*

Next page:
76. *It was in this study at
Montbard that Buffon worked,
surrounded by bird drawings
up until his death in 1788.
It was in 1744 when working
for Louis XV that he thought
up the idea of his "Histoire
naturelle générale et particulière".*

G. DE RABUTIN-S⁺ DE BUSSY- LIEUTENANT GÉNÉRAL DU ROY

...TUS AB ORIGINE ALTA

DE MI AMORI ME CANTO

DE SOLIDITE QUE D'ECLAT

LA CAUSE EN EST CACHÉE

QUIETO FUORI E SI MOVE D'INTRO

Bussy-Rabutin

at Bussy Castle

In order to amuse a mistress he loved dearly, Bussy wrote his work *L'Histoire amoureuse des Gaules*. A rival for his affections copied out the manuscript and had it put at the bedside of Louis XIV. The result: thirteen months in the Bastille for Bussy followed by permanent exile to his castle in Burgundy.

He was forty-eight when he left the Bastille and was to live for another twenty-seven years. During these years he painted on the panelling of his castle, representations of his happy moments, his great achievements, his loves, and his disgraces—indeed his whole whimsical philosophy of life. These paintings in the form of anecdotes make the Bussy castle an extraordinary place, almost a monument to the glory of derogatory sentiments.

Yet, Roger himself was by no means an outstanding person. He was, it is true, from a long line of eccentrics. As far back as the twelfth century, the wit of Amédée de Rabutin (killed at the age of seventy-two in combat) was so celebrated that his name was to become a verb in the French language: "rabutiner", meaning "original". Later, Claude Rabutin enchanted Louis XII with his lively talk. François was well-known because of his two illegitimate sons, who read Caesar and Salluste in the original text when they were quite young. Another example from the family is Sainte Jeanne Chantal, a widow who had the word "Jesus" marked on her bosom with a red hot iron. She aban-doned her children to enter a convent. Her youngest son wept and tried to block her way; she looked on him as the Devil who assumed an angelic face to defeat her will, and ignored his entreaties. Finally there was Madame de Sévigné, *née* Rabutin. She was entirely of Rabutin stock and had more gifts than her cousin Roger; indeed, her spirited correspondance is the joy of posterity.

Bussy-Rabutin was well-born, and since his brothers had died, he bore the title from the early age of sixteen, just as he left a college at Clermont. He soon acquired a taste for battle, and fought in his first campaign. He was sent to college again at Autun, but had no liking for study. He joined up with Condé, an opponent of the young Louis XIV who was amused by the young man until Bussy left the regiment to run after a lady in Dijon, and then returned to find that the enemy had overrun the area. Condé reprimanded him then forgave him and won Bussy's affection.

In 1636, we find Roger fighting in Picardy. Sickness swept away 500 of his regiment, and he had them buried in a single vast trench.

His father, mortally ill at the time, bestowed his blessing upon his son and gave Roger 3,000 piastres. Bussy spent them in the company of a Parisian woman, but unfortunately the old man recovered and he had to explain where the money had gone. Now a poor man, he, more than anyone else, felt the *mal du siècle*,

93

which ran through the nobility of the times. Rents brought but little, and high ranks were expensive to obtain. War produced no money either, so all that remained was marriage. The difficulty was that, for the moment, he had no desire for wedlock.

At the age of twenty, Cardinal Richelieu, Minister of War, promoted Bussy to colonel. Shortly afterwards he fought a duel which Richelieu had prohibited and killed his opponent. He again fled to Condé for protection. The prince had a new favourite whom Bussy insulted and consequently fell into disfavour with his leader.

Amatory interludes were Bussy's downfall, and he had them frequently. Out of favour with Condé, he chased after a *petite bourgeoise*, luckily escaping serious scandal because the husband proved understanding. An affair with a fifteen-year-old cousin, whom he spirited away to his castle with him, kept him away from his troops, who spent their time looting and ravaging the countryside. The king sent for him and demanded an explanation. "It wasn't my fault", was Bussy's ingenuous reply, "I was away at the time".

This little adventure cost the twenty-three-year-old Bussy a five-month term in the Bastille where he met the Marshal de Bassompierre, the man who was to become his master and guiding spirit. The marshal had been a fashionable young man during the reign of Henry IV, and his tales of his gallant adventures so enchanted Roger that he tried to live in his image for the rest of his life—with some success. Like Bassompierre, Roger was put in the Bastille for a long period and was later exiled to his distant estate.

This sixty-year-old jail companion was brilliant in Bussy's eyes : before entering the Bastille he had burned 6,000 love letters so as not to compromise his lady friends. He told yarns to Bussy who listened open-mouthed and saw in him the prince of loose living whom he vowed to imitate. Bassompierre had been Henri IV's rival with Isabelle de Montmorency, but at the request of the monarch he withdrew from the contest.

When the king died, he became the queen's lover and had the audacity to say in front of her : "All women are whores."

She demanded : "What's that. And what about me ?"

"Oh, you are the queen," he ambiguously replied.

She liked Saint-Germain-en-Laye as much as Paris, and once remarked : "I should like to have foot in each place." To which Bassompierre promptly replied : "In that case I shall not move from Nanterre." (Nanterre is midway between the two.)

These lessons in the art of love, which he learned in prison, were the undoing of young Bussy. He was to learn dearly that one cannot joke under Louis XIV as was the fashion at the time of Henri IV. Bussy also relished his hero's altercations with the king. After the intervention of Luynes, who disliked him, Bassompierre was appointed ambassador to Spain and entered Madrid on a mule.

Louis XIII chortled : "How fine it was to see an ass on a mule."

Bassompierre quipped back : "Indeed, Sire, I was representing you." Who else would have dared to make that reply to the king ?

Bassompierre left the Bastille after ten years as an inmate, when Richelieu died. He appeared again at Versailles, as Bussy was to do forty years later. He was greeted as something of a ghost from the past, but prison had not dulled his wit. Nevertheless, he made use of it with greater discretion than before.

Louis XIII asked him : "What age are you ?"

"Fifty, Sire."

"You must be wrong."

"I am not counting my ten years in the Bastille when I was not serving Your Majesty."

He was on the point of being made governor of the young Louis XIV when he died. This was a great sorrow for Bussy. The child monarch might have learned something from the old man and treated Bussy better in due course. In reality, he was the last survivor of the feudal epoch. Between 1641 and 1654, Bussy was still able to find a place in society owing to the mood of the times. Under Mazarin, duels, pranks and his type of humour were still fashionable. But he failed to move into the second half of the seventeenth century. He was neither prudent, nor religious nor diplomatic, and right up to the age of forty he believed that personal worth, wit and conquest of women were sufficient to see him through. He remained twenty years of age and kept the view of life he imbibed from Bassompierre at the Bastille. Consequently, even his marriages—made for money—came to nothing. His first major office as lieutenant in the Duke of Enghien's Light Horse had to be bought with the remains of his first wife, Gabrielle de Toulongeon's money, but Condé who had replaced him by a favourite forced him to sell the position. His second post, purchased with the fortune from his second wife, was frittered away while he wrote his book, a satire on manners at Versailles.

This second marriage won him a big black mark in the dossier being drawn up against him. Misinformed about the feelings of a young bourgeois widow toward himself, he tried to kidnap her in a carriage in order to marry her, thus restoring his financial position. The incident grew into a scandal. Once again, he had acted rashly, when he only wanted to get his affairs in order. However, as a result of his second marriage, Bussy was better off for money and won a little breathing space financially speaking.

He was reputed to be such a ladies' man that people imagined him worse than he really was. In reality, it is probable that his two wives were not too unhappy in their marriages to him. His first wife produced three daughters for him in the four years of their life together, then died while he was away at war. His second wife gave him two sons, the first in 1660 and the second in 1670. However, his visits must have been fleeting for he is known to have spent but a year at the Castle of Bussy with the former and a month only there with the latter. So he amused himself, played for time and courted Madame de Sévigné. "They rocked with laughter together," it was said. They were both Rabutins and had the same turn of mind. Her husband uncovered the first motions of their love, and died in a duel; Madame de Sévigné drew apart from her cousin, but not before she introduced him to Madame de Montglas, who turned out to be a disaster as far as Roger was concerned.

This gallant fellow, who had already experienced so many adventures that came to nothing, was to risk his life with this charming, pretty and intelligent woman, although there were plenty of others just as charming. Destiny for Roger at the age of forty assumed the visage of Madame de Montglas. He was at the time in exile in Burgundy and the writing of *L'Histoire amoureuse des Gaules* had its roots in Good Friday of 1693. Invited by Mademoiselle de Montespan's brother to Roissy Castle, he had been regarded as the accomplice of that libertine who organized a parody on Easter, a kind of Black Mass. Those present were rumoured to have caricatured the religious service, baptized a pig and eaten a man's leg.

Whether it was true or not, this was the century when a man needed to be rather devout to find favour. The way to win a lady was to be a member of the pious faithful and to conceal one's amorous feelings. This Roissy Castle affair would have died down of its own accord if Bussy had purged his crime in a spirit of repentance.

Madame de Montglas remained in Paris, and Bussy could not appear at Versailles. Louis XIV did not care for Bussy, even though the king had shortly beforehand been enchanted by Bussy's sayings. These were some of them:

"Which is the best mistress, the prude or the coquette?... The prude gives more glory and the coquette more pleasure."

"To want to marry a lady is to want to break with her, though a little more honestly than by changing your mind."

"For your husband to make love to you day and night is no longer in the fashion. I suffer from it day and night for, in the end, Iris, his love either pleases you or upsets you."

With these and other sayings Bussy made incursion into the manners of the age. He was funny and nobody really had anything to say against him. His tales and sayings made the king laugh; even the ladies who were wickedly portrayed gladly accepted his attacks, since those who were left out were so jealous that the others were delighted to be included in this guide to great woman lovers. *L'Histoire amoureuse des Gaules* was much superior to his previous works and started a court scandal. It had been written to kill time and amuse his mistress but it proved to be a forceful satire on the court and hit at the very power of the crown. Everyone could recognize themselves. Later La Bruyère wrote that he should be imitated. In scandalous writing of this kind he had the verve of Saint-Simon and of Brantôme. He had a way of digging at his victims and a way of expressing himself that would be disallowed today. Before writing this book he had produced *La Carte du pays de Braquerie*, a guide to a land of libertines where towns are shown as women (a code enabled them to be identified) and the governors of the towns were their lovers. For example, Pont-sur-Carogne, was Mademoiselle de Pons, Count de la Caze's daughter, the queen's lady in waiting, who was mistress to both the Duke of Guise and Monsieur de Morticone at the same time.

Bussy wrote: "For a long time there were two governors simultaneously in this town, of very different type, yet they lived on the best terms in the world. The function of one was to provide pleasure. The first nearly wrecked his home and the second badly upset his health. This place is now a republic." The humor in *L'Histoire amoureuse des Gaules* is in much the same style. Bussy wrote it to amuse a few close friends in the know, and to occupy his time. Then Madame de Montglas had smallpox and he ran to her side thinking she was dying. She recovered and came to meet him but had a relapse. It was then that he read her his manuscript, and she laughed immensely, the more so since she recognized herself among the characters. Bussy had not wasted his time in the castle because as a result of this book he was able to dominate Madame de Montglas. Nobody could have offered her such delightful entertainment. Unfortunately Madame de la Beaume, a friend

of Madame de Montespan, by flattery managed to get a look at the manuscript.

Bussy yielded to temptation and showed his manuscript to Madame de la Beaume, an evil genius whose father and husband had both put her in convents. She was beside the sick Madame de Montglas when Bussy read passages from the manuscript. She flattered him and used his vanity to lead him astray, which was no hard task. In the end she got him to read it out to her through convent bars, as prayers were intoned near by. She asked to borrow it and gave it back the next day, having copied it out during the night. She had copies circulated in Paris, songs were made out of the words and jibes invented against the king. Bussy was out on a limb.

This is how he describes his own downfall: "Five years ago not knowing how to amuse myself where I was, I well justified the proverb that idleness is the mother of all vice; for I set myself to write a story, or rather a satirical novel, truly without intending to make evil use of it against the people concerned, but only to pass the time, and at the most to show to some of my good friends, and give them pleasure, and receive from them some little praise for the achievement.

"However, with the innocence of my intentions, I cut the throats of people who had never done me wrong, as you shall see by what follows.

"Since true events are never extraordinary enough to amuse very much, I had recourse to invention, believing it would please the more, and, without the least scruple of the offense I gave to those concerned (since I did it half for myself alone), I wrote a thousand things that I had never heard told. I made happy people who were not listened to, and another who had never wished to be. And since it would have been ridiculous to choose women of no birth or merit as the main heroines of my novel, I picked two who lacked nothing in qualities, and who even had so many that envy was able to make credible all the evil I could invent.

"Returning to Paris, I read this history to five friends, one of whom pressed me to leave it with her twice for twenty-four hours, and I could not refuse; several days later I was told it had been seen abroad. I was in despair, and was assured that she to whom I lent the story and who copied it did so through simple curiosity without intending to harm me; but she had for another the same weakness as I had regarding her own request. I went to see her at once and complained; instead of plainly admitting her imprudence and joining with me to remedy the ill, she openly denied that she had ever made a copy and claimed it was not made public and that, if it was, I myself must have lent it to others. The assurance with which she spoke and the natural desire I have that my friends are never at variance with me, removed my suspicion. Yet I do not know how she acted. In the end the scandal of this story ended for a while, after which one of my friends, after quarelling with her, showed me a copy of this manuscript which she had obtained.

"It was the spleen of having been so often deceived by one of my lady friends that made me go against her. And, since one can never bear to suffer without vengeance the resentment of people one has offended, she added or substracted from this story whatever pleased her so that I should evoke the hatred of most of those whom I spoke of. The first copies circulated were not falsified, but as soon as the others appeared, since people will run after the strongest satire, they found the true ones insipid and eliminated them as false.

"I do not presume to excuse myself by this, because although in fact I said only good of people whom this friend maltreated, I am nevertheless the cause of the ill she spread. Not content with having spoilt this story in many places, she later composed others at full length on a thousand peculiarities she knew about me when we were friends, which peculiarities she seasoned with all the venom she could raise.

"However, when I found out that a story was circulating under my name and that my enemies had even given it to the king, even though I needed only to deny them, I preferred that the king should see the original and preferred to acknowledge my real offense, rather than allow myself to be suspected of what I had not done.

"You know, that on return from Chartres, when the king had read this story, I asked to give his majesty the original written with my own hand and bound. He took the trouble to read it; but although he found a great difference between it and the copy, he saw fit to decide that the offense I rendered to two women of quality, and that which I had originally caused to be done to others, merited punishment. Thus he had me arrested, and while giving this example to the public, he satisfied at the same time the resentment of those concerned and also his own justice."

In vain did Bussy throw himself at the king's feet, assuring him that it was all lies. Foreign publishers produced editions of the trafficked work. Bussy was seized, searched and thrown into the Bastille for a year. Madame de la Beaume disappeared, so did Madame de Montglas—for a disgraced lover was a matter for shame. The only person who came to see him daily was his own wife, whom he had seen only one month in so many years. She moved heaven and earth to get him out of the Bastille. He was eventually released when thought to be almost dead. His proud office was taken away without being paid for, on the grounds that he would never again have enough strength to carry out his duties.

At the age of forty-nine, he thus returned to his castle in Burgundy ruined, dishonoured and abandoned by Madame de Montglas and her friend. He had written *L'Histoire amoureuse des Gaules* at the age of forty-two in 1660. The scandal erupted at nearly forty-seven when he had just been elected to the Académie Française, an honour due to the greatness of his family name. He was forty-eight when he began his thirteen months in the Bastille.

This time there was no Bassompierre to divert him in the Bastille. The scandal had taken seven years to reach him and kill his spirit. In 1666 he returned to Burgundy to end his days writing memoirs and looking after his children, his land and castle. He had nothing more to lose and it is evident from the maxims and scenes he got painted on the walls that he no longer feared anyone.

The castle is not very well known, lying as it does in the middle of valleys near Alésia. It differs from many others by its position in a low-lying area surrounded by forests, in contrast to most castles which are on high ground. Its fortified parts are fifteenth-century and the balustrades and bridge Louis-Treize. The two wings are François-Premier and the interior paintings seventeenth-century. The main structure of the castle was built by Bussy's father and Bussy himself between 1610 and 1665. The decoration of the grounds and on the walls was the work of himself or artisans. On the walls of the cylindrical tower's *salon* he had painted Madame d'Olonne, Madame de Fiesque, Madame de Châtillon, Madame de la Ferté, Madame de Montglas, Madame de la Beaume, Madame de Sévigné, Madame de Grignan and the Countess of Bussy herself. They are shown frolicking under the gilding and at the feet of each lady is a maxim.

Under Madame d'Olonne, who successfully led a scandalous life in an age when it was very difficult to do this, he wrote : "She was famed less for her beauty than for the use she made of it."

Under Madame de la Beaume who lost him is written : "The most lovable and the prettiest had she not been the most disloyal."

Under Marie de Beauvoir is written : "Very sparing of her friendship but sparing nought for those to whom she grants it." She was the wife of Choiseul du Plessis and was pretty, lively, intelligent and particularly knowledgeable on the activities of other people.

Under Magdelaine d'Angennes de la Ferté we can see : "Beautiful and with good intentions, but the attention of a husband, a hostile man, has not been unconnected with her behaviour."

Under Isabelle Angélique de Montmorency is written : "To whom one could refuse neither one's purse nor one's heart, but who did not value the adventure."

Under Madame de Montglas he inscribed the words : "By her inconstancy she re-

stored to the Mother of the Church her place of honour."

This lady, his mistress, was really the most harshly treated because he loved her still. On the windows in the heraldic room, he had her shown as the moon because the moon "has more than one face", and as a siren rising from the water—"he who listens is lost"—and as a rainbow—"less Iris, less ephemeral and less changing than mine"—and as a swallow fleeing winter (because she abandoned him in his exile)—"who is seeking warm lands at the end of autumn". Underneath a head and shoulders portrait she is depicted as Zephyr and placed on one scale of a balance, the other being empty. Despite this, the scale carrying Madame de Montglas is going upwards and he wrote : "Lighter than the air", thus alluding to her lack of constancy.

So it was that Madame de Montglas ended up bitterly in all the rooms of this fantastic castle. Bussy did not forget the past and now there could be no love nor friendship between them. Madame de Scudéry at one point attempted to bring the two together again but Bussy was afraid of suffering any more. "Ah let me alone to laugh about her. She has already made me weep so", he wailed. This man who had played with love to the full was to remain so affected by her that he was unable to leave a single wall in the castle without its portrait of Madame de Montglas. Occasionally they used to write to each other, but her letters were accounts of her problems. Bussy cried out : "I love her no longer" but he spoke of her in all the letters he wrote to friends. Madame de Sévigné observed : "You do not write so much about somebody you do not love... It is untrue that you speak of her to me only because you have also written of her to Mademoiselle Dupré. I even think you speak of her to the woods, to the echoes and the rocks."

When Bussy learned that his former mistresses Madame d'Olonne, Madame de Montmorency and Madame de Montglas whom he had loved so much, saw each other regularly —no doubt to talk about love—he wrote of them : "You know that they called the union between Augustus, Lepidus and Mark Anthony a triumvirate. I call their's a *triumputat* (meaning in French : 'trinity of whores')".

At seventy-six years of age, he was still writing verses about her : "The air she breathes out is purer than the air she breathes in." Love had not ceased to invigorate him and cause suffering, after thirty years.

In the window frames of the "golden tower", Bussy inscribed other adventures such as the kidnapping of Europe, or the kidnapping of Madame de Miramion by Bussy. Two lovers are shown hanging from a ribbon : "Lovers' quarrels increase their love".

Other loved ones float about in a different window with the accompanying maxim : "He who gives is master of hearts. Tears in love hide many words. If you were as fine as the sun, be certain that if you lack fortune you will be unhappy in love."

Further along is written : "As in war so in love, you must watch day and night. It is sweet to live as lovers; if you do not love too much you do not love enough." Again : "Love and you will be loved", "Without jealousy love will languish". On the plinth of the golden tower is : "Shame, regret and death are the normal wages of temerity."

Elsewhere can be seen the words : "Women have a thousand ways of duping poor lads and the lads pretend a thousand flames to catch young girls". There is a yellow ivory woman in the arms of Pygmalion with the advice : "If you wish to love and never be deceived, love an ivory woman."

Bussy turned his red damask room into a museum of feminine charm. The walls were decorated with paintings showing all the women he had been involved with, whom he had loved or who had given him their portraits so that he would talk about them in exile. But these have all gone now and there remain only the portraits of his cousin Madame de Sévigné, his daughter, his wife and a few others. To him these are women who happened to live at the same time as he did and mean nothing to him.

He had a room painted with the great people of his world, to recall past glories no doubt. There are no fewer than sixty-five portraits of celebrated military figures : Du Guesclin, Gaston de Foix, Bayard, Montmorency, the High Constable Bourbon, the Duke of Bellegarde ; we can see Condé and Turenne (badly placed in one corner and with the inscription ; "Henri de la Tour, Viscount Turenne, monarch of Sedan celebrated on account of his wife"), also "Henri de Lorraine, Count Hauvert, Great Equerry of France whose extraordinary actions in war under Louis XIII surpass all belief". Bussy, who looks very much like Molière when young, has a glint in his eye. He has the same look at the age of thirty, in another painting to be seen in the "golden tower".

Finally there is the famous heraldic room of the castle. Every castle where he stayed is shown on wall panelling. They include : Versailles, Rueil, Saint-Germain-en-Laye, Chambord, Vincennes, Saint-Cyr, Saint-Cloud, Luxembourg, Marly and many others. Here too are a series of "jokes" in typically Bussy manner. A portrait of the author is fitted in place of the usual mirror over the mantel piece ; he is surrounded by five smaller paintings. There is also a fountain painted on a narrow tall section of panelling with the inscription : "high like my birth". There is a bird with an open beak perched on a tree —"I sing my love"—and supposed to be Madame de Montglas. Under the portrait is an erupting volcano plus the words : "The cause is hidden, the reason for my disgrace with the king is unknown to me." A peculiar watch is painted closed and with the keys adjacent : "Outside it is motionless but inside it moves" —a reference to the author's own head. A diamond is shown on red velvet : "More substance than brilliance" ; this means that Bussy is highborn, he likes love, is as reliable as a diamond and active inside like a watch spring.

Having learned what he thought of himself, we are drawn further round these walls in the hope of finding out what he thinks about life and what it has done to him. We see a picture of a cottage behind an enormous onion set on a table with the Italian inscription :

99

"*Chi mi morderà piangerà*" ("Whoever bites me will weep"). This is a jibe against Boileau who attacked him on his own ground. There is a lone tree : "*Miscent automni et veris honores*" and a sun-dial with the sun shining on it : "*Si me mira me miran*" ("If the sun looks at me, so will others"). This signifies that Bussy is no longer esteemed by the king, nobody cares for him any more. A lone sun is shining. He wrote : "*Mus virtud que lux*" ("More virtue than glory"). A snail is shown moving across Burgundy country-side : it is Bussy : "*In me me involgo*" ("I creep into myself") and a chesnut tree says : "*Vetantur mollia duris*" ("Softness hides under hardness"), also Bussy. The stars say "*Non mille quod absens*" ("The number doesn't matter if one is absent"), meaning that he cares little for all his conquests if Madame de Montglas has left him. A field of corn under raindrops : "*Collicit ut spargat*" ("It receives in order to share") ; here Bussy is thinking of all the favours he ought to have received from Louis XIV but did not.

To Bussy, life "*Decepit et plaut*" ("deceives and pleases"). Our hero in the form of a reed "bends but does not break". A flower blooms and "The sight of it gives me life". Another dies and "Its absence kills me", another direct allusion to Madame de Montglas. There is a dove : "*Piango la sua morte e mia vita*" ("I weep her life and my love") which recalls his first wife. A flaming phoenix : "*Morir per non morir*" which is doubtless our friend rising from the ashes.

A fire is depicted with the words : "*Splendes cum du materiam*" ("I will be splendid, give me fuel")—but unfortunately the king failed to provide any. Madame de Montglas is once again shown as the moon : "*Offerte cum luce quitem*" ("She brings rest as well as light"). Water is thrown on a container of quicklime : "*E frieda ses accende*" ("She is cold and she bursts into flame"), a reference to Madame de Sévigné. A hive is surrounded with bees : "*Spont faros e que spienta*" (which means in Rabutin's terms that anyone who comes too near the hive will be stung. A torn flag is stirred by the wind : "*E lacero o qui virtu spira*" ("From shreds he won glory")—Bussy after his battles.

The left wing of the castle has a gallery given over to the kings of France, also the Rabutins and the dukes of Burgundy. Here also are exemples of Roger's irrepressible humour. Sébastien Rabutin, elder son of Brother Hugues de Rabutin, is shown killing a wolf; the king had the painting copied and placed in the Swiss room at Fontainebleau. Brother Hugues acknowledged his two bastard sons and Bussy promptly had them painted.

After Roger de Bussy died, his successors carried on the gallery out of a desire to continue the spirit of Roger. Marshal de Montrevel was added with the inscription : "Dead in 1717 from the shock of an overturned salt-cellar," and also : "Charles de Fieux, a more than mediocre author but very fecund; he died in 1784 aged eighty-three."

The castle grounds were not spared the art of Roger de Bussy, who caricatured the great pools and waterfalls of Versailles. He had a very small rockery built from which sprang a tiny jet of water about ten inches wide and at least one hundred yards long, which fell into the central pool in the grounds. Bussy, defying the king's vengeance, was heaping ridicule on the only place he would have really liked to be : Versailles. "The grapes are too green", he remarked.

To prove it, he conveyed to Louis XIV that he was still friends with plenty of the ladies and that others often wrote to him. At the end of his life (which came gently to a close at the castle in the company of his eldest daughter), he returned for a short while to Paris after the king at last contacted him. But by now he found the capital greatly changed; it gave him no pleasure and he returned home, glad to have a final look at the panelling on the castle walls and the inscriptions that spelt out so appropriately the story of his eventful life.

78. A naïve painting in the heraldry room ▷ depicts an onion on a table and cottage, with the caption in Italian: "Chi mi mordera piangerà" ("Whoever eats me will cry"). This was a retort against Boileau who attacked Bussy.

79. Bussy-Rabutin's little-known castle in Burgundy near Alésia was built by Bussy's father and continued by himself, between 1610 and 1665. Bussy personally supervised the decorating and in each room had scenes painted of people or allegories on Louis XIV's court. He had said too much about court life and was banished to his own property. ▽

80. "Apollo's Chariot", and "The Lady Astride ▷
a Bull" were painted on the walls. The works
signify that Bussy's future was destroyed and
that the beautiful Madame de Montglas had
lost none of her power.

◁ 81. Bussy de Rabutin's bed wa
hung with a red gold-trimmed mate
rial. On the walls he fixed portrait.
of women he had loved or who stil
loved him. Some sent their portrai
to him after he was exiled, to mak.
sure they were among the celebritie
in his room. In a sense, this wa
an art gallery of his love life whic
was said to have actually mad.
Louis XIV jealous. Works are ar
ranged chronologically.

82. Bottom left to right among the
portraits above the table is Madame
de Sévigné, a cousin Bussy loved at
one stage, also Madame de Grignan,
her daughter.

LEVES AMBO, AMBO INGRATÆ.

CHANGEANTES TOVTES DEVX, ET TOVTES DEVX INGRATES

84

84. *An allegorical representation of Madame de Montglas, depicts her with one foot on the moon, because she and the moon were "both fickle and both ungrateful".*

LEVIOR AVRA.

PLVS LEGERE QVE LE VENT.

85

85. *The bust of Madame de Montglas, Bussy's mistress, sits in a scale. It weighs less than the empty balance because she is "lighter than air", an allusion to her disloyalty.*

◁ 83. *This room features sixty-five famous military figures: Du Guesclin, Gaston de Foix, Bayard and others. Bussy was malicious in his placing of the portraits or the mottoes underneath. Condé is poked into a corner, so is "Henri de la Tour, Viscount Turenne, monarch of Sedan—noteworthy because of his wife...".*

Preceeding page:
86. This heraldic room is probably the only one in Europe with a satirical decorated fresco with symbolical scenes reflecting the misfortunes and the pride of the owner. He was a noble lord rejected by his king because he loved too often and said too much.

87. In the tower room Bussy had many women he knew painted around portraits of himself and Madame de Montglas. The motto with the picture of Madame d'Olonne says that "she was less famed for her beauty than for the use she made of it". Of his mistress Madame de Montglas he said "her inconstancy has restored honour to the Mother of the Church". A recess sums up the spirit of the tower: it contains a picture of an ivory woman in the arms of Pygmalion with the motto: "If you want to love and remain undeceived, then love a woman of ivory."

87

ALLICIT UT PERDAT

MINVS IRIS QVAM MEA

89

90

△ 89. Madame de Montglas as a siren: "He who listens to her is lost."

△ 90. Madame de Montglas again, depicted as a rainbow over Bussy's castle with the bitter comment: "Less Iris, less ephemeral, less changing than mine."

91-92. Bussy de Rabutin was ▷ received in these two castles by Louis XIV: Saint-Germain-en-Laye and Vincennes.

93-94. Allegories in the heraldic room. The torn flag is supposed to be Bussy's future of which he said: "From the shreds he brought forth glory." Here too is a phoenix in flames: "To die and thus not to die." This is Bussy rising from the ashes and finding a new taste for life.

ST GERMAIN EN LAYE

VINCENNES

91-92

88. This tower is dedicated to some of Bussy's amorous recollections. His own portrait as a young man is in the center. On his right is the Marquise de Montglas, the cause of his exile by the king.

E LACERO OGNI VIRTV SPIRA

MORIR PER NO MORIR

93-94

95. *Left to right, in London: Dr Carlyle, Thomas Carlyle, Miss M.G. Aitken and Mr. P. Swan.*

Carlyle

in London

The Thomas Carlyles moved into their London house in 1834. It is a tall narrow building now designated 5 Cheyne Row, Chelsea.

They had previously occupied a house in Edinburgh which was an open door to writers on the *Edinburgh Review*. The editor was an admirer of Mrs. Carlyle and his support enabled them to keep body and soul together.

Thomas was thirty-nine when they moved. Eight years earlier he had married Jane Baillie Welsh, a rich intelligent young girl, but not very pretty. Thomas stole her from a friend of his to whom she was engaged. She preferred this son of a Scottish farmer who was all set for a career in the church. But he lost his faith after reading the works of Herder, Fichte, Kant and above all Goethe, whose writings he translated. He never forgave them for causing him to lose him his vocation and a good deal of religious sentiment continued in him. Carlyle might even be termed a mystical puritan. He regarded himself as a bit of a "guide", and it was the "guide" whom this physically and morally unbalanced young lady married. During their period of engagement she told him she saw a future "great man" or tutor in him, but that she did not love him. She was to regret this remark in due course.

Carlyle made a living out of teaching, tutoring and journalism. He wrote an essay, *Sartor Resartus*, accusing philosophers of destroying the spontaneity which alone enabled man to communicate with the forces of nature hidden under the cloak of appearances.

In London, he found it hard to get his work published. *Sartor Resartus* is important because it contains the germ of the ideas he developed in later writings. Carlyle treats nature from a subjective and unconscious viewpoint. He was haunted like all the English symbolists (Coleridge, for example) by the mystery of a life in which he felt demiurgic communications. For him, a few *élite* beings serve as revelations for humanity; they are incarnations of the eternal in the temporal. They include prophets, great heads of state, representing totality. The very words he uses make the modern reader cautious in his approach : he puts forward vague and blustery ideas, half way between poetry and theosophy, and rages against his epoch, suggesting hero-worship as an answer. James Joyce said that history was a "nightmare" from which he was trying to awake : this correlation between history and a dream, or rather a nightmare, this disarray, the desire to seek some unity where none exists, this abandonment of reason in The Word, is a characteristic of a whole family of British writers dating from Carlyle.

It was, we recall, in 1834 that Carlyle set out with his wife to conquer London. His immediate interest was in its libraries where he planned to direct his research toward the French Revolution.

He was ambitious and kept his eye on the road to success. He believed that his century was to be an important one on the stage of history.

The Carlyles had to wait three years before the appeerence of *The French Revolution*, a work into which they put all their hopes. They used to receive visitors in the same small drawing room where their shiny piano stands today. Carlyle the idealist, ranting against the morals of the profit motive, against factory life and banks, would welcome his guests in the dark hallway of the house; they included a few young liberal disciples of John Stuart Mill who had just produced his *Logic*. Mill's was a mechanical system of thought; he had a nervous breakdown at one stage and came round to accepting the laws of affectivity, which pleased Carlyle more than somewhat. Other guests at the house were foreigners including Ralph Waldo Emerson, who was to make Carlyle known in America.

But in 1836 an unfortunate incident threatened to reduce to ashes Carlyle's careful ground-work for success. The manuscript of *The French Revolution*, which was at the time with a friend, was partly destroyed by fire. Thomas was obliged to write the book again from notes and the work finally appeared in 1837.

The results came up to the young couple's highest expectations. Within a few months Carlyle had become England's "literary lion". London society thronged to his Chelsea home to see and listen to the author of this great work, very hostile to the French and their Revolution, more anecdotic and melodramatic than historical.

Jane, however, could hardly keep up with their busy new life, and in 1840 Thomas was forced to seek a bigger "hall" than his own Chelsea lounge. Fashionable London bought tickets to hear him in their clubs. Thomas Carlyle, adding a touch of play-acting to his nervy style, and with his handsome northern features and peasant stance, spoke in violent tones which thrilled the ladies. Some ladies declared themselves to be his fervent disciples, and were either rejected or accepted by him depending on their standing in life. The future Lady Ashburton, daughter of a rich banker, was among those allowed to join the group, but she later offended Mrs. Carlyle.

The natures of the two gifted Carlyles grew in intensity with their arrival in London. Jane Welsh was impulsive, anything but Victorian, given to taking lone walks in the streets and climbing on the top of double-decker buses, inquisitive about art and literature, and laughing at her husband's pipes. She had already surrendered her own independent judgment and any hope of a separate literary career. She gave up her interests to those of Thomas who lost all thought for his wife's intellectual formation and wanted her to be just a typically Victorian wife. She had nothing against this and was pleased to demonstrate her own weakness. They were affectionate to each other, but there was something missing.

Today, the Carlyle couple have become a veritable legend. Some regard them as a typically incompatible pair, and others see in them a pattern for the ideal marriage. Still others believe they represented everything that a home should be. Closer study reveals that Carlyle himself was impotent and that Jane desired children. Hence the complexes she had arising from frustrations that made her a jealous and unbalanced woman.

When she heard her husband talking to the ladies about heroes and the admiration they merited, she would lower her eyes. Thomas would declaim about the universe, asking repeatedly what it was and then declaring it to be made up of power beyond ourselves. On the platform he looked quite pale. He returned home nervous, often telling Jane he had a stomach ache. She bestowed her maternal love on him.

These lectures are contained in *On Heroes and Hero Worship* (1841). They enabled the Carlyles to live comfortably. Jane furnished the Chelsea house in the style of the times: wallpaper which was a novelty then, screens of the kind so dear to Goethe (Thomas's favourite writer), heavy curtains to protect the privacy of the happy few allowed into the presence of the man of the moment. This is the décor Thomas had as the background to his role of "great man". Here it was that Carlyle endeavoured to draw unto himself the worship due to gods, prophets, poets, priests, men of letters and kings.

These are the chapter headings of his book. Carlyle believed history was solely the story of great men, and their achievements. Twenty years later Tolstoy, describing the story of a great man vanquished by the Russian armies and steppes, wrote in *War and Peace :* "One man alone is never the cause of a whole series of events." History's episodes are rich in outstanding gifted personalities : princes, kings, conquerors, prophets and thinkers. But history is also the story of peoples without whom great personalities, outstanding figures could not have played their parts. The vast scenes of history have in the end been played out by the masses, and through the spirit of the masses. The heroes to which Carlyle wants us to render exclusive worship may indeed be representative of a popular movement—Mahomet, Dante, Shakespeare, Luther, Knox, Rousseau, Cromwell and Napoleon—but they were swept along in a collective, popular event. For example the conquest of America was an epic achievement by Spaniards of low extraction, from their country's poorest provinces, Estramadura. The Crusades are another example. Even so the notion of providential figures to act as an example for others and to shape their destinies, appeals to a certain type of thinker. Such people will find their guide in Carlyle's book, a work abounding in suitable formulas, rich in comments on man's living relationship with the mysteries of the universe, and redolent of German romanticism—magic source of all violence.

He wrote of life as a whirlwind of limitless power, all-enveloping and never at rest, as old as eternity. Beyond science all that remained for us was fear, pity, humility and adoration, expressed either in words or in silence.

Carlyle's thought moved on from a basis of religious fact to adoration founded on complete wonder. From this he switched easily to the admiration and deification of great men. For him there existed no nobler sentiment in the heart of a man than admiration for his superior. Loyalty is mixed with faith, and society is founded on the cult of the hero. He believed that the social hierarchy, degrees of dignity and rank could be termed "hero-archy" or government by heroes. Carlyle recalls that the word "duke" comes from the latin *dux,* meaning "leader".

Naturally, worship must be directed toward men who are "truly great and wise". The dignitaries in a society are like banknotes backed by gold, but there are also some forged notes about. This state of affairs can be accepted if there are not too many. But not if all the notes are forgeries ! This, says Carlyle, is the moment for revolutions with "cries of democracy, freedom, equality !" The people then claim there is no gold and never has been, he wrote. Besides, he added, hero worship had always existed.

As Eric Bentley observed in 1947, there are many absurdities in Carlyle and we can no longer accept his charges against Negroes, Jews, French and "the people". We cannot praise Bismarck, Frederick the Great and the Germans quite as he did, calling them the premier nation of the world. Bentley wrote that the moral danger in such views was evident in 1947.

Yet there was another Carlyle. The man whom Engels was to translate, whom Dickens, Ruskin, Emerson and Walt Whitman praised. These were followed by others no less worthy in subsequent generations : Nietzche, George Bernard Shaw, Oswald Spengler, Stefan George and D. H. Lawrence.

Thomas Carlyle's rigid views did nothing to soften the character of the poet and prophet whom his wife worshipped. In vain did she watch over the comfort of the great man; in vain did she yield to his every desire. By now he had become famous and blasé, subject to insomnia, irritable, dyspeptic, jealous of the talents of all his contemporaries (even of Dickens), a conformist and henceforth champion of strong government despite his former liberal notions. He came out against the rich because of their privileges and the poor because of their vulgarity, and against the decadence of the century over which he nevertheless had visions of reigning.

Such is the man who used to recline in a deep black leather armchair, which Jane fitted up with a book-rest. She arranged a studio for him away from the noise, high up in the house, where he retired to meditate on the coming extension of his empire. One Englishman, and one only, escaped his ire : Robert Peel, head of the new Conservative Party. Carlyle sent him his volume of Cromwell's *Letters*, but unfortunately Peel died shortly afterward of heart trouble and Carlyle saw only one remaining individual worthy of his attention : Bismarck.

In 1857, Thomas Carlyle completed his *History of Frederick the Great*. In the same year King Frederick Wilhelm IV of Prussia sank into madness and handed over the regency to his son Wilhelm. Throughout Germany there resounded Carlyle's new panegyric glorifying the founder of Prussia's greatness. Its keenest reader was the man who was to make of the new Prussian monarch a German emperor—his minister Bismarck. The influence of Carlyle, whose work was utilized by the Fascists and Nazis half a century later, was beginning to be felt in the world.

From 1858 to 1865, while Jane was slowly recovering from nervous breakdown, Carlyle produced further volumes of the *History of Frederick the Great*. He was at his zenith, and in 1865 went back to Edinburgh for election as rector of the University. Perhaps he saw again their house on the quayside, but one questions whether he thought at all of the wife he left behind in their London house. Jane herself was happy only in the city which Thomas was so sick of.

Jane consequently bestowed on her dog the love bursting out from inside her, but an accident to this new companion upset her badly. The very next day while driving her carriage she let go of the reins and fell dead into the road.

On the first floor of the house in their room Thomas Carlyle regarded the sad, hurt face, illuminated by candles she had kept for this very purpose since her childhood. Carlyle spent his last years annotating their correspondance. But this pious task did not take up all his time. He became involved in business and furthering his own reputation. He accepted an Order of Merit from Bismarck (Carlyle had produced an article against France in 1870). He refused the Order of the Bath because it was offered by a Jew, Disraeli, and on February 4, 1881, the bell tolled for this prophet of the personality cult and spiritual father of National Socialism.

96. This stairway led to Carlyle's room where Jane died, and to the study above which she arranged for her "great man" so he would not be disturbed by noise.

◁ *97. The Carlyles' bedroom.*

98. Nº 5 Cheyne Row in Chelsea where the Carlyles lived after arrival in London in 1834 until they died, she in 1867 and the author in 1881.

100. Statue of Thomas Carlyle in his study. ▷

99. In this lounge the Carlyles entertained John Stuart Mill and young liberals. Jane chose the furniture. Thomas used to read out passages from his first successful work: "The French Revolution" (1837). The room soon became too small for the throng of admirers.

101. The study at the top of the house where Carlyle withdrew to work.

102. The washroom next to Carlyle's study.

103. *Jane Carlyle chose wall-paper, which was a novelty at the time. She also fixed a book-rest to the armchair for Thomas. The whole house was designed for his comfort.*

Cervantes

in Valladolid

The trail of Miguel de Cervantes Saavedra might logically lead to a windmill rather than the house of a sedentary writer. Perhaps this genius of adventure and dreams dwelt in one of the thirty or fourty windmills that Don Quixote mistook for giants as he rode along with Sancho—the character who attached himself to the valiant hero believing he would perhaps change his destiny and the face of the earth.

Sancho was even more convinced he would succeed, when he saw Don Quixote charge the giants (the incarnation for him of Power and Injustice) so furiously that his lance broke. As Miguel de Unamuno said : "That's all the giants threatening Cervantes could do : break his weapon but not his heart."

Cervantes, poet and soldier, was born in 1547 of a poor New Castille family. His birth-place became known to the world at large only 200 years after his death. He went off to seek fame and fortune in Italy in the service of Cardinal Julius Acquaviva ; he later fought for Venice against the Turkish Sultan, took part in the Cypriot Expedition, lost his left hand at Lepanto ("for the glory of the right", he said) and was finally captured by a corsair and became slave to a Greek in Algiers.

His only homes might appear to have been camps, wayside inns and the prisons of Seville, Algiers and Valladolid.

A biography of Cervantes could well bear the title of one of his chapter headings : "How so many adventures rained down on Don Quixote, that there was no breathing space between them." This is the chapter in which the noble hidalgo pronounces these memorable words : "Freedom, Sancho, is one of the most precious gifts that heaven has given to men. Nothing is the equal of it, neither the treasures the earth holds in its bosom, nor those the sea hides in its depths. For freedom, and for honour, one can and should risk one's life ; on the other hand, slavery is the greatest ill that can befall men. I say this, Sancho, because you have well noted the abundance and delights that we enjoyed in the castle we have just left. Well, in the midst of those exquisite dishes and cooled drinks, I seemed to suffer the pangs of hunger, for I did not relish them with the same freedom as if they belonged to me. The obligation to acknowledge the benefits and graces one receives is like a set of shackles that do not leave the spirit free to roam. Happy the man who receives a piece of bread from heaven, with only heaven to thank for it."

To which Sancho, forewarned by earlier experiences, merely replies : "But we shall not always find castles where we can feast ourselves !"

Freedom ! Life without fetters, and free "exercise" of the mind. These were keen demands, more difficult to satisfy than in other ages than the times of Miguel de Cervantes

104. Cervantes and his family lived at Valladolid in 1605. They had four humble first-floor rooms over-looking a garden and marble fountain such as we see here.

Saavedra. He knew the reign of Philip II and half that of Philip III. He was a contemporary of El Greco, Lope de Vega and the senior of Velasquez and Murillo. The wandering existence he had differed little from that of many strong-minded figures of his age, when the narrow system of the Middle Ages was breaking up : Christopher Columbus, Camoens and El Greco, not to mention a host of humanist travellers who had only temporary homes.

Cervantes' family itself had no fixed address in Spain. The father, who was a doctor-surgeon, took his family from Valladolid to Seville and then to Madrid, where the boy studied a little. Later he went to Rome and learned the basic concepts of humanism, in the service of Cardinal Acquaviva. There he drank in the treasures that Italy offered Renaissance man. Many critics in France, Italy and Spain have brushed aside the judgement that Cervantes was, in the words of a Spanish critic of 1624, "a soul of no culture but the gayest in Spain." We know for certain that Cervantes had his fill of Italian thinking and in particular that he carefully studied Erasmus. His idealism and neoplatonicism have been well emphasized and some interpretations of his philosophy go as far as to compare him with Pirandello.

Indeed, how could a man who has left behind such striking evidence of his sensivity and lucidity, have stayed in the Venice of the fifteenth century without knowing the most important contemporary works and encountering the new vision of the world ? Besides, *Don Quixote* shows clearly that he was a great reader of king-in-armour type stories. He was to declare : "My book is entirely an invective against the knightly tale."

As we know, it was of course another one. Familiarity breeds contempt and it is quite possible that this satire hides a painful chagrin. Before he began laughing at himself, Cervantes took everything quite seriously ; he genuinely meant to adopt the virtues of one of those fearless and irreproachable knights he read about. He took part in the biggest naval battle of the times, Lepanto, where Don Juan of Austria emerged victorious, in 1571, against the Turks.

The event rang in his mind, we may be certain.

Yet this triumph of Cross over Crescent was a short-lived, pompous victory whose consequences Cervantes discovered in a hospital at Messina. Perhaps he thought the loss of one hand was worth the rank of captain. He went off again to obtain this promotion, but his galleon was seized by Berbers and he spent five years captive in Algiers. His captors found on him some documents signed by Don Juan lauding his prowess at Lepanto. He was reckoned a prize catch, and thereafter carefully watched. He began plotting his escape only to end up in a closely guarded jail.

Near Valladolid one can visit a house that Cervantes might well have loved to stay in. It contains a simple table, white walls, a canopied bed with orange and blue curtaining, a map of the world just like so many the Spaniards of the time studied dreamingly, and a statue of Christ that could have received the gaze of Cervantes and the touch of his nervous fingers.

A house bears witness to the constant fight of man against wind, rain, sun and fatigue. Before ever he sought shelter against the elements of nature, Cervantes had felt them in all their strength ; he had known hunger, cold and thirst in camps, ships, battles and African scrub.

We can imagine him huddled of an evening on one of the benches recessed into the kitchen walls, silent and meditating like any peasant. Cervantes was a man of the poor with all the characteristics of a man of the people. He was, too, a man of the Spanish countryside, naïve, adventurous and thinking of glory. He is the possessor of every popular and provincial virtue and is the incarnation of the Spanish soul. We have only to read him to know exactly what the peasants thought of the king, of Christ and the human adventure. Did this house in Valladolid really house the genius whose mind gave birth to the extraordinary dialogue between Don Quixote and Sancho Panza ? The house seems to be every bit as authentic as the windmills, roads and inns in the book *Don Quixote*. Here Cervantes might easily have broken off bits of bread and munched them, and swallowed back his wine. We can see the eternal Spanish water or wine jug, and any Spaniard today would feel at ease there.

We can feel Cervantes' presence. To this kind of dwelling came a defeated adventurer, ransomed by the Trinity Fathers in 1580 from the corsair who had him prisoner and slave for five years. Gone for ever were glory and action. He was just a ransomed soldier, with only one hand, poverty stricken.

But hardly had this thirty-four-year-old veteran returned from his trials and humiliations, than we find him writing a romantic novel. This is an accurate description of *Galatea* which he wrote in 1584 as a present for Catherine Salazar y Palacios of Toledo. She read this ambitious love letter and agreed to marry him. But she was its only reader.

He now turned to the theatre. All his life Cervantes resembled a rat in a trap seeking escape. He had dreamed about the theatre as a boy. Even in prison he composed sketches like those he had seen played on the simple stages of his own land : they were five-day dramas or mixtures of ballet, dances and comic scenes. He claimed with confidence : "I was the first person to show in play form the secret movements of the soul and depict moral scenes." Critics are not entirely in agreement with this. His type of theatre is drama only in the sense of the noble thoughts he inspires. Nevertheless *Numance* has breadth ; it is the story of the city of Numance, beseiged in 134 B. C. by Scipio and Jugurtha. The play was a flop, and his comedy sketches were preferred.

Since he had to produce these in order to live, he turned them out copiously. In a sense he was similarly placed to Hogarth, whose public demanded cartoons which brought him a small fortune, whereas he only really wanted to be a serious painter.

Three years after he got married, Cervantes attempted to take part in the "invincible" Armada, defeated in due course by Sir Francis Drake. Miguel ended up as a galley master. He vainly requested the king to send him to the distant "land of gold", America. From this period we still have a loan note bearing his signature relating to the purchase of clothes. His whole life seems to be staked out in a series of requests that were turned down, promissory notes, unpaid invoices for comedies he wrote, bad deals. He won a literary prize in 1595, but finally he ended up in prison again.

The trouble began in 1594 when he held the job of Andalusian tax collector. As he said himself, it was a despised profession. Certain irregularities were discovered in his accounts and he was thrown into Seville prison for three months. He was called to Valladolid, where the court was, to explain his accounts. He stayed there several months, living a sordid impecunious existence in a suburb. It remained to be seen whether *Don Quixote* (written in prison) would bring him fame and security and in September 1604 he was licenced to go ahead with printing the first part.

First mention of this work is found in a letter Lope de Vega wrote in the same year 1604 : "There is no worse poet than Cervantes and nothing more ridiculous than his Don Quixote," he declared. The two men did not care for each other.

Philip II had died in 1598 and he would certainly not have tolerated a work that alleged religious and social hypocrisy in Spain... Philip III allowed it to be published and, it is said, even laughed at the book.

In the course of the festivities connected with the baptism of the Infanta, Don Quixote was portrayed together with his equerry Sancho Panza, a detail indicating that the opinion of Lope de Vega was not that of the people. A taste for *Don Quixote* grew rapidly throughout the country and wherever Spanish was spoken. Even in far away Peru, the two characters turned up at masked balls. Cervantes had not even finished the second part of the work when forgeries of the first part began appearing.

The second part was officially published in 1615, ten years after the first. This also was an immense success. The work as a whole became known and appreciated in France. A member of the Spanish nobility, questioned about Cervantes by French gentlemen in the ambassador's suite, said : "I was obliged to tell them that he was old, a soldier, hidalgo and poor. At this one of them replied : 'How is it that Spain has not poured riches on such a man ? Surely he should be kept by the State Treasury !' Alas he is maintained, but in prison."

At number 14 Rostro Street in Seville, visitors today are shown a house where Cervantes is said to have lived at one time. He was also thrown into prison with eleven other citizens on suspicion of killing a gentleman found near by. Besides, a man who was perpetually talking about justice and who thought it worth telling how a hidalgo sent men to the galleys "by force and not of their own free will" was always regarded as a spoil-sport and simpleton. As Don Quixote said : "Let every man live with his sin. God is in his heaven and he does not forget to chastise the wicked and reward the good. It is not right that men should make themselves the executioners of others." Such was the case of Don Quixote's author who thenceforth moved along the path to martyrdom.

In 1613 his *Novelas Ejemplares* was published and in 1615 eight comedies and the second part of *Don Quixote*. But despite this there is not the slightest evidence of wealth or fame in his household. There is no sign of anything demonstrating a desire to please or surprise, which was so much in the nature of the ingenious hidalgo. There was not even a false coat of arms. Not a single relic of Lepanto. He was a solitary prince of the absurd who contemplated his own ridiculous position, deliberately chose it and lived it ; he would leave the kitchen and without a glance at the canopied bed, raise his eye toward the crucifix.

His must have been a wan smile. He once wrote a pamphlet attacking himself, so as to incite curiosity and get his works read. In it he wrote : "This book in the name of an imaginary hero conceals a satire on some most distinguished court personalities."

On 19 Avril, 1616, he completed the dedication of his *Persiles and Sigismonde* to the Count of Lemos :

"That old song which begins :

'Already my foot is in the stirrup...'

I would like for it not to fall so correctly and so precisely in time with my epistle, because I might well begin it almost in the same way and say :

'Already my foot is in the stirrup
In the heart of anguish at death
Great Lord, I write you this.'

Yesterday they gave me extreme unction and today I write you this. Time is short, anguish grows, hope flees..."

He died on April 23 and was buried in the convent of the Discalced Trinitarians in Cantarranas Street, Madrid, which today is the Lope de Vega Street.

Spain was to "discover" Cervantes in 1780 well after several other countries. From then on Miguel de Cervantes Saavedra was to Spain what Shakespeare is to England, Dante to Italy and Pascal to France. Is it the result of the justice in which he so fervently believed ?

105. Balconies overlook an inside courtyard in the house at Valladolid.

◁ 106. One of the rooms in
Valladolid house.

107. Cervantes' d

106

108. Writer's room in restored state.

109

110

109. *Cervantes' portrait.*

110. *"Don Quixote and Sancho", by Daumier.*

III

112. *Don Quixote dreaming, by Goya.* ▷

111. *In Seville, this house has been reconstituted as a museum in Cervantes' memory.*

113. *This white-walled kitchen with azulejos tiles is in the Cervantes Museum.*
▽

112

Chateaubriand

from Combourg to La Vallée-aux-Loups

Combourg or a two years' long dream.

The feudal castle at Combourg, in Brittany, had been acquired in 1761 by Chateaubriand's father, René-Auguste de Chateaubriand, youngest son of a large family. He had looked to the sea. He owned an independent shipping line, and gained enough money to buy a home that was able to give him the roots appropriate to his aristocratic origin.

He chose Combourg, a castle that sustained eighteen parishes. The land at Combourg was poor and the management of the property had been neglected by the previous owners. Monsieur de Chateaubriand was to restore the estate to its former heathly condition.

There it was that René, living alone with his sister Lucile—the other sisters being now married—discovered the exciting moments that can be experienced by two people together. Lucile and René, sitting before the great fire on the ground floor, would feel at the centre of a drama played out by ghosts and storied figures of the past. Madame de Chateaubriand had resigned herself early in marriage to bringing up their children on her own. Monsieur de Chateaubriand used the place as a ship more than as a castle, tramping along its corridors at night-time much as an officer keeps watch on the bridge. Lucile and René played at being afraid, and were delighted a the connivance it generated between them.

René wrote : "At eight o'clock the bell rang for supper. After supper, on fine days, we sat out on the steps. My father, armed with his shotgun, fired at the owls as they came out of the battlements with the fall of the night. My mother, Lucile and I looked at the sky, the woods, the last rays of the sun, and the first few stars. At ten o'clock we would all go to bed.

"The evenings in autumn and winter were of quite another kind. With supper over, the four of us would move from the table to the fire-place and my mother would throw herself with a sigh onto an old sofa of flaming Siamese material, and we placed an occasional table beside her with a candle on it. I would sit next to the fire with Lucile ; the servants cleared the table and withdrew. My father would then begin his walking about which continued until bedtime.

"He wore a white ratteen robe, or rather a kind of coat the like of which I have seen only on him. His half-bald head was covered with a large white bonnet which he wore bolt upright. During his walk, he went away from the fire, and the huge room was so badly lit that we could see him no longer, but could only hear him striding in the shadows. Then he would slowly come back into the glow and emerge gradually from the dark, like some ghost with his white robe and bonnet, and his long pale face. Lucile and I would exchange a few words in a low tone when he was at the other

135

114. This portrait of a debonair François-René de Chateaubriand is in the romantic style so loved by the writer. It certainly belies the com- *ment made by Napoleon Bonaparte after seing another portrait: "He looks like a conspirator who has come down the chimney."*

end of the room, but we kept silent when he approached us. He would say to us as he went by : 'What are you talking about ?' And seized with terror we would not reply. He went on with his striding. The only sounds striking the eardrum were his measured beat, my mother's sighs and the murmuring of the wind. Ten o'clock would sound out from the castle clock and my father would stop. The same spring that actuated the hammer of the clock seemed to have halted him in his steps..."

It is hardly possible to change the outside of a great bulk like Combourg. But *La Belle Époque* managed to add some balustrades to the stairs and entirely transformed the inside of the big room Chateaubriand described, dividing it into two, painting and carving Renaissance styles there.

In his *Mémoires* Chateaubriand said that on entering the castle one was immediately inside a courtyard with views of the battlements "where scolopendrium grew and a wild plum tree flourished." This courtyard was covered over and used thereafter as an entrance vestibule. On the ceiling of the doorway, formerly plain, shields of the crusader knights have since been painted, the companions of Geoffroy de Chateaubriand in the army of King Saint Louis. But this decoration, false Renaissance of 1880, has not entirely obliterated the old Combourg. The amounts lavished in the later period did not hide it all. In the upper levels, gained via a narrow staircase leading to the roofs, the visitor traverses a pathway hidden by the crenellated walls to a tower where a small bedroom now exists. This was the room used by François-René. "It was hidden," he wrote, "in a sort of isolated cell up in the top of a staircase leading from the inside courtyard to the various parts of the castle... A few swifts in Summer buried themselves in the walls and were my only companions. At night I saw only a small piece of the sky and a few stars..."

The furniture in this room all belonged to Chateaubriand. The Restauration iron bed with its canopy in white cambric is the very one on which he died at the Rue du Bac in Paris. A tiny window lets in the light and reveals how thick the walls are. In this lordly cell is a portrait of the Duchesse de Berry and another of the Count of Chambord, which recall Chateaubriand's liking for royalty. In the castle library the personal belongings of René de Chateaubriand are still unchanged : his desk, pens and books, even a mummified cat wich was found during repairs. Perhaps it was this cat that René and Lucile thought they heard mewing in the night.

Eventually, three of Chateaubriand's sisters married and Chateaubriand himself stayed alone with Lucile. "Our friendship lasted all our lives," he wrote. "The existence we led at Combourg, my sister and I, increased the exhilaration due to our age and character. Our chief pastime was to go for walks."

A book called *René, or The Wave of Passions* appeared in 1805. This was a description of the romantic life and confused passion they felt for each other at Combourg. The novel immediately triggered off the depression of the age (the *mal du siècle*). Chateaubriand, by writing it, had buried his memories, but Lucile was unable to sublimate them and suddenly agreed to marry at the age of thirty-one a knight of Caud, a septuagenarian who shortly died. She believed later that she had found her brother again in the shape of a young poet called Chênedollé who loved her, but she learned that he had married during the Revolution and had a child, so she rejected him. Less than a year afterwards, Lucile committed suicide in a small room in the Rue d'Orléans-Saint-Marcel in Paris, between Rue Mouffetard and the Jardin des Plantes. Her brother, who lived in Paris at the time, did nothing for her. He did not even attempt to keep her out of the common burial ground.

La Vallée-aux-Loups.

In 1803, he had re-written a work called *Le Génie du Christianisme*, in which he added a dedication "to the First Consul Citizen, for whom thirty million French pray at the foot of the altars he has returned to them." In acknowledgment, Bonaparte appointed him secretary-writer at the legation in Rome. But the new diplomat committed a number of blunders and in the same year was named chargé d'affaires in the Swiss Republic of Le Valais. He had only to await an appropriate moment at which to hand in his resignation. Following the execution of the Duke of Enghien the next year, Chateaubriand resigned his post in a double protest. Shortly afterwards he wrote in the *Mercure de France* the now famous critique of tyranny, beginning : "When in the silence of abjection can be heard only the chains of slavery and the voices of the informer..." The publication was suspended at once and Napoleon burst out : "Does Chateaubriand think I am an imbecile, that I do not understand ? I'll have him cut down on the steps of the Tuileries."

It was only a word in anger, and as a result of the compensation he received, Chateaubriand bought La Vallée-aux-Loups a few miles from Paris. Napoleon had told him to go far away. "It is to the great desert of Atala that I owe the small desert of Aulnay," Chateaubriand wrote. It was in fact to the emperor that he owed it, although no doubt it was his book *Atala* which provided the money for the repairs and foolhardy expenditure he undertook. What was La Vallée-aux-Loups like when in 1807 Monsieur and Madame de Chateaubriand bought it for 24,000 francs ? A farm surrounded by an orchard situated at Aulnay, near Sceaux and Chatenay. It was the immense park that seized the imagination of Chateaubriand. The farm building itself he turned into a residence of several storeys, flanked by a bell tower. The façades are a mixture of neoclassicism and troubadour-romanticism.

The way in is up a pathway over mossy banks bearing century-old trees, and the house is entered by a door hidden by an ivy-covered minstrel balcony. This is the north façade which contains Gothic windows and is as striking as the noble frontage with its huge Greek portico supported by caryatids and columns that would certainly feel happier in Athens. A slate-roofed tower abuts on to the right wing of the house, and a small iron staircase gave access to the first floor. These are the contradictions of an epoch which was discovering several styles and wanted to use them all at the same time. Chateaubriand translated into the decorations his whims as a romantic writer and historian.

The author's yellow drawing room has been turned into a Chateaubriand museum containing busts, engravings and books recalling his life. The small *salon* with its large windows, which the ivy has finally conquered, has a filtered light. On a chest of drawers stands a bust of Madame Récamier, as if laid on an altar for her greater glory. The *salon* next door overlooks the vast park which may be seen between pilasters and caryatids through the Greek portico. The world of a simple country gentleman is reflected in the piano, the old screens, bouquets of wild flowers, *crapaud* armchairs covered in red velvet, pink cretonne curtains, Directoire furniture, *moiré* wallpaper of artificial blue, objects of recollection in their golden frames, *The Burial of Atala*. A double-turn iron staircase designed by Chateaubriand which leads to the first-floor bedrooms is perhaps the most surprising feature of the house. Its shape resembles that of the finer staircase in the entrance hall of Broglie Castle in Normandy. This iron material heralds the metallic architecture of the Second Empire.

This was the atmosphere in which the author of *Les Martyrs* thought up the characters of Blanca, Cymodocée and Velleda. It was also at La Vallée-aux-Loups that he wrote *Voyage en Orient* and began his *Mémoires*.

At La Vallée-aux-Loups Chateaubriand realized at last some of the consequences of a marriage which had taken place years before. In 1792, when he was twenty-four years old, he was married off by his mother to Céleste Buisson de La Vigne. The wedding to this supposedly rich young lady took place just as he was leaving for England, and he never quite realized what had happened. He tried at a later stage to make up for his indifference, and laconically wrote in his *Mémoires* : "Madame de Chateaubriand is a better person than I am, although not so easy to get on with. Have I been irreproachable toward her ?" Madame de Chateaubriand was, in any cases, joint ruler over La Vallée-aux-Loups. She found, at a late stage, that she could play a useful role in her writer-husband's life. She was never an inspiration to him, but at La Vallée-aux-Loups she became a "colleague" by planting the trees.

Chateaubriand brought back from his voyages a nostalgia for trees of other climes, and friends were to help him obtain them. The Duchess of Duras kept him informed of her discoveries at a nursery in Mérinville. Joséphine herself sent him a magnolia exactly like the example she had at Malmaison. Chateaubriand seemed for ever planting things.

Even today, this residence on the outside of Paris, which has now grown up around it, is an astonishing romantic jungle, laid out by a retired couple. All places where famous people lived have a mystery somewhere; the one at La Vallée-aux-Loups is in the form of a small octagonal brick cottage called La Tour de Velleda, which is a rather sad eighteenth-century folly in which Chateaubriand liked to write. It was built in seventy-two hours for a rich brewer of Rue Saint-Antoine and it is said that this man, having at the start of the Revolution done a valuable service to the royal family, was thanked by the queen who promised to visit him at his Aulnay home. He considered his house was not worthy enough to receive Marie-Antoinette and had the new cottage built in three days. Chateaubriand restored it but time has made it a ruin again. It is located in a hollow of the grounds but from its balcony can be seen the entire property. It was converted into an "oratory" by Madame de Chateaubriand, who is thought to have got wind of certain persons visiting her husband. The conversion would in that case amount to a witty revenge, but we have a somewhat gloomy picture of Madame de Chateaubriand and one wonders if she was in fact capable of showing much spirit?

From 1807 and to 1818, Chateaubriand was enamoured in turn of Delphine de Custine, for whom he had "delirious" passion, Nathalie de Laborde and then Madame Récamier.

Juliette Récamier, ruined by her husband, was forty-two and lively. She lived in a small third-floor appartment "tiled, uncomfortable and with a crude staircase", in a convent, the Abbaye-au-Bois, that took in lodgers. Chateaubriand describes this modest apartment in his *Mémoires*. There she used to receive everyone who counted in Paris society, as she had formerly done in the Rue d'Anjou-Saint-Honoré. She would wear "a dress in grey silk with flying pleats, and a black belt and chaste tunic up to her neck" (Lamartine).

Of all the beauties Chateaubriand attracted, Madame Récamier is the most famous. We shall probably never know what exactly their love relationship was. She was the only love he returned to, despite a thousand infidelities. His *Mémoires* and the Abbaye-au-Bois, in the end, meant everything to him.

Under the Restauration, Chateaubriand was named a Peer of France, a title he later dropped under the newly-elected "Chambre Introuvable". Deprived of this income he had to sell his library at La Vallée-aux-Loups in order to keep alive. Then he had scheme to dispose of the whole property with a lottery. Only a few tickets were bought, sixteen out of ninety tickets at 1,000 francs each. Three were bought by the Duchesse of Orléans, ten by Monsieur le Comte d'Artois. The lottery generally met with an indifferent royalist public so Chateaubriand returned all the ticket money and put the residence up for auction. The starting price was covered by Mathieu de Montmorency-Laval, who got it for 100 francs more. He added to the property a small chapel which is now buried in creepers, colocynth and ivy. He let Madame Récamier use it for two years. Thus, one of the women Chateaubriand loved most of all found peace and contentment at La Vallée-aux-Loups. Madame de Chateaubriand's oratory could not keep the feminine influence out of the place in the end.

115. An oil painting framed in pearls shows Combourg ▷
Castle in the 1880's.

116. René de Chateaubriand and his sister, Lucile, spent
"two years of delight" in this feudal Castle of Combourg,
the family seat acquired by the author's father in 1761.
The memory of his romantic existence here and the troubled
love that developed between him and his sister inspired
him to write "René", a strongly romantic work.   The Mal
du Siècle felt in its pages was in his case that of lost youth.
▽

117

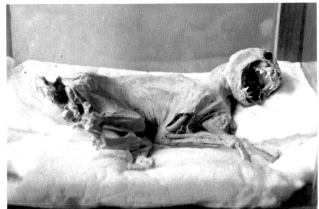

◁ *117. Lucile de Chateaubriand.*

118

119

118. While repairing the walls of Combourg, workmen found this immured cat which René and Lucile thought they had heard at night.

119. The writer's table, Restoration period chair and books have been kept in the library in one of the Combourg towers. The "Combourg cat" preserved under glass is on a bookshelf.

120. Chateaubriand died in this bed in July 4, 1848, while in Paris at Rue du Bac. It was then taken back to the castle.

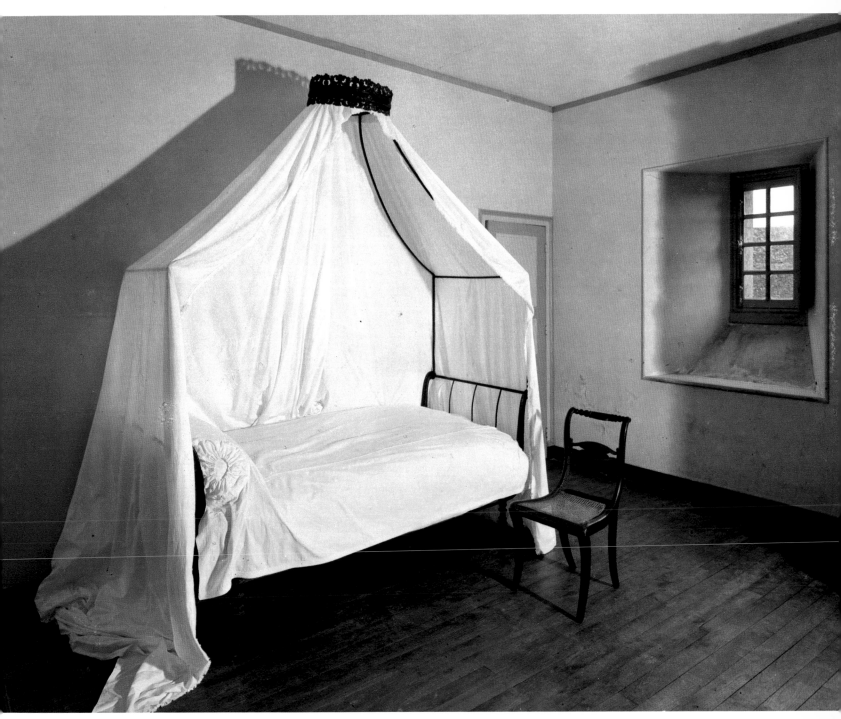

121. Madame Récamier was the great love in Chateaubriand's life. "Everything I have ever loved, I have loved in Juliette." She was beautiful and coquettish, with a marked taste for platonic relationships. Sainte-Beuve said of her: "In love, she liked everything to come to a halt in April."

122. Madame de Chateaubriand.

123. Delphine de Custine.

124. Pauline de Beaumont.

125. La Vallée-aux-Loups lies near Châtenay-Malabry, a few miles from Paris.

126

◁ 126. As an older man, Chateaubriand loved Nathalie de Laborde ardently. She is believed to have been his Cymodocée, and Blanca in "Le Dernier Abencérage".

128. This chapel in the grounds of La Vallée-aux-Loups ▷ was built after Chateaubriand sold the property. Madame de Récamier who lived on after his death used to meditate here.

127. Porch at northern side of La Vallée-aux-Loups. Chateaubriand remodelled this façade in the style of the troubadour Gothic style current in the 1830's.

▽

127

129. *Chateaubriand's gardener saw Napoleon steal into* ▷
the grounds of La Vallée-aux-Loups and climb up this tower,
known as the Velléda Tower, in order to see how his "exile"
was faring. The next day, the gardener found a yellow
glove belonging to him.

130. *The writer had this double stairway built for him.*
It led to the first-floor bedrooms.
▽

◁ 131. The entrance hall in La Vallée-aux-Loups has a terracotta bust of Madame Récamier on the chest of drawers.

132. The small salon has blue moiré paper, the large one chintz. Many belongings of Chateaubriand are seen here, Madame Récamier holding first place in his life. Furniture, cretonnes, red velvet tuffets are those he used. La Vallée-aux-Loups, so near Paris, has been miraculously preserved.

▽

Chopin

from Warsaw to Paris

At the age of nineteen Frederick Chopin had only one object in mind : to see his gifts recognized outside Warsaw. He went to Vienna leaving behind those he loved : his parents, his sisters, his best friend Titus and the memory of a love affair with a girl called Constance.

He was born February 22, 1810 a few miles from Warsaw, in a house attached to the Zelazowa manor where his father Nicholas Chopin was tutor of the five children of Countess Skarbek. Chopin's father had married Justyna Krzyzanowska, one of the ladies-in-waiting and a relative of the countess. Justyna loved playing the piano.

From a distance the residence of the Chopin family might have been taken for a farm, were it not for the two-column portico in front. The house had a huge roof. When Frederick, the future composer, came into the world he was welcomed by local violin players who had come through the snow in a sledge, to play outside the window. The countess agreed to be godmother. In the autumn of that year, 1810, Nicholas Chopin was appointed teacher of French at Warsaw College. The Chopin family henceforth kept the house, which is still standing, for summer visits and went to live in an appartment in Warsaw. They took in several lodgers to help out with their finances. When Madame Chopin started playing the piano, her son in his cradle would begin having convulsions. But when he began to walk it was noticed that he liked to curl up under the keyboard when his mother played.

One night he was found in front of the piano improvising music and from that moment he was given a teacher, Zwyny, of Czechoslovakian origin, who taught him Bach and Mozart. He had an intuition about the child's gifts and allowed him to seek his style himself without imposing a definite method on him. Frederick soon played in public. He produced his *Gyrowitz Concerto* and a polonaise which was published dedicated to the Countess Victoire Skarbek. He was still only eight years old. It was already clear that he was a genius, and he was invited to play his polonaises to the tsar's mother who visited his school.

Later the Chopins set up home in a bigger apartment and took in more lodgers including some who became friends with Frederick : the Wodzinskis, Fontana Slowaki and particularly Titus Woyciechowski.

The family was in no way pretentious and their interior was simple. The drawing room had light-coloured wood furniture, chairs with pierced designs, a romantic sofa, a large occasional table, prints on the wall in wooden frames, simple curtains in white linen. The Chopin family met often. Chopin had three sisters, one of whom, Emilie, died at an early age of tuberculosis. Extra care was taken over Frederick who had the same complaint. The Chopin home in Warsaw was destroyed in the

149

Second World War and has recently been reconstructed. In a small museum in memory of the great musician, furniture and personal belongings have been collected together.

During his Warsaw period, Chopin was a gay young spark who liked plenty of jokes. He was noisy, keen to play theatrical roles and imitate people.

In 1825 he published his *First Rondo in C sharp minor* and, following a visit to Silesia, entered the Warsaw Conservatory. His gifts were quickly detected by his professors; already he had been acknowledged by his own circle. At this time, Chopin was in search of friendship. Titus, his confidential friend, knew him when he was a lodger with Chopin's parents, in the Warsaw apartment. Frederick made demands on his affection and his presence. In order to get him to come and live with him, he used to assume a tone that was very similar to one he used twenty years later to evoke more love from a woman who was growing weary. As a young man, Frederick already had a despairing kind of sensitivity which was to make him suffer so much when he lived with George Sand.

The first girl he fell in love with was Constance Gladkowska, who apparently did not respond to his approaches. Frederick confessed to Titus: "I have perhaps, unfortunately for me, found my ideal. I venerate her with all my soul. It is six months now since I began dreaming of her every night and I have not spoken to her yet. It was while thinking of her that I wrote the *Adagio* of my concerto... Note the passage marked by a cross. You are the only person who knows what it means." And in another letter to his friend, when he felt abandoned by him and by the girl, he said: "You can imagine how sad Warsaw seems to me. If I did not feel happy in the family circle, I would not like to live here."

Titus was, from then on, the close confident of the highly sensitive and shy Frederick. Titus accompanied him when, on the advice of his father, he went to Vienna to finish his musical education. But when revolution broke out in Warsaw, Titus took the first coach back to get into the thick of the fighting. Chopin thought of returning with his friend, but his father advised him against this. With Titus gone, Chopin vainly sought ways of joining up with him but to no avail. Although Chopin had to remain alone in Vienna and Providence separated them, their friendship was to remain strong for their whole lives. In due course Chopin left for Paris, and with the uprising over in Poland, he succeeded in recontacting Titus, much relieved that he had not been slaughtered at the barricades.

On arrival in Paris, Chopin played before the Polish aristocracy. He was greatly admired but studiously avoided all show of facile patriotism, preferring not to take part in fund-raising operations for Polish insurrectional movements. He gladly wrote polonaises but carefully stayed unconnected with any faction. Possibly this reticence sprang from his own father, who was himself a French expatriate in Poland. Chopin refused to support the French revolutionaries who chased out his father, or revolution itself, or the abuse of freedom at the time. The crudeness of those demanding liberties revolted him. Later he criticized George Sand for being hostess to revolutionaries at her Nohant home.

These included Louis Blanc and his left-wing colleagues—"so vulgar". Nor could he stand the loquacious Balzac with his ostentatious ways. Chopin was too sensitive, too delicate, too lucid. Glory itself made him shrug his shoulders. When at one point, after a great success, there was a move to publish his picture, the composer refused saying: "What, to wrap up butter?"

One day, he met Prince Radziwill on a Paris Boulevard and that same evening was playing in a Rothschild drawing room. Chopin's triumph was immediate, but it did not prevent him from remarking: "If I were more stupid than I am, I would image that I was at the summit of my career."

In order to make a living he gave piano lessons. This meant he could avoid giving recitals, and thus have time to compose. He was able to live in style with a four-wheeled carriage, horses and servants. He wore a frockcoat.

Meanwhile in Warsaw, his father Nicholas was worried. He said : "My son, I am going to speak frankly to you. Try to get a little money together, particularly in view of the times we live in... If you share lodgings with anyone, be careful and make sure of his behaviour..."

His father need not have worried. In previous times the grand duke needed to hear Chopin play to calm his moments of fury. Now, in Paris, the Countess of Agoult, who married Liszt, asked him to play to cure her woes. She wrote to him : "If you could come tomorrow, I should much appreciate it. I have just been ill and still suffer ; I am sure one of your nocturnes would complete my recovery."

A few years later, furious with Chopin for becoming the lover of her own rival George Sand, she said of him : "That oyster sprinkled with sugar !" When Nicholas Chopin warned his son about bad friendships, he did not think of bitter tongues. Orlowski commented : "Chopin is in good health and vigorous ; he turns all the women's heads and the men are quite jealous. He is very much in the fashion and doubtless we shall all soon be wearing gloves *à la Chopin*. He is consumed only by homesickness."

The last really living link holding him to Poland was Maria Wodzinska, a girl he met at Karlsbad one summer when he was spending a short while there with his parents. This was an entirely platonic affair. After Chopin's death an envelope was discovered bearing the words *Moia Bieda!* ("my Misfortune !"). The girl had earlier promised to love him, perhaps, but her mother wanted them to wait a year before marrying. In the end Maria married a Pole, although the union was later annulled in Rome. Chopin was for some time inconsolable. It needed the strong will of a George Sand—and she did not lack willpower when she wanted to be loved—to make Chopin finally forget Maria, and become disinterested in simple creatures.

The first meeting between Chopin and George Sand was a disappointment. Frederick said : "How unlikeable she is, that Sand person. Is she really a woman ? I have my doubts." She was eight years his senior, and she invited him to Nohant, but he refused to go. So she set out to win over the Polish circle he frequented, and aimed her main attack at his friend Count Albert Grzymola.

"He must come. It is my ultimatum," she wrote. "I demand to know which of us he must forget or abandon in order to be at rest, for his well-being, for his very life. I am not Bertram de Meyerbeer and I will not fight against a childhood friend if she is a beautiful and untainted Alice... As to the little chap, he will come if he wants to..."

Chopin and George Sand, defying the predictions of their pessimistic friends, were to experience deep passion. Unfortunately for posterity, Sand burned all his letters referring to the early days of their affair. We know only that in an extraordinary chartreuse-type house, at Valdemosa on Majorca, they loved each other and that he nearly died of a TB relapse. The Majorca adventures brought their passion to an end. In *Lucrezia Floriani*, George Sand writes of the early flames of love she inspired in Chopin (who is Prince Karl in the book) : "He had never felt the heart of a woman beat against his own, and the first experiences of this kind were for him more vivid and deeper than they usually are in adolescents faced with the awakening of their senses... His desires had germinated within him for a long time without him wanting to realize it. He had cheated them by means of poetry and religious sentiment for a fiancée whose hand had scarcely touched his own..."

The crazed love which died so soon at Majorca was followed by eight years of "married" bliss at Nohant. Chopin became attached to George as a son to a mother. She, however, wanted only the passion of the early days, for her militant feminism was complete.

Whether it was with Sandeau, Musset or Chopin, once the period of mutual discovery was over, leaving the partners dazed, she preferred solitude or a return to friendship devoid of all love relationship. Chopin's delicate health in this case provided a pretext, because in reality the violent passion George had for Chopin was dead. The inevitable quarrel came over the subject of marrying off George's daughter

Solange, who was determined to wed a somewhat crude sculptor called Clésinger. George, knowing that this was virtually bound to happen, avoided telling Chopin who was in Paris at the time, for fear he might intervene and oppose the idea. Chopin considered that after eight years' life together this amounted to a lack of trust. He felt hurt and had no wish to see Sand again. He died amid his Polish friends and in the company of Solange.

The last meeting between Frederick and George was a chance one on March 4, 1848, in Paris in the entrance to a house in Rue de la Ville-l'Évêque where Carlotta Marliani, their former kind-hearted cook, was living. It was her visiting day and Chopin had been to see her. On leaving the house he bumped right into George. A few years earlier they would not have imagined they would one day come across each other and exchange a few vague words in an indifferent tone of wounded pride.

Chopin asked : "Have you any recent news of your daughter?"

"Not for a week now," she said.

"You had none yesterday or the day before, then?"

"No."

"Well, then, I can inform you that you are a grandmother. Solange has had a baby girl. I am glad to be the first to give you the news."

Whereupon Chopin bid good-bye to Sand and continued on his way.

She thought quickly and had an urge to follow up the exchange, intending to ask him some more. She put to him a number of questions about her daughter's health, and about his own. Chopin avoided lengthy answers and merely replied : "Very well, thank you."

Later Sand said : "I wanted to speak with him, but he got away. It was my turn to say he loved me no longer. I never saw him again. There was bad feeling between us."

Chopin in point of fact died a few months later in an apartment he took on doctor's orders because it faced south. It was at 12 Place Vendôme in Paris. At the end of 1848 he returned exhausted from a visit to London and Scotland, and had up till then rested at a house in Chaillot, which was then a suburb of Paris. The idea of living at Place Vendôme had restored his zest and he had chosen the wallpapers. Stretched out on a bed in the sunny room he listened as the moving men brought in the furniture. He would rise occasionally and look round the apartment. But he was to enjoy it for only three weeks. His friends stayed by his side until the end, and in the evening on October 12, 1849, he received extreme unction. Afterward his friends came back into the room and Poles and French joined in litanies for the dying. Chopin began to feel better and at his request Princess Marceline and Franchomme played the beginning of the *Sonata in G minor*. They stopped when Chopin started coughing.

He was four days dying, and in the end he desired death. Father Alexander, a childhood friend, advised him to pray and he replied in Polish : "Thanks to you I shall not die like a pig." On October 15, Delphine Potocka, his latest love, arrived from Nice and Chopin told her : "God has left me the pleasure of seeing you." He asked her to sing. She picked *Hymn to the Virgin* by Stradella and a Psalm by Marcello.

That night Chopin made his final requests to friends. He asked Pleyel not to publish any of his recent works and to burn his private papers. He asked for his heart to be returned to Warsaw and for Mozart's *Requiem* to be sung at his funeral.

During the night of October 16 he tried to speak but had lost his voice. He was given a piece of paper and wrote on it : "Since this cough will suffocate me, I ask you to have my body opened up so that I am not buried alive." This piece of paper has been preserved ; he had written down the same request his father had made on his deathbed. Only the word "alive" is not clearly visible.

Some people who were present later said that before losing his voice he murmured : "She always said I would die in her arms..." Did he mean George Sand? He himself had once said when leaving his Warsaw home : "To die far from one's country must be quite sad." He passed away in Paris, far from the woman he had loved the most.

134

134. *The original manuscript of the E minor Concerto lies on a table in the Chopin family's Warsaw apartment. The composer wrote this the summer before his departure for Vienna and Paris. The apartment was restored after its destruction in the Second World War.*

135

136

137

◁ 135. Nicholas Chopin, the composer's father.

138. Chopin by Götzenberger, Paris, October 1838. ▷

Next page:
139. The romance of Chopin and George Sand ended on March 4, 1848 in this private courtyard on Rue de la Ville-l'Evêque in Paris. It was here that their last meeting took place. "I wanted to talk to him but he escaped," wrote George Sand.

136. Justyna Krzyzanowska, Chopin's mother.

137. Maria Wodzniska.

140. Chopin and George Sand often walked in the garden of La Chartreuse, during their stay in Valdemosa, Majorca.

141. The walls of La Chartreuse, Valdemosa, sheltered ▷ the early months of their romance. George Sand later wrote in Lucrezia Floriani, recalling these moments: "He had never felt the heart of a woman beat against his, and these first emotions were for him more vivid and deeper than they generally are in an adolescent at the awakening of the senses."

Anatole France

at La Béchellerie

The tiny village of Saint-Cyr-sur-Loire in Touraine boasts a large number of famous houses. In addition to La Béchellerie where Anatole France lived toward the close of his life, there are La Grenadière where Balzac lived (he named one of his works after it), La Perraudière occupied by Charles Perrault, author of *Cinderella* and *The Sleeping Beauty*, and La Gaudinière where Henri Bergson lived. The latter is only a few yards from La Béchellerie and separated from it by a large tree-lined road. A few miles away on the other bank of the Loire is Ronsard's Priory of Saint-Côme and nearby, too, is Rancan, the early residence of Elvire, heroine of Lamartine's *Le Lac*.

La Béchellerie, entirely in the country, has only a few houses round it forming the hamlet of La Clarté. It is a sixteenth-century countryseat with a big slate roof and traditional layout, a simple garden and some outhouses. The author of *Le Lys rouge* and *Le Jardin d'Epicure* liked it the moment he caught sight of it. Having fled Paris in 1914 when the Germans were advancing through France, he found himself at a hotel in Tours in the company of his housekeeper and a few other refugees. He could not get used to writing and living there and the atmosphere of the hotel depressed him. He said : "I have a horror of people who do not sleep enough. In former time this was agreable to me but now it causes me unnecessary regrets."

It must be explained that France was never one of those authors who are satisfied with writing alone. Women had held an important place in his life and still did, even in his advanced age. When he used to go into the Tridon bookshop in Touraine, women admirers would recognize him and ask him to write something in their books ; sometimes these booklovers sought more than mere words. Once a lady "publicly implored from him the ultimate outrages" and he took her hands, patted them, and looking to left and right at the witnesses of the scene, demanded in a loud voice : "Well, Madame, have I now sufficiently compromised you ?"

This man liked women too much not to permit himself an occasional joke at their expense. When he was settled in at La Béchellerie, there was not a single room that did not have its torso or face of a Greek woman on a piece of furniture or a mantle piece. Antique collecting, with him, concealed other tastes. In his study was a marble hand on a stand, a copy of Madame de Caillavet's hand ; she was the "goddess" who for a long time held the predominent position in his life.

When war broke out in 1914, France was seventy, famous and member of the Académie Française. Freedom became more necessary to him than anything else. His prolific output already included his most celebrated works. When he left his Villa Saïd in Paris in a hurry

161

and reached Tours, he was revolted by the idea of having to write novels in a provincial hostelry that lacked any comfort, for the duration of a war that showed signs of lasting a long while. His age and fame allowed him to insist on a certain freedom.

Politically he was radically-minded. In religious matters he was a militant non-believer. The day was to come when his free-thinking ideas turned against him, obliging him to marry his housekeeper at La Béchellerie. So he had, then, a vital need for a quiet home where he could carry on writing. He liked to be comfortable and feel at ease, at the same time insisting on freedom for his ideas to develop. He had ideas on everything, and was sometimes wrong: "I like my mistakes", he would say. "I do not want to give up the delicious pleasure of going astray, losing myself and losing my soul. I want to be able to make mistakes when I feel like it."

We shall see how this desire for absolute liberty made him disown his daughter and marry his housekeeper. This lady had worked for him since he arrived in Tours, and she explored the countryside around about seeking a place that would suit her master. She suggested La Béchellerie after a while, and he acquired it. He had known it several years ago in 1871. War brought him back to it and gave him ownership of it.

Anatole France immediately had extensions made so that he could have his friends there. A rabbit shed became a pleasant little house which he called Les Lapins. The washhouse, the wine store and a smaller Béchellerie were all renovated and converted.

The author later acquired a good deal of land around the house. He came just to spend the war there but stayed until his death on October 12, 1924. As Victor Hugo did at Hauteville on the isle of Guernsey, he made La Béchellerie into a retreat and was so pleased with it he spent the rest of his days there. La Béchellerie is a residence produced from whims, junk and antiques, preposterous ideas in decoration and quite a lot of do-it-yourself work. To reconstruct a house at the age of seventy means rebuilding one's own life to some extent. France,

when he took over La Béchellerie, wanted to keep intact its eighteenth-century interior and retain the Louis-Quinze woodwork, the wrought iron staircase, and the neat windows and the little rooms as they were. He carefully restored the panelling and red lamps in the drawing room, introduced Venetian chandeliers and fixed eighteenth-century portraits to the walls together with Italian mirrors. He thus indulged his taste for antiques and quality furniture. The effect was that this Touraine house possessed much of the *fin-de-siècle* atmosphere of the Villa Saïd. For his study, France selected a large table, Louis-Treize chairs, a wing chair covered in *petit-point* with red as the dominant colour. Near to him he placed the marble hand of Madame de Caillavet, which in an almost comical way brought to a climax the memories of a long affair that was the mainspring of his love life.

This young woman was the descendant of an Austrian Jewish banking family, the Koenigswarters, who settled in Paris early in the nineteenth century. She loved the arts, letters and receptions and was a woman of some spirit. She was virtually separated from a husband who had little refinement, a gambler who liked joking. In due course she obtained her independence and started a literary *salon* at 12 Avenue Hoche in Paris. It was as great a success as were the *salons* of Madame Aubernon and the Countess of Loynes to whom Flaubert and Renan dedicated works. Madame de Loynes had a famous lover, the young Jules Lemaître, whereas Madame de Caillavet had only Victor Brochard who was merely a historian of the Greek sceptics, and certainly he did not satisfy her vanity or suit her reputation. The more so since Madame Cahen at Antwerp, in her *salon*, was flaunting Paul Bourget, Madame Pierrebourg in turn reigned with Paul Hervieu and Madame Lecompte had Maupassant.

Madame Armand de Caillavet therefore set about finding a new author-lover, and she finally picked Anatole France. Anatole's family life was profoundly upset by the pretensions of his wife, a descendant of the Guérin de Sauvilles, who constantly reproached her husband for not being well-born. A woman thirteen years older than she now took her place, by esteeming the things of the spirit more than titles. France commented : "Whether bad or good, one day things will always be what they must be."

Madame de Caillavet had blue eyes, grey tinted hair, was *petite* and chubby, but with enough wit to stand up to anyone who came to her *salon*. France began by confiding to her in a friendly way and eventually succumbed. She knew how to listen to him and, to her surprise, found out that he really was the man she was looking for. Their affair remained concealed until 1888, when Anatole and Madame de Caillavet started to realize that their love was dominating their lives. France used the sentiments of his mistress for his heroine in *Le Lys Rouge*: "I want to be quiet. If I cannot be so with you, it will have to be without you... I mean love to be a pleasure for me..."

She was a woman in love but her head was in the right place. She kept her author on the leash as long as she could, as he maintained the tone of the *salon*. She went with him on most of his foreign travels. They would have been very happy if Anatole had not experienced moments of intense jealousy, as when his mistress went for a health cure to Saint-Gervais or to her property in Gironde.

He said on August 12, 1888 : "We met each other too late. I can forgive you nothing, because I can forget nothing." On August 17 the same year he wrote : "Forgive me, but I am jealous to an extent I did not think possible. I bite my knuckles till they bleed ? Oh yes, I hate you. Forgive me." The following year it was : "Forgive my injustice, which is born of love. Excuse my suspicions, I suffer." and : "Tell me that I shall love you as I have loved you."

Some of his expressions can be found in *Le Lys Rouge*. There was not much need to make a travesty of reality, which was itself of a theatrical kind. "Thérèse", he wrote, "in my happiness I suffer from all that is connected with you but escapes me... I love you, you understand, I love you with all the sensations you bring me, and the habits, and everything that comes from your experiences. These are my delights and my torture."

Yet it was Anatole who broke off the affair. He drew away from his muse, and when Madame de Caillavet became aware of this she suffered badly. She had grown quite plump ; some yellowed photographs in France's first-floor room at La Béchellerie show her in Naples as a small woman of no particular age, bloated and almost buried under tulle and the flowers of a *petit-bourgeois* hat, as if she was trying to keep up with a younger man than herself who was walking too fast for her and not waiting for her to catch up.

Madame de Caillavet was the first to die, in a mood of resignation. All that is left for us to contemplate now is the fat little marble hand with its five fingers pointing to heaven. This is all that remains of a love that sprang from vanity, then knew violence and finally became habit. It was the kind of love relationship that more easily developed in the nineteenth century than in our own times.

Next to France's study is a drawing-room devoted to Emma Laprévotte in very eighteenth-century style. Bound volumes line the walls behind green taffeta curtaining. In the garden, which is on a level with the house, are roses and gladioli, daisies and fruit trees—all growing as thickly as the weeds. The windows of the dining room, staircase, billiard room and first-floor rooms all overlook this garden. So not for one moment can the visitor forget that he is in Touraine, where custom decrees that all kinds of flowers are grown in the gardens, leaving nature to produce its own groupings.

The result is that a natural jungle develops of all kinds of flowers, although the number can be controlled. Anatole France's room on the first floor still contains his small bed in Directoire wood and *Toile-de-Jouy* black and yellow wallpaper. The writing desk is only a table but his chair is pure directoire style. Over the chimneypiece is the striking face of a Greek woman. On the walls are some souvenirs from his travels and a few yellow photos of Madame de Caillavet.

163

Nothing could be more delightful than La Béchellerie's courtyard with its pool of water, the iron vases crammed with flowers, the statue of a woman. Nothing could be more curious than the seventeenth-century Bavarian lumber room used as a guest room, where the furniture jostles with a Gothic canopied bed under an Austrian lamp in the shape of a woman's face attached to stag's horns. Yet nothing could be sadder than this room where the half melted candles remain to this day in the chandeliers which cast their glow on the author as he lay so long on his deathbed. This unbeliever of eighty-four years of age expressed to friends his astonishment at death's trials. "So this is what it is like to die... It is a long business."

In a little house at the end of the garden which he could see from his window, he had collected together all his books, including fine editions of Rabelais, Montaigne and Racine which were to deteriorate with the damp and had to be taken back to the Villa Saïd. There, too, were antique busts and his *Mémoires*. It was the den of an upstanding gentleman at the turn of the century who gave his life to literature and love. He would go there in a dressing gown and velvet skull cap. He used to do some writing there. In the house he would move his statues about from place to place, and find new positions for his newly-acquired treasures.

He cared little for the productions of the nineteenth century and would say : "It was a low epoch." He was of the generation that believed more in style than in objects themselves. For him art stopped in the eighteenth century; the older a thing was the better it was. Unrelenting in his rearranging, France told friends : "I should have been an upholsterer." Everything interested him at La Béchellerie, except himself. "Far from attempting to know myself," he wrote, "I have always tried to forget myself. Knowledge of oneself is a source of concern, anxiety and torment. I am in my own company as little as possible. It has seemed to me that wisdom lies in turning away from oneself, from one's image, and in forgetting oneself resolutely. Whether small or grown up, young or old, I have always lived as far away as possible from myself."

This Touraine house was indeed a very good means of distracting his mind from his own person. Although he cared little for his own company, we cannot avoid his presence. He seems to be everywhere ; in his choice of treasures and their grouping. The house was a home for a pagan and freethinker in matters of love, and the presence of women can be keenly detected. His taste was conservative and traditionalist, and the house became a museum of styles from the great ages. The garden might be described as epicurean and could easily have met with Colette's approval.

Anatole France was as vigorous in his tastes as in his views. But this attitude turned against him and led to a tragi-comic situation. France had disowned his daughter when she married the son of an ardent Catholic whose ideas contrasted with Anatole's own ideas and he never saw her again. She died from influenza during the war. She left behind a son. It was the memory of the girl, his remorse at having lost her without "forgiving" her, and the existence of the motherless boy, which tormented him. In 1920, he married Emma Laprévotte, who had been living in his house since the end of 1910. A photograph still exists showing France on the steps of the village hall between two little girls carrying huge bouquets of flowers. He is an old man in the photo with a white beard next to a woman whose bland face is not in the least like that of the passionate and eccentric Madame de Caillavet's. It is a sorry document summing up the irony of a life given over to scepticism and unbelief.

Life affected him at his most vulnerable point—his heart. This happened very late in years and, in accepting the bonds of marriage after a life of unrestricted freedom, he seemed to be trying to make up for having been so hard-hearted in the past.

143. A small salon in La Béchellerie overlooks the garden. France acquired this property during the First World War. He could no longer stand living in a Tours hotel and, in this sixteenth-century manor house, he successfully repeated the atmosphere of his Villa Saïd in Paris.

144

144. *Madame de Caillavet, the writer's beloved. They both suffered in turn from jealousy.   She inspired his heroine in "Le Lys rouge", who said: "I want to be quiet.   If I cannot be so with you, it must be without you; I mean love to be a pleasure for me."*

145

145. *The eighteenth-century staircase at La Béchellerie.*

146. *The main courtyard of La Béchellerie.* ▷

147

148

147. *The writer's library in a garden house at La Béchellerie contains works by Rabelais, Montaigne and Racine. France worked here clad in a dressing gown and velvet skull cap.*

148. *Anatole France liked to be surrounded by the antique objects he collected. He cared little for those of the nineteenth century and used to say: "That was a low period."*

149. *The guest room was in the servant's quarters of the manor: "I should have been an upholsterer," he said.*

150

150. *A 1922 photograph shows Anatole France and his grandson.*

151. *In the writer's study is the furniture selected by Anatole France: a heavy table, Louis-Treize chairs, a petit-point wing chair. Between the panels, he fixed a red lamp and hung eighteenth-century paintings on panelling. Near to him was a marble hand, that of Madame de Caillavet, which recalled to him their long relationship.*

152. Goethe and Schiller were close friends—their friendship is immortalised in this picture. Goethe confided in a letter to Schiller: "In the whole of my life I have never met with an unexpected happiness, a pleasure I did not have to fight hard for."

Goethe

in Frankfurt

Goethe spent his childhood at Frankfurt, in a sad and sombre house in the Grosse Hirschgraben, restored by his family in 1755 and repaired after being destroyed by war in 1945.

Johann Wolfgang was born there on August 28, 1749 and stayed in Frankfurt sixteen years, after which his father sent him to study at Leipzig. He was back home for the period from September 1768 to March 1770, his nineteenth to twenty-first years. Again from September 1772 to October 1775 he spent some time in this house, and there wrote *Werther* and the early *Faust*.

The house tells us more about the character of his father than about Goethe. From the poet's memoirs we know that he preferred the attic to the lower storeys, occupied by the family. To his father, culture was everything. To the son, the analysis of the contradiction inherent in desires was more important that actual knowledge. Wolfgang was taken away from school at an early age due to an exceptional number of illnesses, and given a tutor and private teachers. This is why the Frankfurt house includes, as in a college, some rooms given over entirely to music, painting, reading and theatre.

This birthplace of Goethe in the Grosse Hirschgraben was built in 1591 and joined up with the building next door when he was five years old.

The Goethes fortune derived from the grandfather, Friedrich Georg Goethe, a hotelier and master tailor, who had placed his trade sign on the front of the house—a paschal lamb with banner. Later his son chose a new sign, "three lyres", and his grandson Wolfgang chose "the morning star" after he was given a title in 1782 by the Duke of Weimar. The social rise of the family was thus publicized on the wall of the building.

A large wrought iron staircase and a wooden clock (made by another Goethe of Frankfurt) are at the entrance to the house and suggest the steady bourgeois life of the occupants. The Goethes cultivated the arts as a matter of principle rather than through love.

On the ground floor is a dining room that reflects the father's taste for Flemish style. This room might easily be found in a house at Antwerp or Bruges. The walls are in a so-called "dying blue" colour with gold overprinting; the French *bleu mourant* was to be transformed to the German *blumerant*. A carved mirror of Dutch origin, which greatly impressed Wolfgang on his return from Leipzig, is still there; this mirror suddenly conveyed to him the old-fashioned atmosphere of the house and his father's outdated ideas. A Flemish lamp, heavy German seventeenth-century furniture, high-backed chairs upholstered in black leather—all are no doubt inherited from the Textors, a legal family on Wolfgang's mother's side.

Here, too, are a wing-chair and a large

iron and ceramic stove blackleaded in parts and decorated with the mythological elements of earth, fire, air and water. Pitchers, pewter items and still-life works all add to a Spanish mood that was more common in the interiors of the Charles V epoch rather than of the German Princes. The handiwork cushion of Goethe's mother recalls the realities of daily life in this family seat.

Dating from the time of the hotelier grandfather is the wrought iron gateway between the small courtyard and the garden, and another that gave access to the family vineyard planted in 1725. In the cellars of the house were kept, until 1794, some wines of the good years 1706, 1719 and 1726 which the old grandfather bought. In 1825 a linden tree was planted in the courtyard on Goethe's birthday. Also seen here are a well and some stone figures. The kitchen next to the dining room has been restored and includes collections of copper cakemoulds and wicker baskets of every imaginable size.

The house was destroyed during the Second World War, but fortunately the furniture had been put safely away. Despite the destruction, the stove of Goethe's mother remains intact to this day.

On the first floor are the drawing rooms. During the Seven Years War (1759-1762), the Goethe family hosted there the French Count de Thoranc and his suite. This "occupation" brought a breath of fresh air to the old place for Wolfgang who spoke Italian and Latin. The Count spoke no German. After a while Wolfgang was able to converse in French with the count who took great pains to amuse the boy. Goethe's father was always a little grumpy but the count greatly admired his taste for painting, and while in Germany he amassed a collection that was closely similar to his host's, and took it back to France (later the collection went to the Goethe Museum). What Goethe liked in the count was his views on relations between the bourgeois and soldiers. He was also interested in the inventions. He suggested public lighting be erected in the streets of Frankfurt. The city authorities reported his "good works"

to the emperor and the count was in due course given a title as a result of local pressure.

The presence of the French was for Wolfgang a welcome change from the irritating ways of his father, who spent his time raising silk worms in the loft and constantly watched the comings and goings of his son through the library window. When Wolfgang used to enter the house, he took good care not to catch sight of his father and went straight up to his French friends on the first floor.

The Count de Thoranc was the first person to extend young Goethe's vision beyond the conventional studious existence he was living. Another important influence was a man called Behrisch, whom he met later in Leipzig.

The first floor of the building comprised three rooms. One of them was called the Peking Room owing to its Chinese-style wallpaper. This is rather severe with its Louis-Quinze armchairs in red damask and a tall ceramic stove from the Hoechst factory. A room facing north still contains portraits of the Textor grandparents and some still-life paintings by Juncker. The south room has portraits of Peter Antony Brentano and his wife Maximilienne. This lady in August 1773 spent some time with the Goethe family, bringing her mother too, and later went to live in Frankfurt in January 1774.

She it was who became Lotte in *Werther;* Goethe gave her dark eyes. The first floor additionally housed the music room which Wolfgang's father arranged. A large red harpsichord which he acquired stands there today. According to Goethe's memoirs, his father spent more time repairing it than using it. He also added a grand piano with a belly at right angles to the keyboard. In *Poetey and Truth,* Wolfgang said the piano lessons his sister Cornelia had were torture, and that he was made to play the 'cello. The landscapes in this room were painted by Hackert, his teacher, with whom he visited Italy. Other paintings were commissioned from another teacher, Krauss. Wolfgang had several art masters.

In the loft were several rooms used by painters and various other artistic guests. The boy Wolfgang used to run errands for them just to have an excuse to be with them. On this floor, too, is a small room (not open to the public) which contains the twenty-eight pleas Wolfgang made over a period of four years in his capacity as lawyer in the court at Roemer. He did not remain a lawyer for long, since the success of *Werther* made him an acknowledged poet.

While the ground floor of the house is in seventeenth-century style, the first floor is German rococo of the 1750's. The second and third floor are Louis-Seize. They have striped tapestries, furniture in polished walnut and simple flooring. On the second floor is a reading room and an art studio: a library and art gallery. A third room here was occupied by Goethe's mother. In the library may still be seen the law books that Goethe's father used to read.

At the age of fifteen Wolfgang met his first love, Gretchen, "of unbelievable beauty". He tried one day to kiss her but she pushed him away. "I pressed my face into her hands and left hurriedly. The sight of this girl and my inclinations toward her had opened up before me a new universe of beauty and perfection," he wrote. Gretchen had become Eternal Woman. Without his father knowing he spent April 3, 1764, in the company of Gretchen and some local lads. "When I took Gretchen to her door, she kissed me on the forehead," he wrote. "This was the first time and the last that she accorded me the favour, for alas, I was not to see her again."

A well-intentioned friend of the family had visited the house to inform Wolfgang's father that he had got in with a gang of forgers and was mixed up in some shady business; young Gretchen's friends had, indeed, been involved in document forgery. Goethe's father flew into a fine rage and Wolfgang was subjected to exhaustive interrogation.

He wrote: "I could not deny that I had returned late home several nights, that I had obtained a key of my own, and had been seen more than once in pleasure spots with lowly persons of suspicious appearance, that girls were involved in the affair—in short, that everything appeared to have been found out, except the names."

Already the imaginative Wolfgang, harassed by his family and separated from Gretchen, pictured his friends "seized, interrogated, convicted and dishonoured".

In reality, Gretchen, questioned by the police about her meetings with Wolfgang, denied any love between them. This was one of Wolfgang's early mortifications, a deep humiliation. The girl told the police: "I must admit that I have seen him often and of my own free will. But I always regarded him as a child and any consideration I had for him was more as a sister."

So it was revealed that this "great love", transformed into the love between the young Faust and Margarete, was nothing more than a brother and sister relationship. Whether the girl denied everything as a means of proving his innocence, we simply do not know. Whatever the reason, the young lover found his illusions dashed to the ground and himself hating Frankfurt and his home.

"I never returned to Gretchen's district, even to the neighbourhood, and just as I gradually became disgusted with my old walls and towers, so the city itself became displeasing to me. Everything that was formerly so venerable, now appeared to me as deformed images."

This ended Goethe's childhood, and the character of Margarete was born. Wolfgang at fifteen was a dejected soul, but even so, his vivid imagination was able to produce of his despair the character of Faust. His father, seeing him so distraught, sent him off to finish his studies at Leipzig college. There, whom should he meet but Mephistopheles in the shape of Behrish, who dragged him into a series of adventures of which Goethe's genius later made good use.

On return to Frankfurt in 1768, at the age of eighteen, he had in his pocket the three main characters he needed for Faust: Margarete (Gretchen), Mephistopheles (Behrisch) and Faust (himself). He began work on the first draft.

The room occupied by Goethe's mother was the intimate centre of the house. The huge

173

wall cupboard is still there with the little work-table decorated with mother-of-pearl figures handed down from the Textor family, also the Empire table of his mother, and some family portraits. Goethe's father, painted in 1800 by Juncker is there and the portrait of Wolfgang as a young man which his mother had done by Schumann, a painter in the court of the Duchess Anne Amélie. The portrait, which shows him with a silhouette in his right hand, was to become famous. The room where the poet was born has since been restorated.

On the landing of the second floor we can see the astronomer's clock owned by Councillor Huesgen whom Goethe mentions in the final pages of *Poetry and Truth*.

Cornelia's old room contains some of her own and Wolfgang's belongings, including some homework books of the year 1757, a few poems he wrote at sixteen, a red pencil portrait of Cornelia by Morgenstern and her death certificate; she died at twenty-six while bringing her second daughter into the world.

Upon the third floor the poet's own light green room has been reconstituted with his desk and other furniture. Silhouettes of the family and of Charlotte, one of his first loves, are hanging on the walls. Wolfgang's room adjoins one turned into a theatre. This was a present from Cornelia's grandmother, and Wolfgang could produce the plays he liked from an early age.

The period at Leipzig enabled Goethe to realize what a gulf existed between his desires and the reality of life. The Goethe we know took form. He had just written: "Since I was in Leipzig I have learned that in order to be anybody at all, you have to be great. I have even had doubts about whether I am a poet" (September 22, 1766). At Leipzig he wrote some poems, but they were not appreciated. In May 1767 he wrote to his sister: "Let me therefore follow my own way. If I have the gift, I shall become a poet, even if nobody guides me; if I have not, all the criticism in the world will be useless."

A further love affair with Kätchen, a lower-class girl, drew him away from the type of friends his father wanted for him. This romantic lover went through the affair to please his new friend, Behrisch, eleven years older than he; Behrisch was admired by Wolfgang, was cynical, strange. Wolfgang served him, just as Faust served Mephistopheles in due course. The raw experience with Gretchen, so pure and distant, was followed in Leipzig by the affair with Kätchen ("Annette") who was a real daughter of the Devil. How else could Wolfgang retain the friendship of Behrisch? But Goethe, ill and spitting blood, was to fly back, terrified, to his father in Frankfurt, believing himself lost.

More than his health, it was his illusions that he left behind in Leipzig. He fell in again with the old family mood; his spirit was cooled by that stay in college and the increasing difference between home life and his own ideas. Little Wolfgang had disappeared for ever. Yet he suffered as much over his new-found cynicism as he had over his former idealism. A mystical crisis developed, during which he wrote: "My love, that unfortunate passion which cost me so very dear, is now buried, interred in the depth of my memory... Oh! tell, can there be any sadder experience? To be old in the body, young in years, half-sick and half-alive!" (November 6, 1768). He felt this notion that he had too much experience for his young years, strongly at Frankfurt; there also he later believed he was too old for his irreparably young soul. Possibly Goethe's ideas on the separation between desires and reality sprang from these two experiences in love, undergone in a world without prejudices between two periods spend in a straight-laced family atmosphere. The difference between the brothels and the paternal home, between the idealistic love for Gretchen and the Leipzig incident, was later to reappear as literature in *Faust* and *Werther*.

Goethe's father naturally wanted him to resume his life exactly as before, when he got back from Leipzig. The notion of the desire-reality gulf came more strikingly than ever to him when he discovered the joys of Shakespeare and Wieland (1733-1813), known as the German Voltaire and the author of the poem

Oberon. Unfortunately, his father wanted him to be influenced primarily by the professors of Frankfurt. Father stuck by his intentions and family life became unbearable. Frau Goethe, to escape her husband's nagging, sought refuge in a religious movement while Wolfgang went through metaphysical agonies : the sacrament of confession no longer gave him any assurance and Communion even worried him. He wrote of this period : "I tried to free myself completely from any links with the Church." He demanded that God, if He existed at all, should reveal Himself and sweep away any doubts he had about His existence. Exactly as Sartre was to do in our time, and probably at the same age, Goethe arranged to fix an appointment with God. But God failed to turn up in both cases. Consequence : their work no longer involved God.

Wolfgang wrote : "Since I was quite young, I have thought to be on good terms with my God ; what is more, I imagined after all kinds of experiences that He might even be indebted to me, and I was bold enough to think that I had something to forgive Him for." Henceforth Goethe's God was a personal God, the kind of All-Loving, All-Powerful notion we find in *Werther*. His deity was a type of pantheistic Nature-God.

He discovered moreover, that "our best convictions cannot be put into words. Language is not suitable for everything." Man is isolated in relation to himself, and in relation to others and a very distant God. The poet was eighteen when he went through this religious crisis and he subsequently sensed a deep contradiction between his own ideas and those of society, particularly people in power in Germany. Frederik II detested Shakespeare, whereas Goethe used him as a priest uses his breviary. The Prussian monarch liked only French literature : Voltaire, Montesquieu, the Encyclopedists. He was of the opinion that "the abominable plays of Shakespeare... are fit for Canadian savages" and that the German language was only to be used on horses.

Wolfgang proved the opposite, and his work became full of contradictions. "It is almost like a game to find them in his works," said Valéry, who wondered whether Goethe had in fact "produced for himself a system by which opposites can be developed."

Wolfgang Goethe was the first man to open the way to the romantic movement which Madame de Staël, under his influence, spread throughout Europe.

In the spring of 1770, Goethe wrote : "I felt that my health had come back, and even more so my youthful ardour. Again I had the overwhelming desire to leave the parental home."

Which he did, to study law at Strasbourg. But a year later he was back in Frankfurt, tagging it "a wretched hole", and declaring : "May God deliver us from this misery, Amen !" In between times, he had fallen in love with Frédérique, a peasant from Alsace aged twenty. He left her in due course.

"They took Gretchen away from me," he wrote, "Annette abandoned me. Here, it was I who was guilty for the first time... I sought solace in poetry once again in my old way." The episode with Frédérique enabled Goethe to imagine Margarete left in the lurch, with her child, by Faust. That other Margarete would never marry and Goethe had no doubts about his own future, so henceforth he sacrificed his love life for his future. Later on, at an advanced age, he wanted to sacrifice his life for a nineteen-year-old girl, but she rejected him.

On his arrival in Frankfurt this time, Wolfgang encountered Merck and became his friend. This was a new Mephistopheles, and the friendship clearly indicated Wolfgang's penchant for cynicism and nature. "Whence would we obtain our knowledge," he asked, "we who from our youth have seen only stiltedness and good manners in ourselves and others ?" Such was the final attack on his upbringing by his father, and he left again.

In 1772 we find him in Wetzlar falling in love with Lotte Kestner, *née* Buff. He then spent another three years in Frankfurt, though the period was broken up by a journey on the Rhine in 1774 and another in Switzerland July-August 1775.

He now began writing a play on Mohammed and took up the legal profession to please his father. He was evidently confident about his gifts and reckoned in due course to gain his freedom and flee for ever from the Frankfurt house. A picture of Prometheus filtered into his mind and he wrote *Titan's Ode* which was quite impertinent toward the gods, and his father. Sentiments in this work include: "Cover your sky, Zeus... Who has aided me against the arrogance of the Titans? Who was it that saved me from death and slavery? Have you not achieved everything yourself, heart filled with a sacred flame? Must I honour you? Why?"

He also read Spinoza who "influenced his whole thought". Close behind Prometheus was Ganymede: "I come, I come, but whither shall I go?"

He was occasionally still tempted by suicide, and one of his friends killed himself for love. Goethe wrote *Werther* in two months as a direct result, and the book was published in 1774, meeting with outstanding success. *Werther* was translated into every known language, including Chinese. People started dressing like Werther, and killing themselves like him. Goethe still lived in the Frankfurt house but separate from his family. "Whilst I felt relief and freedom at having converted reality into poetry, my friends wrongly thought poetry should be changed into reality," he commented. The book was the most celebrated of its time, and also the most criticized as "pernicious".

A visitor wrote that from 1773 to 1775 "Goethe produced manuscripts from every corner of his room". He was referring to *Clavigo, Erwin and Elmire, Faust* in its early form and later incorporated into the complete *Faust*. We recall that it begins: "I have studied enough, alas, philosophy, medicine, law and unfortunately also theology from end to end with immense effort. And here I am now, a poor idiot no more advanced than before..."

Only feeling has any existence now: "Happiness, heart, love, God. I have no name for him. Feeling is all and a name is mere noise and smoke veiling the ardour of the sky with mist."

He took sixty years to complete the work. Wolfgang was to destroy the paternal myth of all-powerful knowledge in favour of sentiment. On writing the early *Faust*, he described a Margarete who embodied the qualities of the two naïve and tender girls he had known, but at the same time he himself was falling in love in Frankfurt with a rich wanton called Lili Schönemann. She could play the harpsichord well, was beautiful and tried her coquettish ways on Wolfgang who responded to the game. But sadly, he was only one pining lover among many. The two families were against their union and Wolfgang fled.

The opportunity for departure came when the Prince of Weimar and his wife invited him to court on October 13, 1775. He went for several months, and in fact remained there all his life, thus definitely ending his Frankfurt phase.

He realized at this time that he would perpetually be torn between two worlds: the brilliant and successful existence so desired for him by his father, and his closed private world to which he remained faithful until the end.

The house in the Grosse Hirschgraben became a mere childhood memory which inevitably became embellished. On February 13, 1775, he said to a distant friend and confident, Augusta of Stolberg: "If you could, my dear, imagine a Goethe in braid clothes from head to foot, elegant, surrounded by a glow from wall and overhead lamps, in the midst of all kinds of people, and who is riveted by two beautiful eyes at the gaming table... with frivolous intent courting a charming blonde—then you would see Goethe as King Carnival. But there is also another dressed in a grey beaver coat, with a brown silk square around his neck and in boots, who sees spring ahead in the February days that pass..."

Goethe's birthplace remains for him only the dear home of young Wolfgang. Its old walls like the grey clothes of the writer are from now on linked to the difficult trials of a poet's early days. At the age of twenty-six John Wolfgang Goethe was sure of himself. He had lived as Werther, Prometheus and Faust all that time, but now he could only smile at the life from which he had suffered so much. By fleeing from it he was in the end able to find his own personality.

153. The little house in the fore-ground is the Frankfurt birthplace of Goethe, August 18, 1749. The adjoining one was bought by his father when Wolfgang was 5 and he knocked them into one. Here the first "Faust" and "Werther" were written before Goethe reached 25 years of age.

154. Goethe and visitor are seen in a detail from a painting by F. Fleischmann illustrating the biographical work by W. Hauff entitled "Mémoires de Satan". The author's grandson said he knew no more faithful portrait of his grandfather.

155. In the entrance, the large staircase of wrought iron and the clock by a Goethe relative in Frankfurt indicate a normal respectable home life.

154

156

156. The façade of Goethe's house.

157

157. The silhouette of Charlotte Buff.

158

158. Goethe as a young man.

159. Silhouettes of the writer's family ▷
hang in the poet's room with its
contemporary furniture.

159

*160-162. These flemish paintings collected by ▷
Goethe's father in Frankfurt influenced Goethe
who preferred Flemish to Italian art throughout
his life.*

*163. Wolfgang played the cello, and his sister
Cornelia the piano, in the music room in Frankfurt; it was torture for her. At rear is her
piano and at right a red harpsichord which
Goethe's father spent much time repairing.*
▽

163

164

165

164. *Goethe is pictured here with his many music teachers. He had a princely education for a bourgeois son. In reaction, he developed a taste for brothels and the bohemian life. He later modified this taste.*

165. *Goethe at 26, by G.M. Kraus.*

166. The Goethe family kitchen in Frankfurt.

166

169. The ground floor dining room with its "dying blue" decoration, large china stove and baroque mirror struck Wolfgang as being old-fashioned.

169

170. Dutch paintings, an 18th century German ▷ clock and Venitian mirrors decorate the drawing room.

167. *This large drawing room on the first floor housed Count Thoranc during the Seven Years War (1759-1762). The French were occupying the city, and the Count brought a strong breath of fresh air into the stuffy Goethe household.*

168

168. *The library in the Goethe home consisted primarily of legal books. But it had one humorous volume: a dictionary of contemporary fraud.*

170

171

171. *The stripes in this late 18th century room recall the style of Louis XVI.*

172. *The bedroom on the top floor of the Goethe house.*

172

173. *Goethe, seated at his desk, talks to a secretary in this painting.*

173

174

*174. In this small drawing room in the Goethe house are
the portraits of the poet's mother and father.*

El Greco

at Toledo

El Greco lived in a house, or rather a group of houses, in Toledo, Spain, which belonged at the time to the Marquis of Villena. They were located near the synagogue in the Transito Promenade which still bears the same name. The houses have all disappeared since then but the furniture and general atmosphere of the place were later reconstituted by a fervent El Greco admirer, the Marquis of La Vega Inclar, in a house a short distance away.

It was in the year 1577 that he decided to rent twenty-four or twenty-six rooms there. The noisy bustle of the Tagus River filtered to the residence across its gardens, patios and terraces.

The Marquis of Villena charged El Greco a high rent of 596 reals a year against the 300 reals at most which his neighbours were paying. He lived a fastidious existence for an émigré from Crete, who had arrived in Toledo via Rome and Venice. One of his early friends, Jusepe Martinez, remarked that he "wasted his ducats in the extraordinary ostentation of his home."

The explanation lies in the very handsome order he received soon after his arrival, from the Santo Domingo el Antiquo Convent. Within a short time he had another order from the Toledo cathedral chapter for Espolio, a work that was to give rise to a court case, in which the chapter demanded and obtained a rebate.

The same friend records another example of El Greco's "need for money and his luxurious taste". He employed musicians at his house to play during meals, so that he could enjoy the delights of existence to the utmost. Barrès observed that he "had a weakness for songs rising up from the stone floor to the hammering of a guitar."

El Greco—Domenikos Theotokopoulos—was born in Crete in 1541. He learned to draw at Candia and when he grew to adolescence he went off to Venice and joined the Greek community there. Like many others of the colony he was tagged "The Greek", by the Venitians. For ten years he studied under Titian after which this ambitious soul moved on to Rome where the reigning Vatican "monarch" was the Dominican Pius the Fifth, a severe and strict man who had Michelangelo's "shocking" statues and paintings covered up. El Greco, boastful and fawning as he was, remarked of Michelangelo's *Last Judgment :* "If this whole work were thrown to the ground, I could do it again with honesty and decency, and certainly it would not be inferior as a painting." Such a claim was bound to wound a good many Roman ears. A Rome doctor, Giulio Cesare Mancini, remarked : "It was because of these words that he had all the painters and art lovers against him, and was obliged to leave Rome for Spain."

Philip II of Spain, made wealthy by the discovery of gold in the Americas, built the Escorial near Madrid about this time. El Greco

189

went to work there after leaving Rome. However he and Philip did not achieve a good relationship for the king did not care for the artist's style. El Greco then went to Toledo where he remained forty years, more than half his lifetime.

El Greco brought with him to Toledo the techniques he had learned from Titian, Tintoretto and Michelangelo. It would have been easy for him to acquire a considerable clientele among the local aristocracy, who liked the Italian style. But he experienced a new liberating influence in Spain, to such an extent that he even began to annoy the rich Spanish nobility, in particular Philip II. The king was dissatisfied with the *Martyrdom of Saint Maurice*, and had the work put in the loft at the Escorial. He never commanded other works from the artist so El Greco stayed on in Toledo, an imperial city rich in spiritual evocations, but now economically and politically decadent. Here was abundant material for El Greco's canvas.

He painted all his greatest works in a house similar and near to the one we can see today. A desk covered in red leather has even been found like the one El Greco painted in the famous portrait of Saint Ildefonso.

His family life remains as mysterious as the face of Donna Geronima de Las Cuevas, a noble daughter of Castile who was the model for all his paintings of the Madonna. In 1578, she bore him a son Jorge Manuel who is depicted in the foreground of the *Burial of the Count of Orgaz*.

Were Domenikos and Geronima married? The question is of little importance beside the fact that in another house, nearer the Tiber, but with a similar ambience, El Greco experienced the providential climax of an artist's life: the year 1580, when he painted the *Burial of the Count of Orgaz*. He was another Greek expatriate, a descendant of Don Pedro Paelologue, third son of the Emperor of Constantinople.

El Greco's house belonged more to his works that to the painter himself. It was designed for him to visualize and house his paintings. Pacheco, a celebrated teacher of the years 1610-1611, tells us how he visited El Greco when he was sick, and saw a studio from whose ceiling hung gilded cherubs brilliantly illuminated. Throughout his life, El Greco used this technique, first learned from Tintoretto, in order to paint angels.

All the works he had painted so far were displayed in miniature form in a long corridor. It was a kind of catalogue of his output. The client had only to look over them and select the work he wanted copied. One of his pupils in Sevilla offered the same "selection" of paintings to clients such as soldiers, priests, sailors and government officials who were scheduled to leave on the perils of an ocean trip without a picture of their favourite saint in their possession. Hence the existence of at least one hundred and twenty-eight paintings of Saint-Francis of Assisi by El Greco.

El Greco's house contains some surprises according to the inventory drawn up by his son. In the entire twenty-six rooms there were only eight chairs, one table, one leather-covered desk, two chests, two sheets, seven towels, one bedcover, three shirts, one item of outer clothing; above a bed was a crimson damask canopy; on a wall, a sword and dagger. The library contained twenty-seven Greek books, sixty-seven Italian, nineteen works on architecture and a book entitled "How to Remain in Good Health". The house had just one fireplace.

This inventory was made in 1614, the year when he died lying under red canopy. Had he really become so poor? It was said that his lavish ways had ruined him. It is even possible he had concealed during all these years a fundamental poverty.

Even his last resting place was only temporary, "that fine monument of the brilliant Porphyrius" as the Spanish writer and poet Gongora was to say in his epitaph.

The painter was buried at the church of the Santo Domingo el Antiguo Convent, which had encouraged him in his early days in Toledo. But his remains were removed when his son quarrelled with the convent directors, and laid to rest in 1619 at the San Torcuato Convent, which was subsequently demolished.

But El Greco had already built himself a mansion that will last for ever.

Next pages:
177. *Saint Ildefonso writing to the Virgin's order.*

178. *In the Toledo House, a desk covered in red leather similar to that of the desk on the painting.*

176. *In one of the rooms of El* ▷ *Greco's house reconstituted at Toledo is a trestle bearing "The Tears of Saint Peter".*

◁ 179. Young men with elongated bodies were painted by El Greco toward the end of his life. Here two of them are watching the strangling of Laocöon and his sons by two snakes.

180   181

182   183

180. This Dominican friar is believed to be a portrait of Juan Bautista Mayno.

181. Don Rodrigue Vasquez.

182. A portrait of El Greco's son, also a painter.

183. A portrait of an unknown man.

184. A replica of one of El Greco's twenty- ▷ four rooms in Toledo: an inventory of his property reveals he had little furniture. Most rooms presumably housed his canvasses.

186

187

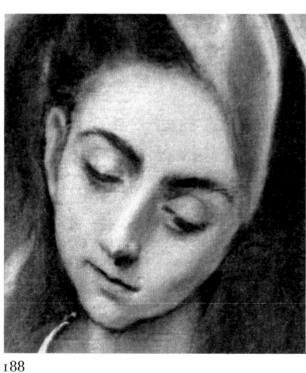

188

189

186. *El Greco used his own wife as model for this Virgin, a detail of a "Pietà" from a private collection.*

187. *The Magdalen, from the same "Pietà".*

188. *This Virgin is from one of the nine "Holy Family" paintings painted in 1597.*

189. *A "Mater Dolorosa" was painted in 1593.*

◁ 185. *El Greco's kitchen: he lived near a synagogue. From his window he could see the grey hill we find in his paintings and also the machine devised by an engineer employed by Charles V to raise the Tagus' waters.*

Haydn

at Eisenstadt

When a friend asked Joseph Haydn on which day in 1732 he was born, he replied: "My brother says it was March 31, but the truth is he doesn't want to reveal that I entered this world as an April fool."

His place of birth was a village called Rohrau, lost in a marshy plain on the frontier between Hungary and Austria.

As a child he had a good voice. His father mentioned this to his cousin Frank, who was chapelmaster and schoolmaster in a neighbouring market town, and Joseph went to live with him for two years learning to read, write, count and bash drums. At the age of eight his fine voice was pointed out by the local priest to Georg Reutter, choirmaster at Saint Stephen's Cathedral in Vienna.

Serving as a choirboy was no sinecure. In a dull four-storey building between the cathedral and the cemetery, the children learned very little musical theory and little attempt was made to develop their minds. The rule of school was that pupils who had completed their education left without a dime when their voices broke. This duly happened to Haydn in November, 1749. There followed ten years of obscure effort of no interest to anyone which ended when he had a fortuitous encounter with a choir member of the cathedral. He borrowed some money from him, put himself to studying music and changed his lodgings.

He went into ecstasies when he discovered the sonatas of C.P.E. Bach.

To earn some money, he taught the harpsichord to the local barber's daughter. The younger girl was charming but she went off into a convent. As to the older one she was little liked thanks to a very difficult personality. Despite this, Joseph Haydn married her in 1760, secretly so as not to break a contract he had just signed with an Austrian, the Count Morzin, who made him his musical director. For forty whole years his life was poisoned by the wretched Maria-Aloysia, whom he later termed the *bestia infernale*.

While with the Count, Haydn was noticed by Prince Paul Anthony Esterhazy, who appointed him his second choirmaster in 1761. From that moment, his homes were to be princely palaces. But we know at what price: a gold braid livery that can be seen on the back of a chair today.

From 1762 to 1766, the Haydns resided in the Eisenstadt Castle of the prince in Austrian Burgerland. After 1766, Prince Nicholas Esterhazy, also known as "The Magnificent", acquired Haydn's services after Paul Antony's death. He had built a summer residence at Esterhazy on Lake Neusiedler, and the Haydns went there with the court when the fine days arrived. Life at the Esterhazy's new home was an imitation of Versailles, and nothing pleased the Prince more than to be told so. It contained a special building for musicians to live in, as well as an opera house. Families occupied two

199

190. Haydn was born in 1732 "in a dirty peasant's hovel", as Beethoven said. From 1761 he was to live in princely residences of the Esterhazy family, whose musical director he was for forty years.

rooms, and bachelors shared lodgings—two or three to a room. Haydn and his wife were the only ones allowed three rooms.

This is a far step indeed from Haydn's "peasant's hovel" at Rohrau that Beethoven laughed about in a moment of ill-humour. It is true that Beethoven could have signed the contract that obliged the deputy choirmaster to wear his employer's livery, and to write out immediately any composition desired by a prince who could prevent his music being played outside the palace, be available for orders in the anti-chamber before and after dinner, to see that his musicians worked hard, check the condition of their instruments and rehearse the singers. For all this, Haydn received four hundred florins a year for three years, had to eat in the kitchen and was housed.

As in his days as a choirboy of Saint Stephen's Cathedral, so as the choirmaster at the Esterhazy residence he performed his duty during visits of notable guests to the Esterhazy Castle.

Any other kind of person might have been put off by such working conditions. But this extraordinary young man, a little cold and starchy, held out. Step by step he beat his way through to victory. With astonishing hard headedness, he worked heroically in the years to come; he composed a great deal and in the end his fame spread beyond the limits that society imposed on his gifts. He became known throughout Europe and this fame outlived the wars and revolutions that overthrew existing society. Goethe wrote: "Without exaltation, he does what he does. His characteristics are inconceivable without deep human warmth. All modern music stems from his work."

And the same author in *Art and Antiquity*, which he dedicated to Haydn, wrote: "He has the two signs of genius, naivety and irony..."

By all appearances, Joseph Haydn led a brilliant life as a paid courtier; in 1772 he wrote the six quartets of *Opus* 20 (the "*Sun*" quartets) which marked the end of a period in which he deliberately sought to perfect his

technical knowledge; he also introduced the fugue style that was to remain latent in his subsequent works. From 1772 to 1782, during what some musicologists have called his romantic period, he wrote more than thirty symphonies which are generally regarded as inferior to his quartets. They are however important because they show the effort he made to give some discipline to the theatrical music in which the Italians were very expert.

In 1785 he met Mozart who dedicated six quartets to him. In 1788 several of his symphonies were performed in Paris.

Prince Nicholas Esterhazy died in 1790. His son Anthony increased the annual pension his father bestowed on Haydn after forty years faithful of service with the family. But Anthony had no musical taste, and he dismissed the orchestra. Haydn went to live in Vienna, where he met a concert promoter from London.

Haydn's London concerts made him a man of fashion at fifty-eight years of age. It was at this moment that he encountered Mrs. Schroeter, an English widow. He said of her: "Although she was nearing sixty, she was a beautiful and likeable woman, whom I might well have married had I been single." However his past rose up to prevent this union.

Ten years earlier, he had gone through a passionate affair that lasted several years. In 1779, a Neapolitan singer working for the prince had set her heart on the man on whom depended the renewal of her contract, and in fact Haydn acted as intermediary with the prince. By 1790, she was not content with letters to Haydn, and considered sending to London her son Pietro and perhaps accompanying him. Joseph Haydn who thought he had eradicated all traces of the past and was now planning an affair of a new kind, became scared and scurried back to Vienna, where the eternal Maria Aloysia was waiting for him.

Haydn's life thereafter took on a rather cotton-wool look, tragic and boringly impersonal, a sorry end to a glorious life.

Joseph Haydn died on May 31, 1809, around one o'clock in the morning.

191. Haydn and Mozart pictured together here met in 1785 and Mozart dedicated six quartets to him. In 1787, Haydn recommended Mozart to the Copenhagen Opera.

192. A contract on May 1, 1761 between Haydn and the secretary of the Prince Esterhazy stipulated that he would see to the musicians livery and eat his meals with the servants.

193. Court life under Empress Maria Theresa and her son Joseph II (mother and brother of Marie-Antoinette) was a copy of Versailles luxury.   Prince Esterhazy who employed Haydn liked to hear his castle compared with Louis XV's magnificent residence.

194. William Hogarth was contemporary with the early novelists featuring English manners. His satire drew inspiration from Puritan attitudes.

Hogarth

in London

William Hogarth, born in London in 1697, began his career in difficult circumstances. Apprenticed at an early age to a metal engraver who produced only ledgers and book titles, he had a hard job paying for his lodgings. His artistic talents saved him on more than one occasion, before it finally enabled him to purchase his own house.

As a young man he depicted his landlady with the features of a shrew, chasing him for the twenty-shilling rent he owed her. The sale of this cartoon won immediate attention and earned him three times the amount he needed to pay her off. However, it took him many years before he finally acquired, in 1733, the house in Leicester Fields where he died.

Hogarth was the son of a schoolmaster from the provinces, who in London finally succeeded in finding work in a bookshop, which just about saved him from starvation. The moment Richard Hogarth saw that his son William had a gift for drawing, he sent him to work for a craftsman who engraved for the aristocracy on silver plate. The workshop was at Leicester Fields, where, it is said, the young apprentice met up with some Huguenot émigrés from France who taught him new engraving techniques.

The trade of engraver was to "bite into" Hogarth's destiny in the same way as the etcher's needle attacks metal in depth so as to give a black-and-white finished work. This job suited the caustic eye of William who would grasp the salient features, shades and highlights rather than the nuances that needed brush flexibility. As Paul Valéry said : "Nature can do nothing with mere ink. She needs literally an infinite store of material. But engravers need but few tools and, if possible, much spirit! *Intelligenti pauca*, says the Latin. Is this not the greater glory of black and white ?"

But in Hogarth's time, the greater glory of which he dreamed was not obtained by the needle, but only by the brush. Although he wanted to be a painter, it was as an engraver and cartoonist that he first, out of necessity, became known. In 1718, his father Richard Hogarth died, and William, who cared little for the job of heraldist, changed jobs and began engraving book illustrations, including those for *Hudibras* by Samuel Butler. Then he attempted a few cartoons in the fashion of the time, which were collected together in a book published under the title *Mascarades and Operas* (1724).

At the time he went to an academy and drew from models but this method gave him no satisfaction. He preferred sketching passers-by when he went for walks, and could reproduce their features from memory.

Notwithstanding his new aims, Hogarth's early training as an engraver pursued him and even hampered him. A tapestry-maker to whom he tried to sell a design refused it when he found out that Hogarth was an engraver and not a painter. This led to a court case which Hogarth won. A year later he did a painting of a scene from an opera that was a current rage. It was so successful he was commissioned to do more.

In 1729, he secretly married the daughter of Sir James Thornhill, the king's painter. The need to support his wife, Jane, meant he had to paint minor subjects that were easy to sell. Several of these works have been preserved and are among his best known examples. They contributed toward establishing his name as a painter. It was easy to sell them but he received little for them, so he set about finding a new style. The idea struck him of painting scenes that were like the several acts in a comedy. The canvas was the stage and the people he painted were the actors. This idea was a huge success and certain of his characters were identified by the London public as celebrities. From that moment onward Hogarth kept to his satirical style, because it enabled him to live and, in 1733, to buy the house in Leicester Fields.

The purchase mainly resulted from the success of his engravings done in 1733 and 1734, from his paintings entitled *The Harlot's Progress*.

His drawings depicted this unhappy creature at her early stages, getting down from a coach outside a London pub tavern, then set up in a superb hotel, then in a garret and finally in prison, before she ended up in hospital. Their success was tremendous and sales soared. The resemblance of one of the characters to a magistrate in office led, it was said, to all the Lords of the Treasury buying it. Pantomimes were based on them. Scenes from *The Harlot's Progress* appeared on fans and china vases. Another series called *The Rake's Progress* was also remarkable but it was a lesser triumph.

Today, the fine house which Hogarth owed to these efforts, squeezed between large buildings, has the stunted look of a suburban house. Even so it was from the date he acquired it that Hogarth began the works that made him truly famous. From that point onward his income was assured and he could cast aside any worries about food, pursue his real vocation, and enjoy life with Jane.

Hogarth's success may be explained by the manners of the day. The preceeding century had been a much disturbed one. The Stuarts had acquired the English throne. A struggle between Parliament and the Crown had ended in the tragic death of Charles the First. Then a civil war followed and the triumph of Cromwell and the puritans, before Charles the Second was put on the throne. With the return of monarchy, a thirst for pleasure seized the population much as it did in France a century later when the Directoire was set up after the Revolution.

Elegance and frivolity were matters of widespread rivalry. The puritans were horrified to see the general licence. Literature with Swift had already poured ridicule on certain excesses. Defoe produced *Moll Flanders, The Story of a Wanton Woman*, but the outstanding question was how the plastic arts would contribute to the trend. England was still unfamiliar with the art of caricature, and even Hogarth had not thought about it, having started out as a student of Sir James Thornhill his father-in-law, who himself had painted decorative panels for the dome of Saint Paul's. Who would have imagined that in 1733 Hogarth was to attack bitterly what he regarded as a major evil of the century, prostitution? This severe critic was not devoid of a strong erotic streak, moreover. After *The Harlot's Progress*, the eight pictures in *The Rake's Progress* confirmed his mastery of the painter's technique. He had found his *métier*. The grace he gives to some of his women recalls the style of Watteau. The scene in the madhouse where the rake ends up shows a sharp contrast between the tragic nude in the foreground and two women in white who flirt with their fans. The mood of the composition, as much as the equivocal charm of the women, makes us think of Goya.

In addition to prostitution, England at that time had another rife scourge, drunkenness, which pervaded all social classes. The punch-drinkers which Hogarth did after he left for Leicester Fields is a truly nightmare scene:

drinkers are depicted around a punch bowl in the middle of a round table, their faces livid with inebriation. The progression to complete drunkenness is shown from left to right in the picture; at first the drinkers seem to be quite normal, later one of them rises and lurches about, finally someone falls. This was another immediate success for Hogarth and once again the public put their own names to the figures in the scenes. Thus was Hogarth's destiny mapped out. It was to stifle him when he tried to seek a different path to fame. So many copies of the punch drinkers were produced that George II granted him a guarantee against forgeries, one of the first protective licences of this kind.

With material needs no longer in the forefront, Hogarth sought another style that was more in keeping with his artistic ambitions, more worthy of an artist's life as it was considered then. In those days painters had to record history in order to win respect. His father-in-law Thornhill was just such a historical painter. In 1735, Hogarth suggested he should at his own expense decorate the walls of a hospital with a biblical scene entitled *The Good Samaritan*. He won polite recognition for this. He was trying to fight against an academic style which he felt was dominating him.

William inherited the school run by his father-in-law when he died in 1734, and converted it into a "salon" where leading artists used to go and discuss painting. Hogarth felt they were too sensitive to European influences.

In due course, money difficulties arose and he had to turn again to the kind of painting that paid off—portraiture. During this period he did *The Graham Children*, *Miss Sulter* and *Garrick in Richard III*. Although he was in fact the best paid portrait-painter of the day, he was still dragging behind his reputation as a caricaturist, and the public continued to regard him as an engraver. A dramatic conflict was on the horizon.

Even so, he accepted matters with a laugh. If they wanted caricatures, they would jolly have them! He produced a series of strolling players which was a huge success and Leices-ter Fields was bustling with life as it filled up with caricatures.

Then he did a series of natural character studies which critics, following Henry Fielding's lead, distinguished from his caricatures. Lavater was later victim of this distinction when he used Hogarth's works to establish a theory of Physiognomy.

Although Hogarth's house became one of the intellectual centres of London in 1743, he was attacked for recording only "popular" scenes. He forthwith hit out at the well-off classes. He paints six pictures which he calls *Mariage à la mode*, showing disputes between a rich, elegant but incompatible couple. They were used as a basis of a comedy play.

Either he lost confidence in his gifts as an engraver, or he still sought to throw off his established reputation. The fact is that he now handed over the engraving to another person, probably to a Parisian engraver since he is known to have visited the French capital. But without result: Hogarth was a slave to his reputation. He put several of his paintings on sale but the London public were not buying any. Even the original paintings for *Mariage à la mode* were rejected by the buying public, and they were sold for a song six years later.

William's spirits then went right down. The *Happy Marriage* sequel to the previous series went no further than the first sketches. He simply could not give up caricature, even though he was one of the finest portrait painters of the time. The caricaturist was lauded and his next series eagerly awaited. Still today, it is his pitiless wit and perspicacity, and his clean lines that we appreciate.

He was a contemporary of the first novelists in England who described the manners of the age: Swift, Defoe, Fielding, and others. Fielding noted that Hogarth's works were to be seen in all decent households. His art, in this puritan rather than art-loving land, was a crusade against vice, gambling, drunkenness, electoral demagogy and cruelty to animals.

The subject matter was more important to the public than the quality of painting. Hogarth flattered public taste in order to make a living; he fully and magnificently responded to a public that was just as dirty-minded as any other, although it read the Bible more. He was their prisoner. He possessed the spiteful humour that seems to be a feature of his race, and which has given a new word to the French—spleen. Elie Faure has asked: "Can one say of a man that he has ruined his vocation as a painter when he has seen the world as a great painter sees it?" Hogarth certainly put the question squarely to himself and concluded that he had lost his vocation. All English caricaturists from Rowlandson to the popular magazine cartoonists might well be regarded as descendants of William Hogarth. But he was to die sadly aware that he was not being venerated for what he wanted to be, a painter. English society was over-interested in criticism, denigration, petty journalism, gossip and story telling.

Before him, there had been in England only Van Dyck and his school, which produced Dutch style portraiture for the high society of Charles II. That century was for a long period virtually unknown to the English themselves who rediscovered it with an exhibition in 1961. It has been suggested that this neglect was due to the fact that Charles II was a catholic and was influenced by Louis XIV.

But in reality the explanation lies rather in purely commercial considerations in the mind of Van Dyck who, after revolutionizing court portraiture and giving it European dimensions, set up a kind of factory in England. He employed Flemish assistants, some of whom specialised in hands, some in hair, others in drapery, architectural background and so on. All this was more or less finished off by Van Dyck and delivered promptly to the client for cash-down payment. That technique was obviously enough to make the English regard the period with indifference.

The 1961 exhibition revealed that, along with Van Dyck's output, there was another English trend in portraiture. It was less conformist, and took more account of the subject's special features. The artists who somewhat gingerly met this demand were miniaturists, or else engravers of whom Hogarth was a highly gifted example. Neither the realism of the miniature portraitist Samuel Cooper nor the romantic style heralded by Peter Lely's paintings of women showed any hint of Hogarth's painting technique. He was the first of the English school of painters but his contemporaries demanded that he reject what was not regarded as "typically English" at the time—caricature engravings.

In a last frantic bid to satisfy his ideals, Hogarth organized a permanent exhibition of works by himself and some colleagues. Titles included *Moses Brought to Pharaoh's Daughter*, a theme that hints of the titles beloved by the romantics later. Once again he had to return to satire afterward.

He abandoned a sequel to the *Happy Marriage* and, discouraged by his "failure" as a painter, bought a country house at Chiswick, now part of London. He fled from the house where he had known the type of success he in no way aspired to, and withdrew to Chiswick where he wrote *Analysis of Beauty*, published in 1753, a book that was as criticized as his historical paintings.

He was appointed painter to the king. This appointment did more for his reputation as a portrait painter, than for the art form he had aimed at, and he now received several portrait commissions. He felt bitterly the injustice of mankind and was sensitive enough to suffer from it. In the mood of a wounded animal, he did a portrait he thought as good as a Correggio, using his wife as a model, and entitled it *Sigismonda*. Horace Walpole commented that it was no more like Sigismonda than he was like Hercules. The work was ridiculed by Hogarth's contemporaries but today's critics are less severe. It was not until 1814, fifty years after his death, that his qualities as a painter began to gain recognition.

In 1764 he painted a picture called *The End of All Things*. In it was shown Time itself dozing among ruined columns. When Hogarth completed this work he declared: "I have finished" and smashed his palette. He died shortly afterwards on October 26, 1764, in his Leicester Fields house and was buried at Chiswick.

195. *Hogarth's Chiswick home is a museum* ▷
honouring the master of British caricature. A
line can be traced from Hogarth to Rowlandson
(1756-1827) and to modern magazine car-
toonists. He personified the comic genius of
the nation.

195

196. *Hogarth campaigned against debauchery,*
gambling, drunkenness, electioneering methods.
He championed Good by narrating Evil. He
himself knew periods of depression and used
grim humour which his contemporaries liked.
▽

197

197. In an illustration from Samuel Butler's "Hudibras",
Sir Hudibras is seen with the supposed astrologer Sidrophel.

199. One of eight works in the series, "The Rake's Progress". ▷

198. This work satirizing good taste in high society *was*
characteristic of his genius, although Hogarth was reluctant
to execute the work.

198

199

Victor Hugo

at Hauteville House

Victor Hugo the exile spent fifteen years on the Island of Guernsey, from October 1855 to September 1870. In one sense, it was a long time for an expatriate who did not expect the Second Empire to last so long. But in retrospect is must have seemed quite short to him, since he later returned there of his own will.

Hugo the exile was rather like a poet cast up on a sea-battered rock. "If there were to be only one poet", he declared, "I would be he". But Hugo was also the poet of the red damask *salon* at Hauteville House. "I thank destiny for my banishment," he said. "I enjoy exiled life more and more; I shall die here perhaps, richer... Decidedly I like this exile : no people to receive, no visits to pay, happiness at being alone, quiet reading, working and dreaming in peace, the savage state."

In Paris, Hugo was producing less and less. He was not at all himself, as Balzac said of him. Hugo realized this : "I am a submerged La Pérouse... One can die a long time before reaching the grave." If Hugo had died before 1848, he would have been merely a distinguished poet. It was the events of that year that saved him from himself. A peer of France under Louis-Philippe, Hugo found after the dissolution of the Chamber that he was no longer a conservative. He was a member of the Fronde in 1830. On July 5, 1845, he was caught in the act of committing adultery with Madame Biard and she was locked up in prison.

Louis Bonaparte later attempted to convert him but Hugo became anxious about Bonaparte's ambitions and ended up his adversary. After a historic argument in the Assembly on July 17, 1851, he commented : "We have had Napoleon the Great, but not so that we could now have Napoleon the Little."

The right-wing Hugo, the conservative, wrote *Lucrèce Borgia, Le Roi s'amuse, Les Chants du crépuscule, Ruy Blas, Les Burgraves;* Hugo the expatriate was to write *Les Châtiments, Les Misérables* and *La Légende des siècles,* by which we know him best.

He was obliged to flee after taking part in an abortive *coup d'état* against Napoleon III. He left Paris hurriedly on December 11, 1851, bound for Brussels, with forged papers and a false name, convinced that a price had been put on his head. All this was possibly pure invention on his part, but the upshot was that the fifty-one-year-old poet-*académicien*, together with his four children, was to begin his life again outside France.

On arrival in Brussels in December 1851, Hugo wrote *Napoléon le Petit.* But he could not stay long in Belgium, since he was officially expelled by decree from France in January 1852 and had promised the Belgian government that he would not do anything to tarnish Franco-Belgian relations.

He was thus obliged to have his rebel works published in London. He later went to

200. Victor Hugo is seen here with his grandchildren, Jeanne and Georges. Later he wrote "The Art of Being a Grandfather".

England and thence to Jersey, whose climate reminded him of Normandy and Villequier.

French exiles already established in the island received him with open arms and he was obliged to adopt their extremism and some of their stupid ways. The exiles published in their opposition newspaper an insulting open letter to Queen Victoria who was paying an official visit to Napoléon III. The result was they were expelled from the island and Hugo followed them. He ended up at the neighbouring English island of Guernsey and almost at once acquired Hauteville House; since he was now a property owner under English law, he was protected from possible expulsion.

In the whole of Europe there was nothing to compare with Hauteville House, a residence that owed everything to the imagination and fancy of Hugo. It was a veritable palace arranged in five years with the proceeds from *Les Châtiments*. It was a curious cottage type of place, with mainly drawing rooms and mirrors, a residence almost without bedrooms, virtually without books apart from those giving vital information; a mix-up of rooms arranged all anyhow. The walls were covered in carpets, the ceilings adorned with Gobelin tapestries, the floors appeared to merge into sofas covered with Shiraz carpets. Cupboards could be dismantled to form Gothic panelling, ship's chests became cupboards, armchairs were large, medium or small to suit father, mother or children, and were engraved with mysterious signs.

The whole house was a strange assorted jumble of things found at antiques dealers in Guernsey, receivers of goods who worked with privateers who for many years made the island their refuge.

The astonishing visual effect of Hauteville House inside is augmented by the quite ordinary narrow façade on the street, exactly similar to that of the other houses. Surprising also is the small house like a station-master's hut occupied by Juliette Drouet, with its pointed roof and the green shutters where every morning Juliette signalled her awakening by hanging up a white hankerchief, to which Hugo replied by putting one out of his window.

Why such precautions and secrecy, when Hugo could simply go to see Juliette through their adjoining gardens; why such mystery when Madame Hugo had as far back as February 1833—twenty years earlier—admitted that Juliette was her husband's "official" mistress, reserving for herself the role of friendly wife, while she bestowed more violent sentiments on the critic Sainte-Beuve? Why, too, must he hide himself from her when she was in fact always away? Was this the way Hugo and Juliette preserved the freshness of their long love? Madame Hugo had never really accepted the idea of going into exile with Victor, at any rate not to this small island he picked. "She hates me less than she hates the exile", he used to say, and she on her side wrote to him in 1858: "The house is yours, and you can stay alone in it."

She had for a long time kept with her their two sons, either in Paris or in Brussels. "We love our children more than they love us," he noted after they had left him. As to Madame Hugo—Adèle Foucher—he had loved her passionately to the point of remaining virgin for their marriage; for years he looked back to their marriage night, but after their fourth child, she decreed there would be only strictly polite relations between them. In return she promised to turn a blind eye to all her husband's future adventures. Hugo, in *Le Tas de pierres* was to write in 1830: "Woe to him who loves without being loved... Look at this woman: she is charming, gentle and candid; she is joy and love in the home. But she doesn't love you... All your loving thoughts come to rest on her but she lets them slip away again exactly as they came, without repulsing or retaining them."

This is Adèle, the wife who leaves the home first and goes off with Sainte-Beuve, finding in him what George Sand, the great woman lover, was unable to find—passion.

Contemporary documents indicate that Madame Hugo was more matronly than muse-like; even so, the dwarf Andersen, who visited Hugo in Paris, departed in a troubled state of mind and left behind some verses for her.

Doubtless she had the appearance and the soul of a lover; she willingly gave up her place in the home to Juliette Drouet, who was really a wifely soul with the appearance of a theatrical actress.

During the fifteen years of exile, Madame Hugo spent more or less lengthy periods at Hauteville House, but stayed away on the slightest pretext. As for Juliette, she stayed the whole fifteen years in Guernsey and never left Hugo. Each time Victor Hugo went travelling, she grew quite forlorn, as he journeyed through Belgium, France and Italy. She wept, too, when she found note books and diaries belonging to Hugo which she ought not to have seen. She was to forgive everything.

When at the age of seventy-one she discovered that Hugo loved Blanche, his chambermaid, she fled from Guernsey. But she was back again before long and forgave all. She told a friend: "His most intimate desire was to remain the gay spark and he made an energetic show of it." Hugo wrote: "I erase one adventure with another."

When Hugo felt remorse he used to give to the poor. The duration of his last infidelity is documented in his diary: "March 29, 350 francs for the poor", then "April 8, 1,100 francs for the poor." In the final analysis Juliette cared less about his adultery than about the state of his health.

After suffering a stroke in June 1878, he was advised by doctors to stay in Guernsey. He worked in quiet and Juliette, looking after him, partly shielded him from the temptation of love affairs. She had a curious role to play, this young actress who the moment she saw Hugo knew that her life was no longer her own. She gave up her profession and stayed faithful to him until the end.

How did Hugo come to be interested in spiritualism while on this island? It was Madame de Girardin who during a visit to Guernsey initiated him into the secrets of "table-tipping". In them, French *émigrés* found just what they wanted: they could read the future, keep in touch with the dead and with past history, they could believe in the future, predict it even. Hauteville House contained an atmosphere invented and built up by Hugo; this atmosphere seemed to be closely linked to the visions he had of the unseen world. It was the house of a seer, and itself gained from the holding of spiritualist seances. Hugo had always been sensitive to night life. When he awoke from a dream he would make notes on what he had seen or felt. When he heard a noise, he thought he was in touch with some invisible presence, and the walls made of ship's chests and cupboards did everything to encourage this illusion. A hand would touch his shoulder and he would not say anything about it to the family, preferring to confide it to Juliette. This believer in the spirits was the son of an atheist soldier and of a mother who followed Voltaire's ideas. As a boy he was sent to the College of Nobles in Madrid as a Protestant pupil so that the Catholics could not "deform" him and he could later choose his own religion. The destinies of the father and son were so similar that one is tempted to think their lives were made up. But they were both authentic. Both men were forsaken by their wives, both kept until death the mistresses they took to replace the wives. Hugo's own daughter Adèle had Sainte-Beuve as godfather just as Hugo's father had as civilian witness the future lover of his own mother.

The Christianity of Victor Hugo was permanently tinged with paganism. Yet he was not deeply involved in the vast anticlerical movement of the age, any more than he was totally allied to the left in 1871. He judged the Commune "idiotic" and the Assembly "savage". He was a man of the Right with his heart on the Left, like many since.

The sea beat against the Guernsey rocks that bore the garden of Hauteville. Palm trees and giant camellias grew there. Hugo had a mast erected to fly the French flag, and from the end of the red drawing room whose mirrors repeatedly reflected the same scene including his own face, he could catch sight of both the flag and coast of France. He had chosen an eagle's nest to live in, but he swathed it in velvet and then wrote *Les Misérables*. In the

215

same way, Andersen had paradoxically written the story *The Little Match Girl* during a hunt meeting held "in princely luxury," as he said, at Graastin Castle.

In the entrance hall to Hauteville House, the visitor is struck by a vast number of moving patches of light. They are merely the ends of bottles mounted in woodwork on which Hugo had engraved : "V. Hugo. Notre-Dame de Paris". On each side of this inscription he hung two medallions of the master and mistress of the house, as if they were two donors of the sixteenth century.

Glass lamps of the Second Empire give but a slight illumination and doors lead to rooms whose exact use is hard to judge from first appearances. A mirror hides a secret door which in its turn conceals a jigsaw puzzle, the broken pieces of some old pottery. There are Sèvres tableware which Charles X had given him, together with soup tureens, bowl covers, Chinese dishes and plates from the East India Company which he found at the antique shops. Here, everything is allowed to parody reality.

The dining room is also lined with pottery : Delft collector's pieces he picked up while in Amsterdam. The letters V and H in violet and blue are interlaced in Delft china.

Between two windows stands a large ancestral armchair marked *Cella Patrium Defunctorum*, opposite the dining table. Nobody is allowed to sit in it ; inscribed on the uprights are the words *Absentes Adsunt*, and *Ego Hugo*, together with the date 1534, possibly the year in which a noble title was granted to the Lorraine family Hugo thought he was descended from. In point of fact, Hugo was a descendant of a small market grower of Beaudricourt in the Vosges, although his father was a brilliant officer under the Empire.

This armchair was the embodiment of Hugo's pride and superstition, and the family ate before its invisible occupant who was supposed to be there during meals.

The meat joint was cut and conversation doubtless continued accompanied by manners befitting such a presence. There was no doubt much play acting in this custom, but in Guern-sey people lived for the *émigré* "gallery" and for the idea one had of oneself. Hugo wanted to feel something of a martyr and on the dining room door lintel he had written : *Exilium Vita Est* — "Life is an Exile".

Above the glazed chimney piece, he placed like some freedom lamp one of the finds he made at the antique shops—Notre-Dame-de-Bon-Secours, and next to her he had written : "The people are small but will be great in your sacred arms, Oh fruitful Mother, Oh holy freedom, with conquering step, you carry the Child that bears the world."

On the ground floor in the tapestry room leading to a small smoking room and the garden, an enormous chimney piece in Gothic style, engraved with anti-clerical and socialist slogans, right under a statuette of Bishop Aframus referred to in "La Défiance d'Onfroy".

Lower down next to the earth itself are written in the wood the names of the people Victor Hugo regarded as the light of the world : Moses, Socrates, Christ, Columbus, Luther, Washington, Job, Isaiah, Homer, Aeschylus, Lucretia, Dante, Shakespeare, Molière. They are similarly written on a chimney in Lamartine's room at Saint-Point Castle. In the nineteenth century people readily modelled themselves on great forerunners. The remainder of this room consists entirely of Aubusson tapestries representing a hunt departure and a Flanders contryside.

The divan, laid out on three sides of the room like some railway carriage seat, is in Persian carpet material. It is a deep divan and twenty people could meditate there on the geniuses of the past listed just opposite. Visitors to this *salon* consisted of a few bearded expatriates ever-willing to plot some conspiracy, always ready to talk about revolts and street massacres in 1848, or about "Napoléon le Petit", the marked man. Who today would remember these exiled warriors had not Hugo, with a feeling for their obscure destiny, painted their faces and names around a photo in the entrance hall ?

Colourless victims of freedom with unknown names, these Guernsey *émigrés* were buried on the island for the most part. They lived in exile as if practising a religious cult with Hugo as the high priest. It seems almost natural that one of their widows should desire at all costs to have a child by Hugo, who was courting her. There was about the place a partisan blood relationship in which the heroism, misfortune and pleasure joined forces.

The billiard room was gay where the smoking room was impressive and sad. Upholstered in blue-green, it had against its walls lines of huge benches, designed by Hugo and covered in flowered cretonne. Light from a gas chandelier was reflected in the wood of the billiard table, and illuminated the family portraits in their vast gold frames. There was plenty of laughter in this room in 1870 where play continued all day. Hugo had novices apart from billiards. He neither smoked nor drank. He walked a lot, swam and had fixed hours ; as he would say : "Rise at six, lunch at ten, supper at six, and bed at ten, makes a man live ten times ten."

Billiards was an English game but Hugo changed it into French billiards by doing away with the pockets. He was a gay man by nature ; in a photograph of him taken after publication of *Les Châtiments* at Jersey, there is no doubt that he had forced himself to produce a special face for the occasion. At the time Juliette wrote to him (January 1833) : "I find you laugh quite frequently for a serious man who has such beautiful teeth." He also laughed a lot with his sons, and the joys of fatherhood outweighed the sorrows of exile. He wrote to Charles who had gone hunting round the London antique dealers in May 1859 : "In the group apart that we are, it is always a hard drag to separate, even for a short while. On this earth, what is best for us, is us. There is nothing outside that worth loving."

On the ground floor of his house Victor Hugo was the family man. On the first floor he dreamed in fantastic drawing rooms. On the third floor he saw his life as linked to that of a great Italian who loved political freedom ; he gave over a room specially for Garibaldi, who never came. The higher one goes in this house, the more one feels Hugo sought solitude. Following the Montana affair of 1867 he wrote to Garibaldi : "Come, you who have not conquered and who cannot be crushed. We shall seek to know the name of hope, and we shall look ahead, because the evening makes dreamers..."

The bedroom contains a monumental Gothic bed and a forty-eight-candle chandelier part of which Hugo sculptured himself. It is an abandoned room attributed to the hero of freedom in the same way as in castles of his noblemen the king is symbolically given a room in the hope that one day he will actually visit and use it.

The red damask *salon* would be merely a Napoleon III drawing room except that Hugo incorporated a dome which used to be on the vessel of a Venetian Doge, the *Bucentaure*. From the dome, he believed, men had thrown into the sea some gold rings to symbolize the wedding of Venice and the Adriatic Sea. The dome is held up by four life-size Chinese statues. These golden Chinamen were brought back by Hugo from his Paris apartment in Rue de la Tour d'Auvergne. He also had brought over five flower-and-bird decorated, black-pearl broideries which he bought in the Rue de Lappe. He claimed they were from the apartments of Queen Christina of Sweden at Fontainebleau. He used them as a basis for this red *salon*.

The blue *salon*, full of mirrors, has a top to it as celebrated as that of the red rooms. It was the canopy of Madame de Maintenon's bed. These acquisitions, which he bought as historic items, are lost in yards of old golden plush. The light comes from its reflection, the windows themselves being narrow ; they are those of the original Hauteville House cottage. The mirrors and Murano chandeliers add a theatrical light.

A staircase lined with glass bookshelves bordered with black leads to a narrow stepladder by which one enters Hugo's personal rooms, lit from the ceiling by a single large round lamp. Everything is dark except for a yellow Luna Park mirror which returns a deformed image.

Up in the third floor Hugo wrote standing

up under a glass casing in the cold to keep in good health. He installed a ceramic stove with a base of blue Deft china. But the stove was never lit. The room contains steps that lead nowhere except to the glass ceiling under which Hugo used to throw his still wet manuscripts for the sun to dry. This room was a bridge, or rather a sort of greenhouse, from which Hugo could see the sea off Guernsey. In order to write he merely had to drop down a plank from the wall. He would stay there five or six hours a day standing all the time. Among works he wrote there were : *La Légende des siècles* in 1859, *William Shakespeare* in 1860, *Les Misérables* in 1862, *Les Chansons des rues et des bois* in 1865, *Les Travailleurs de la mer* in 1866, *L'Homme qui rit* in 1869, *Les Quatre Vents de l'esprit, Toute la Lyre, Le Théâtre en liberté, La Dernière Gerbe, Océan, Dieu* and *La Fin de Satan.*

Next to this room was his bedroom, which communicated with it. The bedroom's walls are in gold and red velvet and conceal a number of secret cupboards. Everything was arranged so that he could conceal a file, a memorandum or notes on his nocturnal dreams and amorous adventures. Hugo drew **a** princess and a knight on a triangular door leading to a ship's washroom and shower.

This is a sailor's room from which Hugo could gaze out over the sea. He slept on the floor on a red velvet pallet. On rising in the morning he could see the Atlantic, or Juliette's house, or the French coast.

On the ground floor, Hugo the family man was easily distracted. During meals when his son François Victor read aloud from the newspapers, according to Adèle's diary in 1855, "while everyone was gasping, he was not even listening and seemed absorbed with something else. He remarked that the asparagus was badly served, that the tails heads ends were mixed up... François Victor jumped from the Crimea to France. He referred to the high cost of food and to the bad harvest. He remained buried in his asparagus. Charles vainly tried to shake him up with a sharp reproach, but he kept out of the conversation and declared that the asparagus situation interested him more than the ever-lasting battle of Malakoff and the bad harvest."

So on the ground floor, Hugo remained the eternal exile who cannot bear political talk on French events or Adèle's piano which he hated. But on the third floor, in the room he made for himself, he could safely say : "I am a man who thinks of other matters."

Paris fell in 1870 together with the Empire. Hugo rushed back, to be fêted and acclaimed, but soon began to miss Hauteville House. He yearned to go back and said to Judith Gautier : "What if we conspire to get Bonaparte back ? We could go away again, back to the island."

Although he died in Paris, he had made three more trips to Guernsey as an expatriate of his own free will.

201. Mirrors, damasks, candelabras fill Hauteville House—the exile's palace of dreams.

202. *Hugo hung his china collection in a corridor.* 202

204. *Azulejos stones are displayed under glass.*

205. *Hugo set this room aside for Garibaldi who never came.*

206. *A drawing room in Hauteville House.*

207. *Hugo had initials inscribed over the fireplace in the dining room.*

203. *In his billiard room, the sofas are of his design.* 203

208

Lamartine

at Saint-Point Castle

The poet Lamartine took up residence at Saint-Point Castle near Mâcon, Burgundy, with his English wife, the former Miss Marianne Eliza Birch, shortly after their marriage in 1818.

He had it as a present from his father who acquired the castle on February 10, 1801. In 1870 the poet's niece Valentine inherited it and her three nieces sold it in 1894 to a Monsieur de Montherd whose grandson is the present owner.

The sixteenth-century structure had a severe beauty to it when Lamartine acquired the castle in 1820. The poet's wife, who was wealthy, had changes made in the English pseudo-Gothic style of the fourteenth century. One of its faces retains the look of a French provincial manor, but another shows distinct similarities with Westminster and English Tudor buildings. Gothic motifs can be seen on windows in stone or ironwork. Buttresses were fitted to the upper mouldings of windows, and turreted towers pierced with loopholes appeared every so often, together with a large Gothic porch. Later an arched terrace was built right around the castle, giving access to banqueting rooms on the ground level. Below, an orchard of orange trees and palm trees reflected an exotic streak in the former Miss Birch.

Lamartine himself seems not to have disapproved of these alterations to the homestead, and he may even have first thought of the idea. His wife planted wistaria and vines to hide the scars from the renovations, thus turning this typical Mâcon castle into an astonishing English-Victorian residence half buried in vegetation and medieval sculpture.

Lamartine had three residences in the area, but Saint-Point was the one he kept longest. His friend Dargaud was to write: "Chateaubriand's house is the cottage of a genius, but the three residences of Lamartine are noble caravanserai. He lived there with guests of his choice." The author of *Méditations* later came into possession of Milly, his birthplace, and of Montceau Castle also near Mâcon. He preferred Saint-Point and usually spent the summer there; it was in this castle that he wrote his *Méditations Poétiques* which brought him immediate fame and caused a friend to remark to Talleyrand: "There's a man indeed." Shortly after his marriage, Lamartine was made attaché at the French embassy in Naples, where he remained until 1821. He subsequently moved to Florence, where he stayed from 1825 to 1828 as secretary at the embassy, being over thirty-five when he took up the appointment. He returned to Saint-Point for the second half of his life. Far away now were the delightful moments he spent with the young Neapolitan Antoniella who ran the home of his mother's cousins. In due course, Antoniella appeared as the character of "Graziella". Past history, too, were his times with Antoniella who was the first Elvire of his *Elégies*. Another mis-

223

208. Elegant and handsome, Lamartine is seen here accompanied by his dogs. Already married to a rich English lady, his real love was now a thing of the past. However, he had not lost everything, for this memory inspired a poetical work in praise of passionate love.

tress, Madame Julie Charles, inspired in him the second Elvire of the *Méditations*. All that remained now for him to do was to engage in political life and write a long work.

Lamartine had said: "I shall marry at thirty or never." This he did when in December 1817 Madame Julie Charles, Elvire of *Le Lac*, died of consumption in Paris. She hoped he would come and see her, because she had been unable to join him that summer in Aix, as planned. But Lamartine preferred to write poems that were to give her immortality. Julie died in Paris as Alphonse de Lamartine poured out his feelings for her in Saint-Point Castle and at Montceau. When a friend handed to him the crucifix and meditation book belonging to Julie, he was deeply shaken and cried out in grief. His sisters said he spent two days and nights in the countryside, and returned pale and unrecognizable. Less than two years later he married his English lady, who was described by a doctor friend as "really ugly".

This marriage was arranged by the Lamartine family, but Alphonse quite liked the idea and a short while afterwards admitted he liked the former Miss Birch considerably: "Decidedly I like my wife", he wrote, "by dint of holding her in esteem and admiration. I am satisfied, perfectly satisfied, with all her qualities, even her looks..." Until the day she died, Madame Lamartine lived in Saint-Point Castle unsuccessfully trying to make him happy. It was in this castle that the quiet hours of their early married life were lived.

She bore a child, Alphonse, who died within eighteen months, and then a daughter, Julia, who took her first hesitant steps on the castle lawns. Little Julia was Lamartine's first love—after Madame Julie Charles. He admitted that it was not pure chance that her name Julia was like Madame Charles's.

In his political *Mémoires*, he subsequently included the phrase: "Julia, the name our daughter acquired through the memory of love." Madame de Lamartine, by some curious connivance stemming from her love for him, agreed to her daughter having the name of the poet's former beloved. Saint-Point must indeed have been the scene of some most peculiar matrimonial discussions. Lamartine always presented himself to the women he fell in love with as a young man who was in despair following some lost love. A Neapolitan girl consoled him after an unfortunate love affair in Mâcon, and the first Elvire soothed his brow after he lost the Neopolitan ("Graziella"), after which Madame Charles enabled him to forget the first Elvire. Next on the scene was Miss Birch who gave back a taste for life to the poet who carried in his heart the eternal memory of Madame Charles. Thus she satisfied both his romantic and his amorous tactics. For Lamartine to be happy at Saint-Point, the place had to be converted and embellished. The castle was transformed so that he could forget, and the little girl named Julia so that he could recall his previous love, with the agreement of an accommodating wife.

Lamartine was also prone to describing his past loves as platonic. Even though they might not have been (and he revealed as much to an inquisitive friend who asked him about Julie Charles), he at least only half concealed the truth. For his passions, in contrast to those of Chateaubriand, were above all the passions of the mind. In this way it is possible perhaps to explain why he was so deeply rent when he saw Madame Charles's crucifix, which she had kissed at the moment of death. Dead, Julie Charles became fully his Elvire; at last he could love her without restraint, could make her divine. Madame de Lamartine understood perfectly well that, between herself and the dream, Alphonse preferred the dream. So she arranged memories for him and piously respected the memory of the deceased mistress. At the same time she animated life at Saint-Point, putting peacocks and other birds on the lawns, laying out flower beds and filling the stables with first-class mounts selected by Lamartine himself.

They had plenty of friends to see them. The Castle was thrown open to Edgar Quinet, Eugène Sue, Madame de Cessiat and her daughters and Madame Coppens. They used to laugh at Madame de Cessiat, who as a good Christian woman gave up reading *Les Mystères de Paris* which made her go wild and neglect her family, but at the same time allowed her daughters to read them, since complete sacrifice of the tales was beyond her abilities. When she came and asked casually "How's everything going on?" her daughter Alix wickedly pretended not to understand and her mother was shamefully obliged to ask outright: "What's happened to La Goualeuse and Rigolette?"

Around 1831, Lamartine's friends used to speak of him with something of devotion. Dargaud, recalling the sight of Lamartine in the woods at Saint-Point, wrote in his memoirs: "We caught a glimpse of Monsieur de Lamartine. Slightly crouched on his white mare, he jumped the gate and arrived at a canter followed by a groom on a white horse and preceded by six greyhounds, also white, who gambolled around with Fido at the lead. A superb Newfoundland dog was also in there with them. It was like something of a Persian fairy tale but it was real enough. The poet had chamois gaiters, brown trousers, an olive green waistcoat, a black buttoned riding coat and a grey hat."

Dargaud also recounted how he toured the estate with Lamartine and visited the stables. "These contained ten horses of various hues and all remarkably beautiful. They quivered and whinnied as their master approached, chatting to them in a voice that was born to echo elsewhere," he wrote. "I shall never forget the timbre of his voice, nor the ardour with which Fido licked his hands, nor the clock decorated with a bronze lyre which struck noon just as I entered the study. The air around the tiled stove was warm, in that room where Monsieur de Lamartine withdrew to write and muse, of a morning before lunch. He would be able for certain to do three or four hours of work, without counting the regular intervals when he left the drawing room for the solitude of the study."

This work room was high up in a tower and adjoined the poet's bedroom, the two rooms being arranged by Madame de Lamartine. She imbued them with English comfort and used some rather special colourings. We know that she could paint very well, and she did two portraits of her daughter Julia which can still be seen in the study, together with medallions of various poets on the chimney piece of the bedroom. No doubt it was she, too, who laid out the large drawing room on the ground floor, furnished in a mixture of eighteenth- and nineteenth-century styles. But one of these rooms has furniture solely in cathedral-like varnished wood; this is a collection unique in France, originally selected and perhaps even specially made for Saint-Point just at the time when this style flourished for a short while.

The tower study and red room are the parts of the castle most reminiscent of the poet. They overlook the countryside and are adjacent to the castle cemetery. Exotic styles mixed with his belongings enable them to escape the influence of the Second Empire caravanserai, although they seem to lead on to this. The furnishings were done in the 1830's and the Cordoba leather on the walls, far from being Spanish, is more of a red-gold flamboyant version of the flowered cretonne the French used in the rooms of their manors. The heavy red Kashmir curtains and the panther skin thrown on the floor are less exotic than they otherwise might be, owing to the Restoration table with its shaped legs and the small wooden tables on which he wrote when he went into the country.

Elvire's crucifix is there in the bedroom on a piece of furniture next to the little statue of the poet's dog Fido. On the wall is a portrait of girl Julia in a romantic kind of dress: the ghost of her and of Madame Charles can be felt here more strongly than the influence of the epoch.

The unusual type of comfort and the belongings are repeated in the vaulted study. The arched ceiling and the walls bear white and blue striped material. This "consular tent" installed inside the tower kept out humidity but, more importantly, broke up the severity of a place that would otherwise have looked more like a hide-out than a study.

Now removed from the study is the tiled stove which Dargaud saw when he first met Lamartine. He was to have a major influence

225

on the poet's religious ideas ; Lamartine's catholicism became less militant and more unsure of itself. His contact with Dargaud swept away his simple beliefs, although he would have liked to retrieve them. Later Dargaud said Lamartine's catholicism was "a hesitant stuttering between a legendary religion and a philosophy, and nothing more." This observation was far from untrue and reflected the friendship he had for the poet ; a freethinker himself, he liked to see Lamartine's humanism gain ground over his christianity.

On the day of their first meeting in the study, the two men forged a deep friendship that lasted a lifetime. We can glean an idea of what it was like from the objects under glass globes, the souvenirs, the poems encircled with flowers, the portraits of little Julia in their Gothic gold frames, the occasional tables, the cradle for Julia's doll.

Lamartine liked to read out on what he had written. All his life he had a public at Saint-Point, mostly women ; it consisted of his nieces and sisters, some noble ladies in the district, a few local priests and Dargaud who acted as a conscience. Dargaud and Lamartine did not always agree in politics and religion, and in a sense Dargaud provided a counterweight to the catholic and feminine influence.

The poet worked hard at Saint-Point, and the bookshops had more works by him than they could sell. He wrote the *Méditations* at the castle and was surprised to find himself famous overnight, and regarded as one of the greatest writers of his time. Although he did not use the romantic and fashionable literary clubs of the time, this was not held against him, and his ability was widely praised. He also wrote *Jocelyn* and *La Chute d'un Ange* at Saint-Point, revealing a special kind of catholicism with which Dargaud was doubtless familiar. In the 1830's, Lamartine virtually isolated himself in his ivory tower, although it must be said that he appeared happy enough when he occasionally went into the park and played with Julia, sometimes giving her a golden coin.

Dargaud recounts that Julia one day offered to pay out of her own savings for a cow which a peasant had lost. The child laughed when she told how she used her golden *louis*. Her father and her friends listened and then she ran all over the lawns, finally disappearing to look for her own white goat. This conjures up a picture of a happy father. But it turns into a sad picture when we realize it did not recur.

Julia was everything to him. She pervades and shines through the *Nouvelles Méditations*, which he wrote in 1823, and *Le Dernier Chant du pèlerinage d'Harold*, written in 1825. All his work in this period is marked by her presence. In 1826 he wrote *Hymne du matin, L'Hymne du soir dans les temples, Milly ou la Terre natale*, and in 1828 *L'Hymne de la Mort* and *L'Hymne du Christ*.

He stood as a parliamentary candidate at Dunkerque in 1830 but lost the contest and returned to Saint-Point.

Lamartine thought he had lost his faith when he wrote *Les Harmonies poétiques et religieuses* in June 1830, and went to Jerusalem in order to regain his faith. He wrote about the Middle East to pay off his numerous debts.

It was in 1832 that he finally set out with his wife and Julia on the ship *Alceste* which he chartered specially for the trip that lasted one year. They visited Egypt, Syria and the Lebanon on the way out. The return journey was a Way of the Cross, since Julia died of consumption and they brought her coffin back to Marseilles.

Julia's burial was described by Dargaud in these words : "The night before the shrouding of Julia in the chapel, Monsieur de Lamartine spent the whole time in supreme intimacy with this angel's body, which he later placed in the grave of his mother."

The tragedy was described in *Gethsémani*. In *Voyage en Orient* he wrote this :

She was the only link in my broken chain
The only pure blue opening on my horizon.
So that her name should ring more softly in the house
We baptized her with a melodious name.
She was my universe, my movement, my noise ;
The voice that enchanted me in all my dwellings ;
The charm and the care of my eyes, of my hours,
My morning, my evening and my night.

Fido the dog who had played with Julia at Saint-Point and on the *Alceste* was immortalized in a statue, and in the *Méditations*, Lamartine wrote:

An organized body that a caress animates,
A deceptive automaton of life and tenderness.

After Julia died, Lamartine left Saint-Point for a while with its memories of her. He launched out into a political career, preaching "liberal and social Christianity" which brought him further fame.

He was elected to the Assembly by the voters of Bergues and political activity saved him from despair. He had written a few years earlier: "Life at Saint-Point does not satisfy me entirely at present." Without Julia it now had no point at all, so he left for Paris.

In the period from 1833 to 1840 he declined to support any one party. "I propose to sit on the ceiling," he declared. In summer he would return to Saint-Point, where Madame de Lamartine carried out more major convertions to eradicate the past. She never again went to Milly where the garden reminded her of Alphonse who died very young. Saint-Point for Madame de Lamartine would always recall little Julia who died at ten years of age. A friend wrote that her daughter's departure was "the death blow". She added: "She was the sole link she had with earthly life, and she has only suffering to undergo now. I pity Alphonse too, although he does not deserve the same compassion as his poor wife does. She must now, more than ever, feel how much a weight she is without giving anything in return."

Alphonse, in reference to Julia and Madame Charles, wrote: "This feeling I have had once in my life has been torn from my heart only by the loss of what I loved. Since then, I have been living in a mood of complete indifference."

In his despair he remained a faithful husband. He wrote at one stage: "I could be amorous but I no longer desire to be." Between the two periods of political activity, there were many visitors to the castle. The reason in the words of Lamartine was that "when I do not suffer I become bored. Such is my life." The poet remained most elegant, hunting and riding. As a young man he had read *La Nouvelle Héloïse* and swore to experience a love as powerful as Rousseau described. But now he had become faithful to his marriage vows, at the same time keeping Voltaire's letters as his bedside reading. He asked his relations and friends to visit him of an evening but found them boring. He would retire to his room, to be nagged later by Madame de Lamartine. He turned against books, throwing them away or giving them away when he he'd finished them. Nord id he care for music—his wife played the piano—nor for flowers. Madame de Lamartine herself wanted more flowers and complained that her husband did not help her buy any.

Their joint solitude, which grew on them despite their many relations, was made bearable by the presence at the castle of Valentine, daughter of one of Lamartine's sisters. She loved him very tenderly, and he returned something of the love he had given to Julia and Madame Charles. This was something of an upsetting experience for both of them, she an adopted daughter and he a famous writer and man of politics.

The trend of his thought at this time (1837-1838) is reflected in the titles of his work: *Les Recueillements* published in 1839, and *La Marseillaise de la Paix* which appeared in 1841. Then came February 1848 when a banned demonstration turned into an insurrection, the Revolution. The insurgents demanded that Louis-Philippe abdicate. A provisional government was set up at the Paris Hôtel de Ville in which Lamartine was a member. Later Blanqui was to remark: "The provisional government killed the Revolution." Blanqui himself had wanted a red flag to be raised, but France was to have the tricolour, which stems from a famous poem Lamartine read out while standing on a chair.

For the first time in French history the Assembly was elected by universal suffrage, but the majority that resulted was not favourable to the Paris working class which proclaimed the Republic. A direct clash followed in June when the Assembly did away with the state workshops. Lamartine named Foreign Minister, found himself harried by a crowd during these momentous times and escaped by jumping on a horse, which he promptly took back to Saint-Point as a souvenir.

Reaction against the Revolution began in earnest with the dictatorship of Cavaignac. From 1849 onward there was talk of ending the *République* by force of arms. This was effected by Louis-Napoléon on December 2, 1851.

The poet-politician returned to Saint-Point a ruined man, and looked back on his days as foreign minister with the phrase: "Three months of poetic hopes." He stood as candidate for the French presidency but gained only 10,000 votes. So it was back to the land. His vineyards were costing a fortune, and he borrowed money. Finally the interest and the payments he was obliged to make to his sisters forced him to sell. So he lost Milly and Montceau Castle in 1861, keeping only Saint-Point.

His friend Manguin listed to him the qualities he regarded as necessary for a statesman. Lamartine commented: "There are only two things that count in a statesman: to avoid being stupid and to draw strength from a principle."

His other friend Dargaud observed that it was also a good thing to be free of debt, to which Lamartine replied: "You are bringing personalities into it." He disliked bourgeois life in which men were well set up with their wealth.

The poet was to end his days forsaken and with a pension from Napoléon III. The City of Paris gave him a house at Passy, but the sale of his Mâcon residences humiliated him so much that he bitterly hated even the man who thought to help by offering to buy one.

Madame de Lamartine died at Saint-Point in May 1863 in her bedroom. Her husband on the floor above was unable to come to her bedside because he himself was stricken with rheumatism. He learned afterwards that she became delirious toward the end and called out for their son Alphonse. In this vast castle where years earlier peacocks sported and friends came and a little girl played, there remained only a couple separated by indifference and illness.

It was Valentine who looked after Lamartine when his wife died. He could no longer stand any friends and avoided them, growing wild and uncommunicative. "I have done enough talking in my lifetime, and have the right to keep quiet now," he would say when urged to take part in conversation.

Oh death, is it your voice that strikes my ear
For the last time? What now, do I awake
On the edge of the tomb?

In 1869, when he had to be taken to Paris, he refused to get into the train, and had to be forced to leave his property. He wanted to die at Saint-Point but he ended this life at the Passy house in Paris on February 28, 1869. Lamartine died kissing the crucifix which Julie Charles had kissed at the moment of her death.

You cry, and already I have drunk from the sweet cup
And forgotten evils. My elated soul
Enters the celestial harbour!

209. Saint-Point, with its neo-Gothic façade, rises up starkly behind the trees of the park.

210. *This little-known portrait in the salon of Saint-Point is of Madame Julie Charles, the Elvire of his poem. He never forgot her and was to name his daughter Julia in her memory.*

210

211

211. *Portraits painted by Madame de Lamartine hang over the chimney in Lamartine's room. Seen also, amidst the glow of Córdoba leather, is the poet's deathbed and the crucifix which "Elvire" kissed in the moment of death.*

212. *The poet's room in the château tower has striped walls* ▷ *and a few books in a small bookcase. A great reader, Lamartine generally disposed of his books to avoid being encumbered by them. At right is a portrait painted by her mother of their daughter Julia when she was five. The child's death was a turning point in the poet's life.*

212

La Varende

at Le Chamblac

Few great homes have managed to preserve the living traditions of the nobility as well as the Château of Le Chamblac in Normandy. The forebears of Jean de La Varende, a twentieth-century regional writer and author of *Nez de Cuir*, wore out three castles, it was said, before they finally handed Le Chamblac down to him. To be able to keep it in his possession, he wrote tales, short stories and novels.

The property was a challenge to its owner to look back on the past and make it live again. For a time he lived there the year around and isolated in the midst of five hundred acres of woods and meadows, La Varende undertook to resurrect the age of the nobility.

"Alas," he wrote, "I have become enslaved by this house. There is not a single room which I have not worked on with my own hands, using my craftsman's skills. I have married a ruin. I cherished this house as soon as I learned to love at all and I now realize my folly. What's the use? For whom, for what? Do the bricks and trees, the drawing rooms and the bedrooms depend on anxious care and jealous concern to acquire a metaphysical existence. This house is part of my life like a venerated declining parent whom one deprives of nothing. I bought the castle from my brother, I felt its pulse, coddled it and sounded its depths. For years, I gave up everything to look after it. I went seven years without visiting Paris... I spoke with its phantoms... I had ghosts as friends... I have not been a man of my times, and that is doubtless an inexpiable sin. The archives were burned and the castle itself is sure to disappear... I am insured for a ridiculously low sum so that if anything serious happens, I shall not be tempted to rebuild it."

He continued : "Let us trust lyrically in the fire of heaven, logically in an Electricité de France short-circuit, bourgeoisly in butane gas—and let us trust in the taxman."

Such are the thoughts of a man for the home he has loved, he admits, as a man loves a woman. Faced with the idea that it might disappear, he tries to imagine every possible way of life he might adopt if one day he is separated from it. But, thanks to him and his descendants, the castle survives today.

To build, for this man of letters, was to write a story. And in the love he bestowed on the decoration of his residence, he reveals the feelings of his soul just as he has in his writings.

Located a few miles from Bernay in the Auge region, Le Chamblac is built in very simple style. "A brick façade with two narrow rising structures, two wings at the rear, lantern type roofs and wrought iron balconies," is how La Varende described it. The castle has attractive pink walls, a pleasing window arrangement and a large park with chess figures in boxwood. La Varende seems to have dreamed up his domain before he created it. A visit to Le Chamblac is an exploration of the dreams of the

233

213. The ship models on display in the corridor of Le Chamblac were built by La Varende himself. "Alas", he wrote of his home, "I am enslaved by this house. There is not a room I have not worked on with my own hands, using my own skill."

writer. He was the man who thought he saw what others are no longer able to see; a provincial gentleman—often in Paris, although he pretended not to be a Parisian—the writer who in his stories sought to evoke the aristocratic traditions of the pre-revolutionary past could, in the usual tradition, have produced here a typical French garden, but he preferred to invent a chess game in the shape of boxwood trees that he had planted. Today they still dominate the castle entry with their tall notched shapes, and give it an eccentric appearance. Only the queens are left out of the game and one wonders why the trees did not suggest these royal shapes to the owner of Le Chamblac. The chessboard was never finished, but it gives the park a striking mystery with its "castles" that continue growing every year. This is the work of someone who could find a human face, the shape of an animal or the hint of a dream, in leaves or in the slits in the plaster. It is a child's game of fantasy, of course, but it amuses all ages. La Varende rejoiced to see the castle as he thought his predecessors saw it. The walls retain the traces of succeeding generations it is true, but the personality of the writer has left the deepest mark of all.

La Varende adored suites of drawing rooms. Those that are small in this castle make the others seem almost vast. The absence of any really valuable furniture has bestowed on the interior the charm of a simple family home.

The beauty of the woodwork, in accordance with his ideas, enabled the rooms to be alive without much furniture. It was as if his imagination was struck dumb before the triumph of shapes to which nothing needed to be added.

Le Chamblac contains so many eighteenth-century items of furniture and other subjects that it is impossible for the visitor to remember them all. They derive their special character from the way they have been selected as a group. The armchairs are provincial eighteenth-century. The tapestries are in fresh colours. The *objets d'art* reveal a lively imagination.

The dining room has a seventeenth-century air about it. The large tapestries were placed there in 1676 and remind the visitor of Monsignor de Laval-Montmorency, first bishop of Quebec. The deed of sale to his brother is still pinned on one of them. La Varende was referring to this family when in *Nez de Cuir* he paints a few traits of the Normandy nobility. He writes of the early nineteenth century: "An incomparable hospitality, a generosity that is disconcerting. At Beaumesnil, where the Laval-Montmorencies lived whose greatness might have intimidated youth, there were during certain months of October as many as sixty people at the residence. And there were no Empire infiltrations, for everyone had the same refined education, taken to the extremity of self-control and social art. So much so that all the *convenances* that still make social life bearable are mere feeble remains of that art : *convenances* is a word with a double meaning, only one of which we retain today—*convenu* ("accepted") which is artificial, whereas it used to be simply what *convenait* (was appropriate) in order to preserve life's joy, *entente* and quality.

"Nothing could have been less arbitrarily built up. On the contrary, a whole line of age-old experience had fashioned these requirements, a long period of trial and error. Even disorder and fancy were controlled in a simultaneous movement of people with respect for their personal dispositions. In such a homogeneous circle, one felt that an acquired position was constantly reinforced, rather than disputed. Thus emerged the provincial laws, which are sometimes so astonishing to the stranger."

Some of this atmosphere still floats in the dining room at Le Chamblac. The nailed chests, the two great lions in old Rouen material, the *petit-point* table cover, the china in the dresser and the hidden oratory give this room a somewhat grim simplicity, which is broken up by the sun's rays as they pass through the damp air.

The drawing rooms on the same level with the park all have hangings in silver-threaded, pink brocade, put up by the present owner's grandmother. These brocades evoke thoughts of those who chose them. The woodwork in these rooms is simple, and the furniture pleasantly reveals the *naïveté* of the local cabinet makers.

The best examples of the furniture were lost in the two world wars, or dispersed in successive wills. But Le Chamblac has not suffered from this.

Perhaps these empty spaces have enabled Jean de La Varende to exercise his own taste in filling them. For example, he has placed a light-coloured clock at the end of a hall; in a bedroom there is a collection of drawings of butterflies from the eighteenth century. All around there are watches and miniatures; he apparently never stopped buying them. A violin that belonged to a dancing master recalls better than anything the century when people sang, recited or played the game of proverbs. Next to the violin are a few perfume boxes.

In one bedroom in the roof, the visitor is surprised to find, in a small eighteenth-century box, seven razors shining like new, one for each day of the week.

La Varende was something of a theatrical producer, and the visitor feels rather like a member of an audience. He bought many things to embellish Le Chamblac, and in many cases the item he brought back found its final resting place only after moving about from top to bottom of the castle. "Two large Chinese cellular vases of the seventeenth century, of incomparable colouring and unique composition" came to rest in the end after being tried in several places "because", as he explained, "Chinese art goes with the eighteenth century but its proportion must not exceed one fifth; a quarter is dangerous."

It is easy to see how a man so sensitive to the harmony of a whole home which only time could produce, felt more than anyone else the disorganizing tragedy that is always associated with inheritance.

He said: "One does not know what laws decide the dividing up of a house which, hitherto, seemed definitive in its furnishings and arrangement. These separations are heart-rending for the person who has charge of the castle and, in fact, it is a considerable indignity to him. He has to bear the whole burden without even the benefit of finding everything intact. He has the secret pain of seeing at his relation's houses the items that were the elegant features of his own cumbersome residence. At Le Chamblac I am almost the only one to see again the nature of former times, I alone suffer to find with others the furniture that has been taken from us.

"There have been cases of much more painful kidnappings, by the dealers; sharing out under inheritance does, after all, bring joy and refinement to the lives of the family. Twenty years ago I found in one of the leading Paris antique dealers an escritoire on which I used to do my homework. In a right-hand drawer I found the red marks of some ink I spilt. The honest fellow dropped 100,000 francs for me, but where could I find the other 300,000 francs I needed? Ah, how beautiful it looked to me!"

We find here all the elements of a drama that Balzac did not fail to detect. The owner and collector betrays La Varende the novelist. These uprootings, the resistance to change arising from the taste for finality, the desire to preserve things, memories, the "secret suffering" at seeing in other's homes the furniture one has been part of, the whole misery, even not being able to buy back what one rediscovers and recognizes as one's own, even things being sold off by a second-hand dealer—so many dramatic experiences lived out under the huge slate roofs of the past age—he felt them all. For La Varende, the past of Le Chamblac lived on in all its furniture, even those pieces that had gone.

To this love of *objets d'art* and things must be added his love of ships. The castle lofts, he admitted himself, are full of them. Over a hundred models, built with his own hands, are preserved there under glass. Rafts, historic vessels and great sailing ships lie together side by side. Modelling them kept him busy and enabled him to dream away.

He recalled: "From earliest childhood I gouged out hulls and rigged up ships under the critical eye of my grandfather, Admiral de Langle... I have kept it up ever since. There is always a hollowed out hull somewhere in the

235

house. To produce marine shapes has always been a matter of complete self-realization for me.

"I am a fervent craftsman, but only a marine craftsman. Above all I have scraped out sailing ships, because of grandfather who was a demigod of those times. From him I have inherited a disdain for engines. One fine day (actually it was a fine evening) I had a daring idea to produce a history of the sea in models, and it exists here today : Egyptian vessels from the time of Pharaoh, Noah's Ark, Greek galleys, eighteenth-century ships, whaling vessels, trawlers, gondolas, yachts and, among all these delicate shapes, the *Le Quevilly*, a Normandy sailing boat, one of the first tanker ships for oil (the English put army tanks in them and these vessels got the name from this)."

When he finished a model, La Varende resumed his passion for the bigger "ship", anchored among the woods and meadows. On the upper floors, each room seems to have received from him a destiny and an atmosphere that distinguishes it from the others : there is a room of Scottish sabres and another lined with red *toile de Jouy*, and another with a green clock and some butterfly collections. A banqueting room is to be seen on the ground floor. The movable head of the Louis XVI canopied bed hides an escape door behind it. There is also a gallery with orange tiled walls, where ships' models are seen under golden angels. This gallery overlooks the park.

There is, too, on a wall in one drawing room, the discovery the writer made at the close of his life : an extraordinary painting purchased at a public sale showing a man with his nose hidden by a band of black leather, attending the presentation of horses to the Duchess of Berry at the Du Pin stud farm. This person is none other than the ancestor of De La Varende, *Nez de Cuir*, who inspired him to write his most famous novel. He had "an open face with a strong blunt jaw, good outlined lips and a square profile." He was wounded by a sabre thrust on the field of battle when the Cossacks first invaded France after the Battle of Leipzig in 1813. " But...

my face ?", the wounded man asked of his surgeon. "You must give me a mirror when you do the bandage again.

" No, it is not pretty.

" Horrible ?

" You will have to live with a mask'.

" Oh. I have no more face. My nose has been cut off, cut off! Two holes, two holes like a dead man ! "

The mutilated hero appeared "upright, slim, wearing diamonds and light clothing. He brandished his proud small head, and a snowy white mask over his wound." He also wore "a *Légion d'Honneur* ribbon which seemed to bleed like a big thumb from his button hole and made women tremble as if it were a wound..."

"After a few years he did not change the mask which thenceforth, in his fastidious way, he matched with his clothes. The mask became his symbol and emblem. Roger used it on his seal."

Finally, there is also a wonderful view over the woods attached to the property, in front of which stands an iron screen with two immense trees, one of which has grown slower than the other. Everywhere in Le Chamblac can be felt the touch of the man who, together with his son, has loved it most of all. He did not hesitate to say that he had made himself the castle's slave for all his life.

"I am my first valet, I admit it honestly. I shut my house every night just as one kisses a child good-night who has captured one's heart. There are even days when I open it up, too. I am never indifferent when I walk round and I offer up a friendly prayer to the great place. She is well looked after and, like women who have known only zealous love, she ages well."

The visitor can feel that the castle has been preserved and embellished with passion. For ever it will remain filled with the spirit of the 1839 aristocracy who still believed in the civilizing role of the Master, and who played that role. If, in a whim, La Varende wished his castle to the devil of destruction and the hasard of an electric short-circuit, he took good care when he was dying to pass on his great love of the past to his successor at Le Chamblac.

214. Seen from the balcony, the clipped trees are a part of the chess game that La Varende started to produce in his park.

215

215. La Varende's model of "Le Quevilly", a ▷
ship that was the forerunner of a large present-
day oil tanker with the same name.

216. This painting which La Varende acquired
at an auction sale, was the climax of a life
devoted to collecting beautiful things. Behind
the horses being shown to the Duchess of
Berry (right) is La Varende's ancestor,
"Nez de Cuir".
▽

216

217

218

◁ 217. *Jean de La Varende is seen here at Le Chamblac.*

◁ 218. *"Nez de Cuir" can be seen in this detail from the painting below. As a young man, he selected patches to match his clothes. Later, he wore only the black one. Women were fascinated by this affliction.*

Preceeding page:
219. For the dining table in Le Chamblac, La Varende chose a petit-point cover. The cupboards contained china that was in the castle before the inheritance was divided up.

◁ *220. When La Varende began to re-create his estate, he became its garderner, caretaker, mason and painter. He was devoted to a past age that escaped his grasp. The chess game he planted in the approaches to Le Chamblac was symbolic of the game he played with the past.*

Leonardo da Vinci

at Cloux

Leonardo da Vinci spent the last two years of his life in French Touraine near the Castle of Amboise at a manor called Cloux.

Due to his residence there France possesses the *Mona Lisa*, now in the Paris Louvre. If it were not for Cloux, and King Francis I, this famed lady would doubtless be in Italy today. It is due to a young monarch of twenty-two years of age that France includes in its art collections *Saint John, The Virgin and Child with Saint Anne,* and the *Mona Lisa.*

Nobody in Italy showed any interest in the old painter. Raphael and Michelangelo, both younger men, had ousted him in the eyes of the pope and the other patrons of the age. Leonardo vainly waited two years for a commission from the Vatican, and accepted the invitation of Francis I on his return from Marignan. The presence of Leonardo da Vinci at his court showed that he, too, could be a patron. So it was that the old painter came to live a few hundred yards from the royal castle at Amboise, in Cloux.

The place is a small manor built in 1471 by Estienne Le Loup, majordomo of Louis XI. It had at the time a chapel which Anne of Brittany had built, a guardroom, and the vaulted rooms where today are shown the models of machines reconstructed by the International Business Machine company, using drawings by Leonardo himself. There are also a few drawing rooms, disfigured by woodwork added in the eighteenth century.

On the first floor, a hanging balcony overlooks a large park with a stream running through it. In Leonardo's room can be seen a canopied bed that used to be in the centre of the floor space. He had fixed to the wall the three paintings of *Saint John, The Virgin and Child with Saint Anne* and the *Mona Lisa* — the only paintings he had kept, and which he brought to France with him.

For a while he found living at Cloux very agreeable indeed. But soon, the young man he had adopted and who came to France with him, left to go back to Italy, and Leonardo turned into a sad, worn-out old man. The King of France was undemanding in his role as patron, and respectful of his protégé's gifts, however much they had eroded with the years. And so Leonardo spent most of his time dreaming up new military and scientific machines which the monarchs of the time did not know what to do with.

When Leonardo da Vinci had any meeting with Francis I it was usually to discuss philosophy or present the monarch with projects that echoed the grandiose schemes of his past. He suggested the king should dry out the marshes of the Sologne region, as he had tried in the case of the Pontine marshes. He proposed the demolition of the Castle of Amboise and its reconstruction. He thought up a scheme for linking all the castles in the Loire Valley by a canal so that his majesty could go from one to the other by boat.

245

221. It was to the manor of Cloux, near the Château of Amboise, that Leonardo da Vinci came as the guest of King Francis I. He spent his two last years there, bringing the "Mona Lisa" with him. This is why it is in the Louvre today.

In return, Francis I made him head of castle festivities, a service which many years before he had performed for Duke Ludovic Sforza of Milan. In that capacity his lively mind had devised colourful pageants, games and fireworks, as well as an awesome array of military weapons and engines for the duke—indeed, he had, at the age of thirty, proposed his services as military engineer to Sforza, sending him a memorandum depicting war machines he had designed, which, he said, would ensure the duke's supremacy in battle. At the end of the note he mentioned casually that, in case the duke did not know, he was also a painter and sculptor.

At the age of sixty-five at Cloux, Leonardo maintained the same attitude. He agreed to be the king's artificer, and painted only a little. He suffered from rheumatism in his right hand but fortunately was left-handed. So it was not this handicap that prevented him painting, but rather his belief that he had nothing left to say as a painter. Nevertheless he considered that he had much to learn in other fields. He preferred knowledge to art, and in Italy such an outlook had made people suspicious of him. At a time when humanism had to give way to the Church, anyone who undertook research was easily taken to be an alchemist and a sorcerer. Overriding such prejudices, Francis I accepted this state of affairs. Possibly he saw the day approaching when he could acquire the three paintings hanging in da Vinci's room. Such a hope certainly gave him the gift of patience.

In some respects, the great man's life at Cloux was almost a reflection of the life he had known in Italy. People had always more faith in his painting than in his research work. They pretended to show interest in the latter in the hope that one day he would provide them with a painting of genius. But money never held any interest for Leonardo and nobody could exercise any pressure on him by means of it. He had chosen freedom. He would never agree to be totally dependent on those who placed orders with him. In 1493 Isabelle d'Este, Marquise of Mantua, had commissioned painters such as Mantegna and Perugino to paint panels in her *studiolo*, one of the rooms in her palace. But she had to write fifty-three letters to da Vinci before he would complete *The Struggle between Love and Chastity*. The subject of this canvas, commissioned by a worldly-minded woman, was uninteresting to him. In 1500, when he had left the court of Sforza, she finally succeeded in getting from him a chalk sketch of her face in profile—the closest she ever came to persuading him to do her portrait. For Leonardo wanted freedom and regarded himself as the equal of any lord.

In an epoch when painters had their meals in the kitchen with the servants, da Vinci made people plead before he would paint a picture; he would dress luxiously, kept horses and servants, and selected his own perfumes. He once returned some money a member of the nobility paid to him. He lived perpetually surrounded by youg men. It was a common thing for painters to have several "disciples" with them.

The existence of this entourage would not have shocked anyone if the painter had not revealed a certain disgust for conventional love, in a era when orgies were quite tolerated. As compared with the Sforzas and the Borgias, Leonardo da Vinci appeared as a secretive kind of person, and nobody could recall him having any love affairs. This, coupled with his reputation as an "alchemist" was enough for him to be left outside the usual circles. He was obliged to refute a charge of sodomy. He was hurt by the accusation and kept even more to himself thereafter.

Yet he was a pleasant enough person, gay, likeable, a vegetarian who respected animals, a pacifist who made war machines.

Young men would accompany him on his journeys. A complete silence veiled his private life. He was not known to have any love life, as in Michelangelo's case. All this, together with his strange drawings, gave him an aura of mystery. Beauty was the only excuse for pleasure he could find, and he said so. Many of his sketches showed old men next to adolescents. One such is now at Florence at the Uffizi Art Gallery, and was done around the year 1500. It is believed the young man depicted was his pupil Salaï when he was twenty years old. Another sketch at the Ecole des Beaux-Arts in Paris shows a man thinking, with a young man, and this is probably a first drawing for the *Adoration of the Magi*. A further drawing in pen shows a naked man with four arms and two heads: one of these twin people is old and the other young, but identification of them has not proved possible; the painter wrote beside the drawing: "Pleasure and pain are shown as twins, as if united, because the one does not exist without the other. If you choose pleasure, remember that behind it lies something else that will give you tribulation and cause repentance."

This was done around 1485. In another sketch in the British Museum can be seen the same old man, but this time he is blowing into a trumpet at the ear of a young lad. In a drawing in a Hamburg gallery, a face spans an old man. Is this, as has been thought, the symbol of intelligence dominated by love? The hypothesis of homosexuality in da Vinci, according to Freud, would explain the mystery surrounding this platonic painter. But posterity has been so anxious to prove this proposition that it has perhaps gone too far. Some have noted that in a sketch where he refers to love he has shown only right hands, he himself being left-handed, and they have sought to prove some hidden significance in this. In another drawing of a man and a woman the woman's body appears to be left deliberately incomplete by contrast to the man's which is shown whole: this is interpreted as showing that the painter wanted to ignore the woman's body. These observers have also noted significantly that the man in the drawing has a pained expression on his face and long hair—does this again, they ask, symbolize a dislike of heterosexual love, and a tendency to homosexuality? People have wanted to comment overmuch on Leonardo's drawings, and in particular have shown too keen a desire to interpret them, perhaps stimulated by Leonardo's own cryptic references to his work.

Notwithstanding this, there do exist in the painter's diary certain passages that lend support to Freud's proposition. His notebooks reveal that he used to buy very good clothes for his pupils. Da Vinci used a familiar tone to himself in the diary as if, by confiding in the paper itself, he was using it as a substitute for some person with whom he liked to imagine he was conducting a dialogue.

Why such mystery? Freud explains Leonardo's behaviour entirely by his childhood experiences. He was an illegitimate child of a public notary and a peasant woman. He was born in 1452 and stayed two or three years alone with his mother. His father was named Pietro da Vinci, married a person of his own rank but had no child from this marriage, and later adopted Leonardo. The boy was to be affected all his life from the absence of his father and the separation from his mother whom he loved. According to Freud, da Vinci was never able to love a woman and the smile of the *Mona Lisa* is his own mother's, which is why he did the smile so often. In the work of *The Virgin and Child with Saint Anne*, Saint Anne is really his first mother because she has a smile very similar to Mona Lisa's, the smile on the lips of the woman who brought him into the world. The Virgin is supposed to be his other mother who married his father, and the Child is Leonardo himself. Another painting shows Saint John with a similar mysterious smile.

Freud has expressed the belief that Leonardo da Vinci perhaps loved a woman once, when he found someone with the same facial expression as his mother's, and that the woman was called Mona Lisa. Da Vinci took four years to paint her and he never parted with the finished work. These three paintings incorporating the famous smile were all at Cloux, for Leonardo would never let them go.

Backing up the hypothesis of homosexuality—which might have been platonic—is a childhood memory which he relates himself: "I appear to have been destined to take a particular interest in vultures, because one of my earliest childhood memories is that I was in my cradle and a vulture approached, opened my mouth with its tail and several times hit me with its tail between my lips." How can this be interpreted? In those times vultures were always thought to be females, and believed fertilized by the wind. Possibly, says Freud, da Vinci's mother or Leonardo read this story, and they were led to believe that destiny had already "picked out" Leonardo. Supposing that he remembered something from this early moment, the incident as he described it is too extraordinary to have really happened. His recollection was merely a fantasy of the mind; Freud explained it by suggesting he had a mother-fixation, that the vulture took the place of his mother, fertilized so to speak by the wind, and that da Vinci's recollection was the sublimated memory of his own illegitimacy.

Other psychoanalysts such as Oscar Pfister, have thought to recognize the face of the vulture that obsessed da Vinci in the folds of the Virgin's dress in *Saint Anne, the Virgin and Child*. The painter, as we know, used to hide faces in the details in his works. It was Mantegna who suggested to him that he could use the veins in rocks for this purpose. Arcimboldo was later to make this trend a fashion but when da Vinci uses it in *Saint Anne*, by painting a man's head using the shapes of reefs, one has the impression it is more to satisfy the complexity of an inquisitive mind than to shock in any way. He liked to see another world behind the apparent one.

Freud believed that his scientific research, his mechanical inventions, hydraulic works and architecture were all merely an attempt at sublimation. Scientific research for Leonardo was a compensation for the disappointment of his love life, according to this theory.

"The instincts and their metamorphoses are the last things psychoanalysts can know. From this point on, it must give place to biological investigation. The tendency to repress and the capacity of sublimation must be related to the organic bases of character, on which the psychic edifice can then be built," said Freud.

Not everything in Leonardo's life can be explained by the fact that his mother was unmarried and a vulture flew over his cradle. He was above all a humanist keen on research. Painting was only one aspect of his work, and for him it was not the most important. On his death bed at Cloux he again confessed to God that he had not done enough for the advance of knowledge. He had nevertheless devoted his life to this ideal, and his painting suffered for it. Leonardo did not regard his life as a success, even though at the early age of twenty it was acknowledged that he overshadowed his own master, Verrocchio. Between 1483 and 1500 he painted *The Virgin of the Rocks* and *The Last Supper* and around the age of fifty he spent four years on the *Mona Lisa*. We cannot but be struck by the intellectual aspect of his work; both the scientific speculation of Leonardo and the cold enigmatic smiles of his paintings stem from the same manner of looking at the world. His painting is intellectual rather than sensual. In the days of the Médicis, the Sforzas and Pope Leo X, they failed to win him any more admiration or official orders. Luck was also against him; an equestrian statue which Sforza ordered was not cast for want of money, and it deteriorated to be finally destroyed by the archers of Louis XII. Michelangelo criticized Leonardo in public. His frescoes were a failure too; he wanted bright tones and endlessly experimented with new mixtures and varnishes with the result that the oil colours he used ran down the wall or disintegrated in a short time.

His experience as an engineer was not much happier. He designed a forerunner in 1479 to the modern machine-gun with his gun-tower, and later produced a glider. He was ahead of Galileo in certain observations. But his thirty-three-gun bombarding device enabling eleven shots to be fired simultaneously was never used, because just as the military were on the point of trying it, peace was signed. Leonardo invented collapsible lightweight bridges like the Bailey Bridges of the Second World War, a large ball which rolled along throwing out long flames, explosive mortar bombs and mines as well as fortresses that could resist these, and the first tank—a protected vehicle on wheels with only the gun mouths showing. But the Sforzas preferred to use his talents for arranging firework displays and designing theatrical machinery.

In Cesare Borgia's service in 1502 Leonardo was appointed "general engineer" and was ordered to visit all fortresses and defenses, but his job lasted only a few months, and the next year he was at Florence.

There, he worked out highly daring urbanization schemes, including houses that could be dismantled, and transportable and superimposable cities so that the governing classes could keep apart from the others. On this point, he was no precursor, but his father did not let him forget that he was himself from the peasant class. Leonardo envisaged the building of ten towns each with 10,000 houses, and planned to pipe the water and waste into the sea, and to make use of smoke from houses by fitting devices in the chimneys.

He even invented a wheelbarrow with a counting unit on it so that the user could calculate the distance and speed he had walked with it. In the course of his mechanical studies, da Vinci examined the behaviour of falling bodies and, a century before Galileo, realized the principle of energy conservation and the relationship between speed loss and its conversion to power. He sought to know how pressure moved within a liquid; to a friend who argued with him, he once said: "Be quiet, you want to hold a mass of water heavier than the weight on it."

He was asked to canalize the river Arno and to paint, in Florence's Palazzo Vecchio, the *Battle of Anghiari*, but he failed in both attempts. He did the fresco with a mixture the formula for which he had found in Pliny; but the painting did not last, the mixture underlying it never having dried. As for the canal, Leonardo made a miscalculation that rendered it useless and he was deemed responsible for this mistake. The canal was abandoned and gradually filled up with sand. Again, in Milan and in Rome, other schemes knew the same misfortunes. Da Vinci's protectors died.

Equally sad was his attempt to fly a glider on Mount Cicero from 1,300 feet up. Of this early aeroplane, da Vinci wrote before the first attempt: "The great bird will for the first time take to the air, filling the universe with stupor and all writings with its renown; giving eternal glory to its birthplace."

A mocking friend recorded afterwards: "Flight did not succeed for the two men who undertook it recently. Leonardo da Vinci tried to fly but he had cause to rue it. He was an excellent painter."

He was always a painter to the engineers and an engineer to the painters. Francis I probably saw more of the painter in him than the engineer, since none of the suggestions Leonardo put to him during his time at Cloux were to be realized. On the death of Leonardo in May 1519, the king, as he doubtless expected, found himself the proud possessor of all the paintings he had his eyes on from the moment Leonardo went to live there.

The death of Leonardo da Vinci has been described in a painting by Ingres. In accordance with reports which are probably apocryphal, the young king is shown leaning over the old painter at Cloux. Romantic style is used to express the unusual. The king who wanted the most sumptuous décors, such as the Field of the Cloth of Gold, had attached himself deliberately to the man who was the most sensitive to beings and things, but the most removed from any desire to have possessions. For Leonardo painting had always been merely "a mental thing", like his research work. He had never possessed anything. To the greatest degree he was aware of his contradictions, and regretted that he had never succeeded in expressing himself in painting. "Sensitivity withdraws when the spirit awakens," he said. He lived constantly with disciples. It was the young monarch who listened to him carefully as he voiced his disappointments about life during his final moments.

Testament of Leonardo da Vinci

Be it known to all present and to come that in the court of our sovereign lord at Amboise, before us personally constituted, Monsieur Leonardo da Vinci, painter to the king, presently dwelling at Cloux near Amboise, knowing the certainty of his death but the uncertainty of his hour, has made known and confessed at the said court before us (in which he is subject and subjects himself in respect of what he has done by the tenor of the present) his testament, and orders his last will as follows :

Firstly, he recommends his soul to our sovereign Lord and Master God, to the glorious Virgin Mary, to Saint Michael and all the good angels and saints in Paradise.

Item : the said testator desires to be buried in the church of Saint-Florentin at Amboise, and his body to be carried there by chaplains thereof.

Item : that his body be accompanied from the said place to the said church of Saint-Florentin, by the college of the said church and also by the rector and prior, or by the vicars and chaplains of the church of Saint-Denis at Amboise, as also by the minors of the said place.

And, before his body is taken into the said church, the testator desires that there should be celebrated in the church of Saint-Florentin three high masses with deacon and subdeacon, and by day should be said thirty low masses of Saint Gregory.

Item : in the said church of Saint-Denis a similar service shall be celebrated, and also in the church of the said friars and minors...

Item : he desires that sixty torches be lit at his burial, carried by sixty poor people who shall be paid to carry them... the torches being shared out in the four above-stated churches.

Item : the testator gives to each church ten pounds of wax in great candles that shall be sent to the said churches to serve at the above services.

Item : that charity be given to the poor at the Hôtel-Dieu and to the poor of Saint-Lazare at Amboise, and, for that, there should be given to the treasurer of each brotherhood the sum of seventy Tours sous...

Given at Cloux in the presence of Maître

Esprit Fléri, vicar of the church of Saint-Denis of Amboise, Monsieur Guillaume Croysant, priest and chaplain, Maître Cyprien Fulchin, Brother François de Courtin and François de Milan, religious of the convent of the minors at Amboise, being witnesses of these demands and called on to accept judgment at the said court. In the presence of the above-said François de Melzi, accepting and commenting, who has, by his faith and bodily sermon, given corporally into our hands, promised never to do, come, say and go to the contrary.

And sealed at his request with the royal seal established by the legal contracts of Amboise, and this as a sign of truth.

Given the 23rd day of April 1518 (before Easter) 1519.

And on the same 23rd of the month of April 1518, in the presence of Maître Guillaume Boreau, notary royal in the court of the Bailiwick of Amboise, the above Monsieur Leonardo da Vinci has given and conceded by his testament and his last will as above, to Baptiste de Villanis, present and agreeing, the right to the water that King Louis XII of happy memory lately dead formerly gave to the said da Vinci of the Canal of Saint-Christopher in the Duchy of Milan, to be enjoyed by the said de Villanis, but in such manner and form as the said lord has given it to him, in the presence of Monsieur François de Melzi and mine.

And on the same day of the same month in the said year 1518, the same Leonardo da Vinci, by his last will and testament as above, has given to the above mentioned Baptiste de Villanis, present and accepting, all the furniture and utensils that belonged to him in the said place of Cloux. In the event, howsomever, that the said de Villanis survive the above Leonardo da Vinci.

In the presence of the said Monsieur François de Melzi and Myself, notary.

Signed : BOREAU.

222

223

224

222. *In the background of this painting of "Saint Anne and the Virgin" are figures hidden among the rocks. This was a favourite trick of the day.*

223. *Freud believed that the illegitimate Leonardo had given "Mona Lisa" his mother's smile.*

224. *Some commentators see in this picture of "The Virgin of the Rocks" the image of a vulture in the folds of her dress. Da Vinci said that a vulture had approached his cradle. Freud thought this story was the invention of a man who could not rise above his illegitimate origins.*

225. *Francis I is seen here with the dying Leonardo in a painting by Ingres. The king acquired the "Mona Lisa", "Saint John" and "Saint Ann and the Virgin" after the artist died. Leonardo had brought them with him from Italy.*

227. Leonardo spent more time thinking up war machines that were rarely used than he did painting. Engineers regarded him as a painter and to painters he was an engineer. ▽

228. Old age and youth are pictured here by ▷ Leonardo. His young followers certainly played a major role in his life. We have no record of any love affair with women.

228

229

226. The outer gallery at Cloux faces the park.

229. The I.B.M. company has produced Leonardo-designed machines at Cloux. They include an early tank, a plumb-line, a metered wheelbarrow to measure distance, the first machine-gun and a glider—the first plane, which was a failure.

Montesquieu

at La Brède Castle

Montesquieu, the eighteenth-century political philosopher, was as a writer as difficult to approach as the castle he owned at La Brède. *De l'Esprit des lois* is not an easy work to grasp. It appeared in 1748 and contains his views on the "separation of powers", and was to inspire reforms in the French Constituent Assembly of 1789.

Yet Catherine the Great and Frederick II made it their bedside reading. This is almost certainly because this thinker from near Bordeaux had a way of putting forward his theories on the separation of political powers without offending the pride of state leaders who held undivided power on a personal basis. Frederick II, it must be added, found he had certain reservations to make with regard to the work. Montesquieu, when he heard about this, remarqued with a wry smile that he knew perfectly well which passages in the book the Prussian king found unacceptable.

Montesquieu was born at La Brède Castle near Bordeaux on January 18, 1689. He was presented at his baptism by a beggar man, with the idea of impressing on the new-born gentleman that all men are brothers. This did not prevent him later marrying a young Calvinist woman, Jeanne de Lartigue, for the simple reason that she brought with her a nice sum of 100,000 pounds. This windfall increased the castle income and permitted the vineyards to be expanded. Montesquieu's attitude was above all inquisitive. His landed fortune mainly consisted of vineyards which he looked after with great care. This enabled him throughout life to live the kind of existence he desired—that is, to write what he thought in complete freedom, although he did so with a good deal of prudence.

He came from a long line of Bordeaux parliamentarians, but grew up amid the peasants of La Brède castle, whom he loved deeply. He was never a regular visitor to Paris nor a courtier. He spent his time cultivating himself rather than being one of the Versailles nobility. He studied law and was accepted at the Bordeaux bar in 1708. Around this time he was already producing at La Brède a treatise on the eternal damnation of pagans. In it, he defended the Greek philosophers, taking the view that they may not have deserved Hell after all. His tolerant ideas pleased Voltaire, who appeared to have similar ideas. Voltaire once said of him: "He is a virile fast-thinking genius." Later Marat wrote: "Montesquieu always respected opinions that implied the good order of society, and attacked only gloomy prejudices in order to rid humanity of them; he never took on the dogmatic tone of a reformer, and preferred a delicate satire whose shafts were the more accurate for being less violent. Montesquieu was a disturbing influence on superstitious writers."

The aristocrat Montesquieu possessed the

230. La Brède lies in the midst of water, woods and vineyards near Bordeaux. Born and raised there, Montesquieu was later to write "L'Esprit des lois" at this tranquil castle.

spirit of his class and the common sense of the peasant he knew so well. He could speak the truth with more malice then anyone of his time. His *Lettres persanes* are a satire on European manners, supposed to have been written by a Persian travelling through France. This litterary form enabled him to say anything he liked without being nasty.

It was in the castle of La Brède that he spent most of his early life, asking himself all kinds of questions about the policy of the Romans over religion (which led to *Considérations sur les causes de la grandeur et de la décadence des Romains*, on which Frederick II made notes carefully with his own hand), and about natural science, drunknenness, intermittent fever, the minds of animals, the causes of echoes; about a child without a brain, shellfish at Sainte-Croix-du-Mont, on the use of the renal glands and reasons for the transparency and weight of bodies (1718). Also at the castle he carried out experiments on mistletoe, oaktree moss, insects, frogs, ducks, and other flora and fauna.

In 1721 he gave up his researches into nature and turned to the study of man. He progressed slowly in this field, studying man's ideas, thoughts, and laws. Through this research, he really established the bases of modern sociology. The *Lettres persanes* were a pretext for these studies, which he had published anonymously. The work was an immediate major success, and he then went to live for some time (1721-1725) in Paris. As in the case of most of the nobility, it was his land that enabled him to live comfortably in the capital city. Each year he returned to the property for the grape harvest and to check up on the management of the castle. He produced white and red *entre-deux-mers* wines and his wife's land produced eaux-de-vie spirits in Armagnac and Agenais.

He was interested in silver and gold and was one of the first people to posit the idea that Spain's wealth was one of the roots of its political collapse. He made many such deductions as a result of his own thinking, and they amounted to a draft version of his later *L'Esprit des lois*.

At this period, Montesquieu was a fully successful author. He applied for membership in the Académie Française and was elected on January 24, 1728, despite the king's view that a provincial could not be a member unless he actually lived in Paris. He sold the resultant position and set about visiting various European cities. He brought back a variety of works from serious observations by legal experts that formed the basis for his later works to odd notes and recorded impressions that appeared as *Cahiers*.

He wrote: "When I was in Florence and saw the country's simple way of live—a senator wearing a straw hat by day and carrying a little lantern by night—I was enchanted. I did as they did and told myself: 'I am like the Great Cosimo.' Indeed, there you are governed by a noble lord who acts like a bourgeois gentleman; elsewhere by bourgeois who act as if they were noble lords."

And again: "The priests of Rome have succeeded in making devotions even delightful by the continual music you can hear, of excellent quality, in the churches. They have produced the best operas and enjoy them. One sees there a freedom of relations between the sexes that magistrates do not allow elsewhere."

From Italy he went to Austria, commenting: "I found very affable men of God at Vienna. I told them: 'You are ministers in the morning and men at night.'"

He moved on to Germany and sailed for England where he stayed until 1731. He admired the English "who like reasoning rather than talking... The English say little but they expect to be listened to. With them, simplicity, modesty and self-control are never ridiculous. They rate personal merit higher than do any other nations. They have their little ways but they get over them. If you send them small-minded people they think you want to deceive them. They are truthful, open and even indiscreet, but they cannot abide being deceived. Everything with an 'air' to it displeases them. They like simplicity and decency; the English like arguing rather than conversing. They are naturally honest people, unless the court or need has corrupted them; worthy people although they do not esteem exploits; they are able to distrust or to love money; but they are incapable of enjoying themselves and prefer to be amused. When foreigners have none of the faults they expect them to have, the English will love them passionately. They admire skill and are in no way jealous. All this is blanketed with a strangeness which is like a cloak that envelops all their virtues."

Wherever he went, Montesquieu discussed everything and saw everyone. In London he became interested in freemasonry, cardinals, prostitutes, sewers and legislation. He demanded explanations on the working of English law, and returned to La Brède with several notebooks and his mind crammed with thoughts, from which he further developed the manuscript of *L'Esprit des lois*. He worked several hours each day and spent the rest of his time looking after the castle and its vineyards. He was a true Gascon and above all loved La Brède. He gave financial explanations for his love of the place but one wonders if money was the only reason. He wrote: "The reason why I like to be at La Brède is that at La Brède I feel that my money is under my feet. In Paris, I feel as if it is lying across my shoulders. In my country I say: 'I must spend all that.'"

Visitors who were often at La Brède included Helvétius, the farmer and author (1715-1771) who wrote *De l'Esprit*, an apologia for sensualism. Like several other friends of Montesquieu he belongs to the Encyclopedist group. They examined social and political problems from a scientific point of view, although they did not stray from the framework of idealistic and metaphysicial conceptions of history. They denounced the concept of feudalism and laid the theoretical groundwork for the 1789 Revolution. Other visitors were Hyde, Barbort and Jean-Jacques Bel. In turn Montesquieu would go for chats with the Duke of Saint-Simon at La Ferté-Vidame; the duke at this time (1734) was writing his *Mémoires* secretly.

In the calm of La Brède castle and the warmth of southern France, the mind feels free, liberally disposed, lively and keenly interested in everything.

The way in to the castle is by three drawbridges over the moats. Montesquieu in his time made many improvements to the property's environs. He cleared away woodland around the castle in order to show it off better, and enriched the library with many books, instructing his secretary to carry out an inventory of the 4,000 volumes during his absences. He was deeply attached to this little fortress. "Why do you not come?" he told an English friend. "It is a fine day and I want to show you how I have tried here to copy the taste of your country and arrange my home in the English style."

In his *Pensées* (contained in the *Cahiers* published by Grasset, 1941), he tells us: "I have had no desire to make my fortune through the court, but have preferred to make money by increasing the worth of my land, accepting my fortune directly from the gods." But when England blocked his wine exports and he saw his main sources of income dry up, he was so upset he did not go to Paris for three years. He accepted frosts, but the English legislation was to have a longer effect on him than bad winters. When he was prohibited from planting on certain land, he fought against the official concerned and won his point in the end. His vineyards were his main concern.

Montesquieu restored the castle. He wrote around 1744 when he was fifty-five: "It is true that I am building a little. One must think about preparing a residence, not to retire in, but to induce oneself to retire." All things considered he was very pleased with his innovations and the woods he had cut down. "I can honestly say that at present this is one of the most agreeable places in France, as far as castles are concerned; nature appears to be in her dressing gown arising from sleep," he wrote.

La Brède is surrounded with flowing water, for a river circumvents the residence. Woods encircle it like a fairy tale castle. On entering the huge hall the visitor is struck by the splendid dark wood spiral columns holding up the ceiling, and by the outstanding candelabras of mirrors and copper arms shedding a glow on the red material on the walls. Some of Montesquieu's trunks in nailed black leather have been kept against the supports of the hall, and some of the author's Bernard Palissy pottery remains on the walls. The colours of the ceramic, the unusual columns, the Dutch lamp and the huge candelabras make this entrance hall one of the finest in the castles of southern France. Next to the hall is a great *salon* with some beautiful furniture, but the true "shrine" of the place is Montesquieu's own bedroom.

This is a very pure seventeenth century. The canopied bed has retained its decoration and curtaining in contemporary green silk. On the large Regency chest of drawers are a Delft ewer and Montesquieu's bust on a red velvet base; they have not been altered since he died. The walls contain family portraits: his favourite daughter and his secretary are side by side in their gold frames. The sunlight falls generously on a white wood table, bearing an old ceramic inkwell, a pen and some of Montesquieu's cards. The floor of simple wood blocks, the heavy partly-open curtains, the windows overlooking the moats and the softness of the air all make this rather austere room a first rate example of a seventeenth century interior. None of the great châteaux of the Loire can offer such intimacy. La Brède is somehow unpretentious yet great.

Montesquieu's room exudes the provincial atmosphere of the southern French gentry. It is easier to understand, after seeing it, something of the sharper side of his southern intelligence, which he exercised so far from the town. A small washroom, hidden in one of the thick walls, may be seen next to the room. It has a table bearing a pewter pitcher. The walls are in green-coloured whitewash. It is unexpected, as is everything else in the castle.

There are some rooms not open to the public, occupied by the Countess of Chabannes, who is, through her maternal grandmother, a descendant of the Montesquieu family.

In the several bedrooms are some twin beds with canopied and panelling, and seven-teenth-century *petit-point* curtaining. The castle appears to have been completely saved from the effects of the Revolution and all the wars since. No split-up of inheritance has led to any losses. During the Revolution, the owners emigrated to England, and the property went through a series of embargos. Montesquieu's manuscripts travelled from La Brède to England, and between the various branches of the family. But at last they returned home. Original new work by Montesquieu continued to be published after the Revolution and right up to 1951, when *Les Carnets* were published.

Most of Montesquieu's books remained in the great library on the first floor where he used to work. There are still several thousand volumes. Some were there when he took over the castle, and he added many himself, for he was a voracious reader. He once remarked: "I have taken the decision to read only good books. Those who read bad ones are like people who spend their lives in bad company." Like Montaigne, his neighbour, he said: "Study has been for me a sovereign remedy against the disappointments of life, and I have never been so depressed that an hour's reading will not remove my sorrow."

In 1926 part of the library was sold and dispersed by public auction. The most precious works, those carrying the *ex libris* seal of Montesquieu and Malebranche, and those bound with the arms of Louis XIII and Colbert, disappeared from the castle. The others are still in the immense latticed cases of the library which, because of its vast size, is occasionaly used for concerts. The room contains a number of Regency armchairs in *petit-point* tapestry, which evoke visions of ease in a family castle such as this.

La Brède is without doubt the most authentic and perhaps one of the most beautiful of French writers' homes, and above all it is a rare example of a seventeenth-century interior. Montesquieu's fame and the good taste of his successors have miraculously preserved the castle.

231. The main entrance hall of the castle has spiral columns. Montesquieu brought back the copper lamp and the wall items from his Flanders tour. His descendants have kept the nailed leather trunks, and the walls still bear his Delft pottery and large Bernard Palissy platter.

◁ 232. From his bed, Montes
quieu could see this Regency
chest of drawers with the
Louis-Treize mirror above.
The chest of drawers now
bears Montesquieu's bust and
a large ewer he owned.

233. The writer's desk in his
room is a simple table that
still holds his books and pen
tray.

Next page:
234. The canopied bed in Montesquieu's room still has contemporary green material. On the
left of the mirror, the family
portrait gallery includes "the
little secretary", as he liked
to call his favourite daughter
who helped him in his work.

235. A medallion of Montesquieu at La Brède.

236. This room leading off Montesquieu's own room was used as a washroom. It contains a seventeenth-century pewter ewer and a small mirror.

236

237. *Typical of La Brède's many bedrooms is this one with its canopied bed and petit-point curtaining. On the mantel shelf is a collection of butterflies from the nineteenth-century.*

J.-J. Rousseau

at Les Charmettes

The crucial years of Jean-Jacques Rousseau's development were those he spent at Les Charmettes as a young man with Madame de Warens. The property she rented lies a few miles from Chambéry.

Born in Geneva, Rousseau was sixteen when he went to France. He was an only child spoilt by a father who never recovered from the loss of his wife, who died bringing Jean-Jacques into the world on June 28, 1712. His father heaped on the boy all the affection pent up inside him, but later he left Switzerland for good and handed the lad over to an uncle on his mother's side.

He went to a boarding school and shortly launched out into life alone as an apprentice engraver. One night he found the gates of Geneva city closed against him when he returned late from a walk. Without more ado he decided not to turn up for work the next day, and went off toward the French border. Arriving in Savoy, he was advised by a certain Monsieur de Pontverre to carry on as far as Chambéry, and given a letter of recommendation adressed to Madame de Warens. She was a recent convert to Catholicism and could find him a job in the area, he was told.

Madame de Warens was a young woman of twenty-eight, living alone in the country, separated from her husband. She had married at the tender age of fourteen.

She won a modicum of security as a result of her conversion, and the clergy at Chambéry provided her with a regular income. She obtained more money from the King of Sardinia, who controlled Savoy at the time. It has been said that Madame de Warens was a secret agent of the king and that the money was for her espionage work. However that may be, it is a sure thing that she was a wide-awake, broad-minded young lady whose religious conversion accompanied by financial profit did not stifle her free thought and spirit.

To the young fellow who on Palm Sunday 1728 knocked on her door she was a veritable revelation, and it was she who gave him his real chance in life.

Rousseau wrote : "I was told she had just gone to the local church... I ran after her. I saw her, reached her and spoke to her... I ought to remember the place ; I have so often flooded it with my tears and covered it with kisses since that moment. Oh, that I could ring with a golden balustrade that happy place ! Oh, to draw the world's homage to that spot ! Those who would honour monuments to men's salvation should go down on their knees : It was on a path behind her house between a stream on the right which separated it from the garden, and a wall on the left that bordered Les Cordeliers church, which had a door in it. I spoke as Madame de Warens was about to go through the door and she turned round. Oh, what became of me at the sight of her !

267

238. Madame de Warens ate with young Rousseau in this dining room at Les Charmettes. She was twenty-eight and he was sixteen. To him she was like a mother. An Italian artist is thought to have decorated the walls with optical illusions.

I had expected Monsieur de Pontverre's lady to be quite different, a sullen old woman. I saw a face steeped in charm, lovely blue eyes full of sweetness, fine colouring, the neck contours of an enchantress. Nothing escaped the keen eye of the young proselyte; because I became in an instant her's, convinced that a religion preached by such missionaries could not fail to lead to paradise..."

Such was the picture Rousseau drew of his adopted mother and the world she opened up for him. This paradise was soon to be Les Charmettes, where Madame de Warens settled a few years afterwards. From their first encounter, she looked on him as a son. He called her *"maman"*, though she was but twelve years his senior. She quickly realized what he sought out of life, and she gave him freedom to dream, seek his own pastures and read when the fancy took him. Jean-Jacques, only yesterday a young working man, suddenly became thanks to her a youth without problems, at liberty to utilize his time and cultivate himself as he thought fit. Yet she advised him to get some kind of work, and for a number of years he was a valet in Turin, later an employee at a seminary in Annecy under supervision of the cathedral.

However, in 1730 he spent a year travelling on foot without aim or money. Returning finally to Chambéry in 1733 he became a music master, found Madame de Warens again and became her lover. As she said, she decided "to treat him as a man" out of a mother's concern and for fear he would succumb to the tender charms of the girls whose music teacher he was.

Jean-Jacques Rousseau had always been frightened of talliing with the other sex and preferred to leave in gatherings of several persons unexpressed the emotions he experienced. In a word, he was not very sure of himself. As to Madame de Warens, she already had in the person of Claude Anet a secretary, a Jack-of-all-trades, gardner and lover. So Rousseau took second place—with the consent of Anet whom Madame de Warens had informed. This triangle was not displeasing to him, and when Claude Anet died in 1734 Rousseau took over as sole possessor of the lady.

They lived together until 1740, spending winters at Chambéry and (from 1736 onward) the summers at Les Charmettes, which she rented. As the name implies, the property was charming. From its windows could be seen the whole of the Chambéry valley, an Alpine range and its foot-hills. Surrounded by woods and meadows, the house also had a garden, in which Jean-Jacques sometimes pottered and dreamed as he sat on a seat in the midst of a labyrinth of hedges. At any time he could go off and stride about the countryside.

The house remains as it was in his time, charming with the attractively coloured walls, the simple decorated panelling and the modest eighteenth-century Savoy furniture. There are only two floors, and a wistaria covered the entire building, until it was killed a few years back by a frost one winter. The entrance hall and staircase recall the arcades of Chambéry. The ground-floor dining room has only a sideboard, some china by Moustiers, a table, and Louis XVI chairs; but it has, too, a striking decorative illusion, a door that seems to be open. The effect is made more extraordinary by the fact that part of it belongs to a real door leading to the cellar. Designs on the orange wallpaper appear as false woodwork. Beams in this room are heavy, coloured blue with wash. The small music room adjoining leads straight onto the garden. Above the doors are areas covered with Japanese flower-and-bird wallpaper, very fresh looking and well preserved. The idea for these would seem to be a woman's; normally one would expect to see conventional subjects painted in oils. The music room contains a few green plants, engravings, a Regency chaise longue, Jean-Jacques' harpsichord and a small green clock; the whole effect an example of eighteenth-century country style rarely found in castles of the period. Although it is true that some of the furniture here today did not belong to Les Charmettes during his time, Rousseau must certainly have felt the effect of the nutwood furniture known to have been there then, of the country chairs and painted walls, the flooring in light wood—and the general way in which Madame de Warens retained the original simplicity of the house.

On the first floor a small baroque oratory in a round structure served as a link between Rousseau and Madame de Warens' rooms. The doors have large round holes in them to let cats go through. One has the impression that the occupants lived confortably. Madame de Warens' room has an eighteenth-century flowered wallpaper similar to *toile de Jouy*. But it has only a few items of furniture : a big rose cretonne-covered bed and a bookcase, with a few contents which have come down to us. Rousseau's room is interesting for the alcove painted with garlands and false marble columns, the grey, blue and black paper and the large Venetian Renaissance mirror between two windows. The atmosphere of the room is created by the paucity of furniture and the green light that penetrates from the woods outside.

Les Charmettes was decorated throughout by an Italian artist. In the Chambéry area, under control of Sardinia at the time, there are several examples of Sardinian baroque, the style which pervades Les Charmettes.

Rousseau wrote : "Here began the short happiness of my life; here occurred the quiet but rapid moments which give me the right to say I have lived. Precious nostalgic moments. Ah! Begin again your lovely course... If it all consisted of facts, actions and words I could describe it and render it in some way; but how to describe what was neither said, nor done nor even thought—but tasted, felt—without mentioning anything except the sentiment of happiness itself? I got up with the sun and was happy; I went for walks, and was happy; I saw *maman*, and was happy; I left her and was happy, I wandered through woods and hillsides, meandered in valleys; I read, hung about; I worked in the garden, gathered fruit, helped in the house—and happiness followed me everywhere."

We may be certain that he was free and happy at Les Charmettes and that Madame de Warens truly provided him with every chance of discovering basic unity in his soul. The result

was that he soon came to believe, after he left her, that the world was badly arranged, that children should be brought up differently, that the existing social order was no good thing.

Emile, an autobiographical work, owed much to his life at Les Charmettes. Rousseau quickly acquired a fervent public in the women who read the book, because he stressed the importance of women as educators, holding that childhood experiences determined the whole life of a man. In this respect, Jean-Jacques was ahead of Freud by a century. Before that, children in well-to-do families were brought up by nurses and were handed over to their mothers as grown-up people. So it was not surprising that women saw in the author of *Emile* the precursor of a new epoch; Madame Necker, Madame de Staël, Madame de Chateaubriand, Madame Andersen and many other women attempted to bring up their children like Emile in the book.

Underlying these ideas were the sentiments and memories Rousseau accumulated during his life with Madame de Warens at Les Charmettes.

During an absence, Jean-Jacques learned that a rival had stepped in to act as gardener and secretary to Madame de Warens. He would not agree to playing second fiddle again and left her, at the same time yearning for the idyllic conditions he had enjoyed with her at the house. All his life he gravitated toward people who could offer him the hospitality of country houses. He attempted to justify his behaviour, which quickly became a habit, by saying it was better to be physically dependent that to possess a skill that was corrupted.

"I felt that to write as a means of earning my living would soon have stifled my genius and killed my talent, which was less in my pen than in my heart, born of a high and proud way of thinking that alone could nourish it. Nothing vigorous, nothing great can emerge from a fully venal pen. No, no, I have always felt that the condition of an author was not and could not be illustrious and respectable unless it escaped being a trade," he said.

So Rousseau, in order to avoid selling his

talent, was the lover of Madame de Warens until 1740, and became the guest of Madame d'Epinay in 1756 who also took in his wife and mother-in-law. He was later with the Prince of Condé who lent him his Mont-Louis house where he began *La Nouvelle Héloïse, Emile* and *Du contrat social*, as well as the guest of Monsieur de Girardin at Ermenonville in 1778. This admirer wanted to give him a house of his own but in fact only provided a tomb. To the end of his life, Rousseau endeavoured to find Les Charmettes again in the homes of other people.

Highly sensitive, sentimental, individualistic, Rousseau was able to protect his easily-wounded feelings by living as much as possible apart from the rest of humanity. He would have liked a career and to have entered society like other people, but he could never have successfully coped with the hubbub of the great. He would have liked to remain with one woman, Thérèse Levasseur, but he could not accept family life and handed over the five children she produced to public assistance. He lived in a world of fancy. At one stage he was close in thought to the Encyclopedists but was put off by their reasoning and their realism. Rousseau always felt himself "the more at home with nature in that he could not bear to be in the company of men". His attempts at sociability were in the end a failure. He spent the first period of his life writing works and living them, and the second in a double life—Jean-Jacques and Rousseau—recorded in *Les Confessions* and *Les Rêveries d'un promeneur solitaire*. The life of dreams won in a battle with real existence.

Once when he was about to go and live with another friend he wrote : "Ever since I was thrown into the world against my will, I have never ceased to love Les Charmettes and the pleasant life I had there. I felt I was made to return to the country. It was impossible for me to live happily elsewhere."

The great romantic movement was certainly partly born out of Rousseau's work. It is no surprise that nineteenth-century travellers went in such numbers on pilgrimages to Les Charmettes. They produced between them no fewer that eighty visitors' books containing strange comments like : "Oh, Jean-Jacques, what would become of our children if we brought them up like your Emile !", "It is decidely unfair to reproach Jean-Jacques with acts which, without *Les Confessions*, would remain unknown", and (by a woman) "I was overcome when I entered this so tranquil house, and I think of you, oh my confessor, whom I understand and love."

When George Sand visited Les Charmettes, she wrote several lines in the book (she tells us) but crossed them out at once. She read "gross insults and stupid attacks" against Rousseau throughout the book and wrote underneath one comment the words : "Rejected, cursed, ever-victim, bless you even so, my poor divine master." Anna de Noailles visited Les Charmettes in 1921 and recounts this in *Les Eblouissements;* Francis James went there in 1903. Lamartine was often there in 1811 and 1815 with his friend Louis de Vignet.

Rousseau succeeded in making personal writings likable. With *Les Confessions, Les Rêveries,* and *Dialogues* he pioneered a new kind of autobiography, a style that concentrated its forms on the author himself. We can see why Bergson regarded him as the master of modern thought.

In fact he has been just this, from the romantic period to our own day. But it is now possible that his reign is coming to an end with the appearance of the so-called "new novel", which shifts the character and his feelings on to objects and the outside world. Rousseau would recognize in these writers' works his own feeling about nature; his descendants see nature and the world reflecting the inner sentiments of a man. The procedure is in reverse, one might say, but it was the lover of Les Charmettes who first proposed escape from the world of the mind and pure reason.

239. *Under arches at the entrance to Les Charmettes is a Louis-Quinze leather sedan chair and an eighteenth-century clock. At the right, is the stairway leading to Rousseau's room and that of Madame de Warens. Between them was the chapel.*

240

241

242

243

244

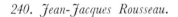

240. *Jean-Jacques Rousseau.*

241. *Madame de Warens in whom young Rousseau saw "a face steeped with charm, lovely blue eyes full of sweetness, fine colouring, the neck of an enchantress. Nothing escaped the keen eye of the young proselyte...".*

242. *Madame d'Epinay.* ▷

◁ 243. *This engraving shows Rousseau standing in front of Les Charmettes.*

244. *Behind the protecting trees* ▷ *lies Les Charmettes. After leaving there, Rousseau wrote: "Ever since I was thrown into the world against my will, I have never ceased to love Les Charmettes and the pleasant life I had there. I felt I was made to retire to the country. It was impossible for me to live elsewhere."*

245. *The music room, with its patterned Japanese wallpaper, green plants, engravings and Regency chaise longue was typical of eighteenth-century French country houses. The harpsichord with its green clock was owned by Jean-Jacques Rousseau.*

246

246. *Jean-Jacques Rousseau's room was on the first floor of Les Charmettes. The alcove woodwork was painted with garlands and false marble columns. Above his desk is a portrait of him in his glorious moments.*

247. *Madame de Warens's room near Rousseau's has eighteenth-century flowered paper. There are few items of furniture: a large bed, bookcases, some books, Louis-Quinze bergère and on a table a small nailed seventeenth-century casket. Rousseau, recalling life here as a young man, wrote: "Precious nostalgic moments. Ah! Begin again your lovely course... If it all consisted of facts, actions and words I could describe and render it in some way; but how to describe what was neither said, nor done nor even thought—but tested, felt—without mentioning anything except the sentiment of happiness itself?"*

Who was Madame de Warens? It is said that she spied for the King of Sardinia, that she lived off money the Church gave her for her good works. We do know that she encouraged young Protestants to convert to Catholicism and in this way met Jean-Jacques. She filled a maternal role and gave him the climate and freedom to discover himself.

248

◁ *248. Rubens is seen here with his young wife, Hélène Fourment, and his son, Nicholas. The garden at Rubens' Antwerp home remains as it appears in the painting by the great master.*

249. This Renaissance gate to Rubens's garden links the painter's residence at right to his studio seen left.
▽

249

Rubens

at Antwerp

Resplendent in the Flemish style of Charles Quint and with a touch of the Italian Farnese period, the princely dwelling where Peter Paul Rubens lived is still to be seen in old Antwerp. After he died, parts of the building that had been dispersed were re-assembled and the painter's furniture brought together again.

This house in the Rubensstraat is indeed more that of a prince that that of a painter with its wealth of antique furniture, medals, bronzes, ivories, rare objets and paintings.

The young Rubens was recommended, by his master Otto Venius, to the Duke of Mantua Vincenzo Conzague, who was a keen admirer of Corregio. He spent eight years in his service and accompagnied him to the court of Spain, vhere he studied the paintings of Madrid and the Escorial. Owing to his post and as a result of his talent, Rubens had the right to sit at the same table with the great painters of his time. Later, on return to Flanders, Rubens became a diplomat, and the house he built in Antwerp after his Italian visit reflects the tastes of a man of the world.

It was in 1609 after his marriage with his first wife Isabelle Brant that he planned this house and acquired land at Antwerp in the Vaartstraat on the Wapper. There, he had constructed a huge residence. The left wing was devoted to private rooms while the right wing, linked to the other by a large baroque gateway, constituted the painter's studio. By its dimensions we infer that the artist painted on large canvasses and at the same time had rooms to house his pupils, who worked in a second studio above his own.

His life, like his home, was not on simple lines, for he had a secret existence lurking behind the one that everybody knows. He himself revealed nothing of it at any time. The tone of his letters is more often that of the public official rather than that of the artist. Rubens spent much time at court and acquired both an easy manner and an impersonal attitude.

His palatial home is laden with reminiscences. The façade and interior of the residential side are primarily Flemish, but the studio belongs to the Italian Renaissance. Humanism however is here only a blind, in view of certain details he selected. He placed his home under the signs of love and wisdom, but the satyrs' heads triumph in the end over those of the Greek philosophers. The Rubens who obtained important official commissions from the courts of Europe was also the man who, under the cover of Humanism, boisterously demonstrated a pagan freedom. On the front of the Renaissance gateway dividing the garden from the main courtyard he had engraved extracts from Juvenal's satyrs.

The walls of his studio gave free play to satyrs, fauns, the God Pan, Bacchus, Silenius, placed in niches at shoulder level. Others,

279

Seneca, Plato and Socrates were placed at the top of the building.

The outside walls of the great studio were decorated with classical scenes by painters but today they have disappeared.

The gateway and the small cottages at the end of the garden were also dedicated to love. Rubens in his paintings frequently showed this scene. For him, outside of his religious commissions, everything was used as a pretext for paganism.

For example, the painting of Marie de Medici disembarking at Marseilles, one of a series he did of the queen between 1621 and 1625, is less a portrayal of a monarch on her vessel's bridge than a group of very fleshy water nymphs.

The painter and his young wife Isabelle Brant set up housekeeping in Antwerp shortly after their marriage, and they had their first child, their son Nicolas in 1818. She died in Antwerp in 1826, after seventeen years of marriage, probably of the plague. Rubens wrote of her : "She was an exquisite companion whom one could, and had to, love because she possessed none of the faults usual to her sex : she was neither weak, nor sullen but all charm and kindness..."

To forget his loss, Rubens left Antwerp and resumed his diplomatic career for a few years. Four years later in December 1630 he married a sixteen-year old girl, Hélène Fourment when he himself was fifty-three years of age, and took her back to the Antwerp house. Judging by the number of paintings he did of his second wife, their life together appears to have been one long dream. This child-wife was soon to bring into the world a son; she restored in Rubens his zest for life, and was hardly much older than Nicholas, product of his first marriage. In this household, youth reigned supreme.

Ruben's young wife was very beautiful and his favourite model. He frequently painted her himself and had her depicted by his friends and adored her. This deep love in the latter phase of his life has apparently been used by some experts as a means of identifying certain of the master's works.

An exemple is a picture of Hélène shown naked in a fur coat which C. R. Bordley declared was a painting by Snyders, Rubens' close friend. But Leo Van Puyvelde on the other hand attributed it to Rubens himself solely because a man of fifty or so would certainly not have allowed his young wife to pose for anyone else in the early years of their marriage. Moral considerations seem to have ousted the rules of expertise in this instance.

The private section of the house was dedicated to Hélène and in almost every room there hangs a portrait of her. She is perpetually beautiful, always dressed and undressed at the same time it seems, wearing feathered or fur hats, pearls and showy dresses with open fronts. A cherubic face looks out at us, above generous breasts. She has naïve open eyes and a fleshy mouth. This is how the old painter saw her, and what his friends sometimes saw in order to please him. She was for Rubens the incarnation of childhood made woman.

The unhoped for entry of this young woman into Rubens' life reads like a fairy tale. A short while after their wedding, he painted himself (in a work now at the Munich Art Gallery) with his wife on his arm with his son Nicholas beside them. Hélène herself is childlike, disguised as a peasant in a light coloured dress, an apron and a large straw hat. To match their happiness, an unreal world surrounds them : the four gardens full of tulips extant today, bushy corners and wooden archways covered in roses, pathways of hoops over which climb wistaria, peacocks picking at corn thrown to them from the summer cottage by a servant. Also there, is the dog owned by Hélène and Nicholas, running to them up the pathway. Rubens himself is in a costume with an enormous black hat, leaning over Hélène who is in white and looks toward Nicholas dressed as a page. Such was Rubens' vision of heaven on earth.

The visitor entering the parlour of the house, hung with its brown and gold Cordoba leather, is struck by the large Dutch copper chandelier, the seventeenth-century red coloured study and the Jacob Jordaens pictures, and especially by the similarity between the old enlarged engravings of Ruben's garden as it was in the seventeenth century and the reality today as perceived through the tiny smoked glass window panels. Nothing has changed, it would seem, since 1631. Yet for more than 100 years after his death, horses trampled there, as the garden was used as a riding school.

The kitchen in mauve and blue azulejos stone and the adjoining scullery, form a passage between the parlour and the ample dining room, also in brown and gold Cordoba leather. At first one sees from the kitchen only its impressive colours and the huge chimney piece, then gradually the components of the room take their place as if they are elements in a still life painting of infinite detail : a dresser with pewter spoons, copper match bearers, hooks for meat and a ceramic Christ. The special charm of the scullery lies also in its everyday objects : for example, in a candle stand of wood are hung together the entire stock of copper candlesticks in the house. In the evening doubtless Rubens, Hélène and Nicholas would together fetch their candles. In the middle stands a sculptured wooden screw press giving the impression of a printing works rather than a domestic clothes press. This appliance gave rectangular folds to linen, such as are visible in tablecloths in engravings by Abraham Bosse.

The dining room and the antiques room are the finest in the house. The dining room paradoxically looks like a Vermeer Flemish interior with its embossed brown leather and generous golden designs, the floor paving, the black and white marble chimney, the light filtering through small windows and falling on a long table bearing a large bouquet of dried flowers in a copper vase. Paintings in this room are seventeenth-century and include a large still life by Snyders showing a basket of fruit on a table covered with game, a flower bouquet by Daniel Seghers and a portrait of Hélène Fourment by Abraham Janssens.

In the art room and the semicircular museum, Rubens endeavoured to keep all his collections. The inventory that he left after his death, which was drawn up in 1640, mentions three hundred paintings some of which

are around the house today : they include early Flemish works and sixteenth-century art by Jan Van Eyck, Hugo Van der Goes, Lucas de Leyde, Aertgen de Leyde, Quentin Massys, Henry Bless, Peter Breughel the Elder, Antonio Moro, Franz Floris, etc. ; Italian masters like Titian, Veronese, Raphael and copies from the Italian by Rubens himself, Van Dyck, Jordaens, Wildens, Snyders, Seghers, Vranckx, Adriaenssens. The painter also owned seventeen paintings by Adrian Brouwer and Dutch contemporaries, works by Heda, Porcelli, Syftleven, Palamede, C. Poelenburgh, Hals, etc.

The inventory also referred to drawings and copies by Rubens to which must be added collections of old medals. The present day museum is more particularly noteworthy for its coloured marble arches than for the antique heads discovered later and placed in the museum. There are seventeenth-century chests including one in red shell, Flemish paintings some of which belonged to Rubens, and the whole effect reconstitutes the mood of the painter's own epoch. A painting by John Breughel called *Walk in a Park* is perhaps the finest painting there and doubtless the least known.

Rooms on the first floor are all similar in size and have large chimneys in them. One of them is particularly worth looking at with Rubens' own bed fitted with a green velvet canopy ; this same room has a portrait of Hélène Fourment attributed to Jan Van Boeckhorst or D. Mytens. Another room contains an exceptionally fine Venetian mirror in gold and silver together with Rubens' chair which on October 20, 1795, was discovered in the Saint Luc studio whence it was taken to Paris by Jacques Luc Berbier, Lieutenant of the 5th Regiment of Hussars.

The lieutenant left a receipt for it. It was not until after Waterloo that the chair returned to Antwerp. There is also an alcove, a former linen room, which contains a black ebony cupboard on which are painted hunting and love scenes of very good quality. The third room is the one where the family met in the evenings. It contains only an art collection of Antwerp works, an old musical instrument ancestor of

281

the harpsichord and a work by Sebastian Vranckx showing an Italian palace. An ancient sculptured doorway lets us through to a balcony overlooking Ruben's studio. The public used to stand on this balcony to watch progress and judge the paintings. There we may see a Jordaens canvass of Neptune and Amphitrite. A wooden staircase leads to the upper floor where a large empty room is situated. There the master's pupils worked.

On the spacious landing giving on to the studio are hung a fine seventeenth-century Brussels tapestry based on a drawing by Rubens, a fragment of the *Death of Achilles*, and also a Snyders painting, one of the best he did, with still life works that are currently in the castle of Fleury-en-Bière.

Rubens used to start work in the large studio very early in the day. He would leave his private rooms, go through the massive gateway and enter this immense room he had fashioned on the lines of the interior to an Italian palace. Certain critics have said that a good many pupils helped him and that in fact he merely retouched a few parts of their canvasses. Others say that the pupils had the right to grind the colours and nothing else.

By 1631 Rubens was the most famous painter of his period. According to his nephew Philip Rubens, he used to rise at 4 a.m. and after hearing mass would have a light meal, prior to starting work. In the late afternoon he would go off on his horse and join a few friends. It was the Dane Otto Sperling who, after visiting him in 1621, gave backing to the rumour that he only finished off the work of his pupils. It was also Sperling who provided posterity with a picture of Rubens at work, at the same time dictating a letter and reading Tacitus.

It is certain that he used to keep several paintings going at the same time. He wrote to his friend the English ambassador Dudley Carleton, concerning a painting similar to *The Last Supper* now in the Brera Museum in Milan: "It has been started by one of my disciples, but I am resolved to take it entirely into my own hands, so that it can count as an original." He himself admitted that he used to be aided sometimes in this studio. There is for example the *Triptych of Saint Ildefonse* painted for the Archduchess Isabella and *The Last Supper* for Catherine Lescuyer of Malines (in this case we know for certain he was not the only painter), *War and Peace* in 1631 with the help of J. Boeckhorst, the unfinished *Triumphal Entry of Henry IV into Paris*, in 1630, and the series (also unfinished) of the great moments in the life of Marie de Medici. In the case of the last works it was not Rubens' fault that it was not finished, but history's.

The order was placed through the Regent and the final confirmation took ten years to come through. Richelieu did not care for the project. When the minister succeeded in removing the queen, Rubens had already painted most of the paintings in the series, and had started the *Battle of Ivry* and *The Triumphal Entry of Henry IV into Paris*. But Marie de Medici in disgrace took refuge at the court of the Archduchess and during that time visited Rubens at Antwerp, not only to look at the works that she was not to take, but also to ask him to lend her money on two crown jewels she had with her.

Rubens may have been tempted that day to add to the series in her life the "great moment" that had just unfolded before him. It was indeed an astonishing age when a painter acquired a fortune so large that he could act as a banker and patron of a queen.

Next page:
251. Rubens used to collect Greek and Roman busts some of which are still to be seen in this semi-circular museum. He owned three hundred paintings of the Flemish and Italian schools, and a collection of old medals.

On the table is a world-globe and there can also be seen some ivory valuables, boxes and newly-found paintings.

250. Rubens and Isabelle Brant. ▷

252. *Hélène Fourment with her* ▷
son.

253. *Marie de Médicis landing* ▷
at Marseilles.

255. *In the dining room, with
its Cordoba leather walls, is
a large still life by Snyders, a
flower bouquet by Daniel Seghers
and a portrait of Hélène Fourment by Abraham Janssens*

254. *Rubens' studio was desgni-
ed to accommodate huge canvasses. The painter was helped
by numerous pupils.*
▽

252

253

254

George Sand

at Nohant

Nohant is a large Louis XVI house on the edge of a village green. Outwardly a peaceful-looking village dwelling of the Loire region, it was the special scene of several passionate love affairs of the romantic woman writer.

Nohant was owned by George Sand's grandmother, Madame Dupin de Francueil, the aristocratic and illegitimate daughter of Maréchal de Saxe, who acquired it after fleeing from the Revolution Terror, and took refuge there with her son Maurice. When George Sand took it over it assumed the character of a refined bohemian interior of the 1830's.

George Sand, in fact, was almost born there. Maurice brought her in one morning, despite the fact that his mother had refused to recognize his marriage. But Madame Dupin de Francueil welcomed the baby girl at once. She bore the name Aurore.

It was Madame Dupin who brought up the girl. Maurice himself was to die a few years later after falling off a horse at Nohant. Aurore's mother was a beautiful dancer who rarely came to see her daughter. So it was perhaps natural for Aurore to develop a wild nature, inheriting her father's adventurous traits, which he in turn had as a descendent of the Maréchal de Saxe. At any rate, her grandmother took to her readily, and relived the times when her son was little. Madame Dupin, adopting the ideas of the times, brought her up without restrictions and allowed all her granddaughter's natural inclinations to blossom forth.

Aurore was lucky to have a woman with advanced ideas as a grandmother. She was raised in the style of Jean-Jacques Rousseau's fictional child "Emile", as were many children of the intelligentsia at that period. Others included Madame de Staël, Balzac, Andersen, Goethe, Lamartine and Tolstoi. It is hard to say whether the method actually produced gifted adults but the technique was widely adopted indeed, judging by the writings of these people. Under the influence of the "progressive" grandmother, Aurore gave free play to all the talents she inherited, and it was at Nohant that they flourished.

Aurore's childhood escapades found full play in the wooded grounds of the house. The same woods were later to conceal her first loves after her grandmother died and she had gone through her unhappy marriage. Nohant is inseparably linked to the passion George Sand felt for Aurélien de Sèze, Stéphane Ajasson de Grandsagne, Jules Sandeau and above all for Frederick Chopin. There is hardly any trace there of husband Casimir Dudevant. Aurore married him because it was natural for every young girl to get married. She had one child by him, Maurice, but persuaded him also to give his name to her second child, Solange, who she in fact had by her lover Stéphane Ajasson de Grandsagne. Aurore was not against

256. George Sand's rooms at Nohant were also used by her as a study. In the evening, Jules Sandeau would arrive through the large window seen here. The medallions over the doors bear the initials of Nohant's first proprietor from whom George's grandmother bought the residence during the Revolution.

marriage, but life was impossible with this unpolished man who hunted all day long and fell asleep over his books during the evenings. Besides, he made love to the servants.

The wedding took place in 1822 and by 1825 she was already in love with Aurélien de Sèze; it needed only three years for her to follow her natural love of the adventurous life. In 1828 Aurore produced Solange, Stéphane's child. A short while later, in 1830, she discovered the life of letters and love with Jules Sandeau. Her first novel was written in 1832; it was called *Indiana* and she signed her name George Sand—first syllable of the name Sandeau, in memory of what he had meant to her. He had loved her and it was he who made her decide to write for a career.

Nearly all her works were written at Nohant. Although her two great experiences in love had started in Paris, it was at Nohant that they reached their culmination. It was as if George Sand went to Paris to find love and bring it back to her country home. To her, genius and love could be found only in Paris, but real experiences had to be lived out far from that city, whence she brought back her latest love in a carriage. Her experience with Musset was in Paris, Fontainebleau and Venice. But it was at Nohant that George Sand was the most fully aware of her love for him.

Desperate at the thought of losing him after a quarrel, she wrote: "I shall now embrace during my ardent nights the trunks of the pine-trees and the rocks in the forests, crying out your name. And when I have dreamed the moment of pleasure, I shall fall exhausted onto the humid earth." The famous incident when George Sand cut off her hair and sent it to Musset, long recounted in Paris, took place at Nohant. She was in love, too much alone and in too big a house.

George Sand needed to give her love life a background and, for company, she collected together the leading figures of Europe on intelligentsia. To Nohant came Liszt, Marie d'Agoult, Balzac, Théophile Gautier, Delacroix and Tolstoi, not to mention a whole series of young revolutionaries of the 1840's whose political merits were often contested by her jealous friends. "She has the politics of her lovers," it was said. George Sand had turned her desires into reality: she wanted the best of Paris at Nohant, to amuse her when she was not working, and she succeeded in her aim. Few dwellings had ever brought together such highly gifted people. Perhaps she realized that the genius of her friends also needed quiet moments, and that she could at the same time obtain such repose for herself. The company of ordinary dull people would not have allowed her this freedom and leisure, or the chance of exchanging ideas.

Every summer Sand came to Nohant, each time accompanied by her children, a lover and some friends. When it was financially impossible to carry out this plan, she simply refused to make the trip and waited until next summer, when her author's royalties enabled her to visit Nohant again with all these people. The house was more than a residence. It was a way of life.

It was, too, the house of a single woman. This fact necessarily meant there were few men there. The men more or less put up with their rivals, depending on how they felt toward their hostess. But the jealous quarrels bore the mark of greatness due to their genius. Delacroix, for example, would flee from Chopin's noisy piano and his college boy pranks. He would take refuge in the studio—an old coach house—to paint. However, he liked the music of Chopin, just as Chopin liked Delacroix's paintings. Often Chopin fled from the room when it was occupied by Sand's untidy revolutionaries. As to Balzac, he was charming but spoke too loudly and tired people out.

Aurore herself was content just to appear at meal times and never took part in conversation. She would work till lunch time and in the afternoon walk in the grounds. Sometimes, the company took Chopin's piano out into the garden and set it up under a tree, where everybody listened as he improvised. These were the happiest times at Nohant.

In the kitchen petty quarrels broke out alongside the arguments of the "masters". Chopin gave his valet a far higher wage than George

Sand gave her cooks. She had some liberals as visitors with whom she discussed social developments; but it was the composer, a more generous employer than she, who gave the kitchen staff their lessons in politics. Chopin was a democrat at heart and she a democrat in spirit. Many more such details could be recounted; they give more reality to the romantic existence at Nohant. Without such details, it might be hard to believe in the charming life there or the passion Chopin had for George Sand, which would seem more like a legend. Moreover, the meanness that sometimes comes out during a great love story makes it somehow more authentic.

Immediately inside the house at Nohant, a world of dreams opens up for the visitor, with the winding staircase in its cylindrical stairwell and wallpaper whose rose and grey coloured clouds give an optical illusion. The Ladoux "bull's eye" lighting it and the doors on the landings, nailed and upholstered and painted to deceive the eye—these details reveal a curious partnership between the practical and the decorative.

A popular woman like George Sand could, when it suited her, get her imaginative lovers to direct the work of the decorators. Because people did not want to hear Chopin's piano-playing coming from the drawing room, she had the doors soundproofed as best as she could. But this was then so evident that she had the upholstery covered in paint and free hand-drawings were done to represent wood fittings. Who drew them? Perhaps a Parisian house-painter, or a friend, or Delacroix. Who can say?

A small theatre emerged in the same rough way, out of a dream. Everybody took a hand at writing and playing comedies. Maurice Sand read them out and made puppets dance. The auditorium participated. As at a real puppet theatre, the audience took part. Liszt, Gautier and Balzac all had their parts to read. Chopin would laugh like a child; he hated the open and adored indoor entertainment. It was her son and her lover who thought up most of the amusements. Later, they were to fight over the

wing of a chicken, but for the present, they were combining to please George Sand.

On the ground floor, behind a padded door, was a panelled dining room which George Sand had decorated with pictures of local legends. The table was under a Venetian lamp and is still there, with plates bearing the names of guests who used to stay at Nohant: Gautier, Balzac, Turgenev, Chopin and the Prince Napoleon, a heavy young man known as "Plon-Plon".

On one side of this room was the ancestral drawing room where, next to the portraits of the past, George Sand put up those of her own children: Solange (the "little pest") and Maurice, whom she adored. Chopin's piano is there no longer, for she sent it back to Paris after they separated, declaring: "I don't want him to let me have his piano." On the other side is the blue bedroom with flowered *cretonne* curtains dominated by a Polish-style bed—a conjugal bed which Aurore Dupin had when she first got married and in which she was so unhappy. This bed inspired her book *Lélia*, the story of a woman insensitive to love. Once, George Sand wrote to a friend whose daughter was getting married: "We bring up girls like saints, to let them loose afterward like fillies." It was certainly in this room that the idea came to her. Later on she gave the room to her children; it was the only one in the house that directly adjoined her "office", a room done in red *toile de Jouy* wallpaper. There, she used to write on a kind of plank let down from the wall, which served as a desk. She slept there too, in a hammock. Jules Sandeau in the 1830's joined her by leaping through the window, after Monsieur Dudevant had chased him out through the door. There, she found "transports of the soul" which nevertheless allowed room for love.

Sandeau, whom she called "little Jules", gave George Sand only a notion of love and literature, and was soon given up. He attempted suicide and failed. It was said of him: "He was merely the jade in this adventure." All his life he tried to get his own back and said nothing but ill of George.

George Sand failed to discover in Sandeau

the straightforward response from her own ancestors. It took her over ten years, until she was about thirty, to find out that she could be truly in love only with childlike men. She was lucky with Musset and Chopin, the two great loves of her life who combined a childlike nature with genius. Men confident in their virility, such as her husband Casimir Dudevant or the critic Sainte-Beuve (whose bid to win George despite herself was a fiasco that went the rounds of the Paris *salons*), did not have a chance with this sentimental woman. What her great grandmother and her own mother had found in hussars, she found in sick and worried men. Musset succeeded with Sand only because he observed : "When I am with you I am a mere child." This remark amounted to a free pass and Musset, like Chopin later, successfully turned her into a human being. The charming wit and exquisite humour of Musset could not have conquered Sand if the child had not emerged from behind the dandy's jesting. Musset, *"mon moussaillon"* (literally "ship-boy"), was a slim young fellow, somewhat pale and many years her junior. He was subject to crises of delirium tremens which frightened them both, but she loved to look after him. She shared with him his youth, his tears and his eroticism : his letters to her at Nohant were in a mystical style that prefigured *Les Nuits*. He wrote : "Tell me that you give me your lips, your teeth, your hair, all these things, this head I have had ; and tell me you embrace me. You and me, Oh God... how thirsty, my George, how thirsty I am for you."

The passion that flared between them was sudden, heartrending and unexpected. Once before somebody wanted to introduce Musset to her but she commented : "He is very much a dandy, we should not suit each other." They met by chance and she discovered that "he is neither a rake nor a fop although he has thought about being both." It was he who first perceived that they loved each other. He told her : "You are going to throw me out and call me a liar but I am in love with you. I have been since the first day I was at your house. I thought I would just get over it and be your friend." They loved and hated each other in turn, they separated and again fell into each other's arms. Finally in 1838 they severed relations for good.

George then turned to Chopin, the sick young exile, sensitive as a skinned animal, and thought he needed her love. It may be that her idea of falling in love with him was not unconnected with the love of Marie d'Agoult for Liszt. If she could have Liszt, George would have Chopin. At the time Chopin was still in love with his Polish *fiancée*. This caused her to draw back but when friends informed her he was free, she took hold of him.

George Sand was thirty-five now. Chopin was vulnerable and aristocratic in his ways and thoughtfulness. In his music he firmly excluded all vulgarity, and while at Nohant he always spoke of Sand as "our hostess". He was very delicate in appearance and weighed less than 100 pounds.

Chopin's piano-playing was characterized by a light touch which he balanced out by pedal work, a strong contrast to the battering Liszt and Beethoven gave their pianos. The technique produced deep sonority in his music.

Their first summer at Nohant in 1839 was one of quiet intimacy. George subsequently wrote to friends : "He always wanted to visit Nohant but could not stand it once he was there... His country-loving was quickly over. He used to go for a few walks, sit under a tree or pick some flowers. Then he would come back and shut himself up in his room."

During that summer he composed his *Sonata in B flat major*, the second *Nocturne* and three mazurkas. During a stay with her in Majorca he wrote some ballads and preludes, several reflecting his anguish when separated from her. He appreciated her musical taste. When Liszt was at Nohant, she even crept under the piano so as to enter more fully into the music and allow it to penetrate right into her until she was deafened. She was a "sensitive listener" in the case of Chopin. On October 19, 1839, he wrote in his diary : "I feel ill deep down in me. Aurore's eyes are veiled. They shine only when I play, when the world is clear and beautiful. My fingers softly flow over the keys and her pen flies over the paper. She can write while listening to the music." For her it was music above and all around her, Chopin's clear music speaking words of love.

He declared : "For you, Aurore, I would creep on the floor. Nothing would be too much for me, I would give you everything. I live only for a look, a caress, a smile from you when I am tired. I want to live only for you, and for you I want to play soft melodies. You will not be too cruel, will you, my dear, with your veiled eyes ?" Chopin's writing contains some affectation that is absent from Musset's. Chopin's love is sensitive only through his music.

A few years later in 1847 Aurore, having induced a certain moderation in Chopin, wrote to her friend Albert Grymal : "I know that several people accuse me either of wearing him out with my violent senses, or of making him desperate with my outbursts. I think you know the truth. He himself complains that I have killed him by privation, but I was sure to have killed him had I acted otherwise."

How often did the love between them rise to a passionate level ? Was George Sand really the masculine partner in the relationship ? It was she who always tired of her lovers first ; she left Musset when in Venice while he was in one of his delirium crises, so that she could chase after the doctor who treated him. In the case of the Chopin affair, it was she who decided that friendship would be better for his health than love. Was the mother in her taking the place of the loved one, or was the cooled-off lover seeking refuge behind the disguise of a mother ?

When George read aloud to Chopin and friends her novel in which Chopin is depicted as Prince Karol who is loved by the heroine as children are loved, Chopin seems not to have recognize the reference to himself. Delacroix, who was among those present, experienced agony during the reading. How could Sand have spoken of her scarcely-concealed love in front of Chopin ? So it was that Sand had Chopin longer as a friend than as a lover, and in the end it was her love for Maurice, her own child, that was victorious over her love for the musician. When Maurice set himself against Chopin and demanded that his mother choose between them, she picked Maurice.

George Sand needed love in order to write. But she found it only with men weaker than herself. The role of sick-nurse, which at one stage was so attractive, eventually weighed heavily on her to the extent that she had to break off the relationship ; the jealousy of Musset in Venice and the touchiness of Chopin were mere pretexts. She was a glutton for work and never allowed passion to dominate the essential element in her creativity—hard work. At an early moment in their love Musset was to say : "I worked all day ; in the evening I did some verses and drunk a bottle of spirits : she had drunk a litre of milk and completed half a book."

Sometimes Chopin failed to receive inspiration and she would encourage him by saying : "Come on, come on, velvet fingers!" "They are just shadows," he would say. And Delacroix would comment : "They are reflections." By obliging him to love her less and compose more, perhaps she prolonged his creative life and forced him to compose more than he would have without her. She worked for Chopin's genius, rather than the man.

After they broke up, Sand destroyed everything at Nohant that reminded her of him. She heartily detested her daughter Solange, who often acted as her rival toward Chopin, with displays of jealousy and coquetry. Chopin sided with her after her marriage with the sculptor Clésinger, and George never forgave him for preferring Solange to herself. George Sand sent Chopin's piano away and destroyed all traces of his former old room, dividing it into two with a partition and converting it into a museum of mineralogy. She brought home hundreds of stones and fossils for it, one by one.

In this way she obliterated the past even to the extent of changing the inside of Nohant. All that remained of the room where they had made love were the walls, now covered with stone-laden shelves. Her own room, on the other hand, stayed the same as it had always been, with its blue and white Persian carpet, her little table, and Restoration mahogany bed. Although she may have changed nothing in her room, she in fact did a little retouching of the past in the sense that she altered public opinion toward her.

Henceforth she was to become "the lady of Nohant", busy with her role of grandmother and 1848 revolutionary. She would have liked to give the impression that her love life had been inspired by charity rather than passion. Did she want to leave to Maurice and her grandchildren, whom she loved, the memory of a woman who was more of the traditional kind than she had actually been? Did she want to reject her past as a passionate lover and replace it with maternal love, or had she really forgotten everything. She was not anti-clerical but rather indifferent. What could have led her to this travesty of the past, other than her love for Maurice?

The answer to this may lie in the studio on the top floor at Nohant, which she had arranged for her son. There in the roof can be found collections of butterflies, Greek and Egyptian archaeological finds, and dried flowers which they both owned; and on a table now under glass can be seen the frightening will under which Solange loses everything, George having bequeathed all to Maurice.

The last years of Sand's life were spent at Nohant, "writing," as she said, "as one does gardening." She was content enough, although her friends were no longer the same ones. Chopin, Musset and Balzac were dead and her new friends were Théophile Gautier, Zola, Turgenev and Flaubert.

She found friendship with Flaubert, whom she called "her Benedictine", astonished as she was that he apparently needed nothing in this life, not even nature. She said to him: "I know not what kind of feeling I have for you, but I do feel a particular tenderness which I have known for nobody else so far... I ask myself why I love you; is it because you are a great man or a charming person? I do not know." (November 1866.)

Now sixty-two, George Sand was no longer sure of the merit of anything she wrote, but it did not mattere since she worked because she had to. "I live like a cabbage and am as patient as a woman of Berry."

She died at the age of seventy-two, surrounded by Molière's doctors who had failed to discover in time that she had an intestinal blockage. She was buried in Nohant's small cemetery next to the castle, in a spot as pretty as the park himself. Most graves of the Dupint de Francueil family in the cemetery are mere ivy-clad rectangles today. Everything remains natural, so that even death is somehow linked to life at Nohant.

On the day of her death, 15 or so people came from Paris, including Prince Napoleon, Flaubert, Renan, Dumas Fils, and the publisher Calmann-Levy. On June 25, 1876, Flaubert wrote to Turgenev: "The death of poor Sand brings me infinite sorrow. I wept like a calf twice at the funeral: first when I embraced her granddaughter Aurore (whose eyes that day were so like George Sand's that it seemed she was risen again), and the second time when I saw her coffin go by. Poor, dear, great woman! You had to know her as I did to see all that was feminine in this great man, the immensity of tenderness in this genius."

With the granddaughter to whom Flaubert referred, with eyes so like those of George, the Sand line comes to an end. The young Aurore lived beyond the Second World War. It is not entirely a surprise to learn that she lived as bohemian a life as George Sand, though she did not win such fame; the granddaughter in fact took up the profession of clairvoyant in Paris.

On her table beside a photograph of Nohant there lies a visiting card bearing the words: "Aurore Sand, granddaughter of George Sand, Heart Counsellor, Rue Ferrandi, Paris."

By making use of her grandmother's name in order to make a living—talking of love to the simpleminded—she courageously refused to sell Nohant, to keep it for us.

257. The stairway in the entrance hall at Nohant shows the effect of time on the rose-cloud colourings painted on the walls. The voices of Delacroix, Chopin, Balzac, Gautier and Liszt were among those resounding within these walls. George Sand had mattress material affixed to doors so that people could work in the quiet.

258. George Sand.

258

259. Casimir Dudevant.

259

260. Ajasson de Grandsagne.

260

261. Jules Sandeau.

261

262. Alfred de Musset.

262

264. *A window in the writer's room,* ▷
in the château.

263. *A window of the small pavillion
in the park at Nohant, along the
main road.*

263

264

265. Frederick Chopin by Delacroix.

265

266

Next page:
267. This mineralogy room is none other than Chopin's former bedroom. After they quarrelled, George Sand deliberately uprooted all memories of their love. She had a partition fixed in the center of this room and placed stones on the shelves, adding new ones throughout the rest of her life.

269. George Sand used this room when Chopin stayed at ▷
Nohant, and again at the close of her life. She had it
decorated in blue and white chintz. Her Louis-XVI
chest of drawers and china water jug, nailed chest, seventeenth-
century bed and covered desk where she wrote memoirs and
letters, are still preserved as they were in her days.

268

268. The ground-floor studio is in toile de Jouy material.
George Sand wrote "Indiana", her first novel which made her
famous, on this plank in a cupboard. Left of the door is
a ring that held her hammock. George Sand was visited
in this room by Sandeau. Their affair did not last but
he left with her a taste for writing and the first syllable of
his name.

270. *The table at Nohant remains laid with George Sand's tableware and nineteenth-century glasses. All regular guests at Nohant sat at the same table, but she did not always have them at the same time. Each plate has a card on it: Balzac, Théophile Gautier, Plon-Plon (Napoleon-the-Third's cousin), Delacroix, Flaubert, Chopin, Turgenev...*

On the wall around the Louis-XVI clock and the eighteenth-century china fountain are engravings of Berry country tales reflecting local fancies and horror stories. Guests were always highly talkative especially Balzac, although George Sand apparently spoke little, preferring to listen.

Next page:
271. *The front of Nohant looks out on the park. At left the drawing room, far right, bedroom, centre, dining room; on the first floor are the windows of George Sand's and Chopin's rooms.*

Sir Walter Scott

at Abbotsford Castle

From generation to generation, both young and old people have loved Sir Walter Scott's *Ivanhoe* and *The Lady of the Lake*—works that also delighted Goethe, Byron, Pushkin and Beethoven.

Byron wrote in 1821 that Scott was the most astonishing writer of the age. He praised his ability to delight the reader, his gentle personality, his agreeable conversation and personal concern for himself.

And Ernest Hoffmann wrote : "What exactly is the skill Sir Walter Scott employs to hold us spellbound as we read his novels, just as a miser gloats over a treasure he fears may grow smaller ? This dexterity, this talent in fact is the art of exciting curiosity, and indeed all the beginnings of his stories are charming ; also he has the ability to keep our attention by unexpected incidents, to nourish our interest by means of episodes that increasingly embarrass his characters and by a mysterious tinge that almost portends the intervention of supernatural beings, although he almost never goes as far as magic."

This mysterious tinge that Hoffmann mentions was also injected by Scott into his castle at Abbotsford.

Scott was born a commoner, the son of an attorney general, lawyer and sollicitor in Edinburgh. He entered this world on August 15, 1771, descendant of a very old Scottish family, and youngest of twelve children. His grandfather on his father's side, Robert Scott, had by marriage acquired for his successors the right to burial within Dryburgh Abbey—an immense honour at the time—and his great-grandfather had passed on to Walter his taste for adventure.

At a very young age, Walter Scott would listen to the story of this great-grandfather's role in the 1715 uprising of the Jacobites in Scotland. The old man vowed not to shave until the day the Stuarts won back the throne of Scotland. Since this desired event never took place, he kept on growing his beard and inevitably gained the tag "Beardie". We can see his portrait today over the dining room table at the Scott residence.

Walter's childhood was spent on his grandfather's farm at Sandyknowe. He was later at Kelso and then moved on to Edinburgh where he completed his law studies and became a lawyer by profession. Thus his early life was entirely within the frontiers of Scotland, whence he derived his inspiration.

At twenty-four he married a Mademoiselle Charlotte Charpentier on December 24, 1797. Born originally in Lyons, she later moved to Great Britain. He found her "elegant and light as a fairy." She was a brown-haired beauty with big dark eyes, and a reserve that was very British. This was however coupled with a certain gay air, which her French accent made even more charming.

Charlotte had a Protestant upbringing, her

307

mother being of that religious persuasion. Her father died shortly before the French Revolution, and having foreseen events, had transferred a tidy fortune to Britain. He had business dealings with a certain Marquis of Downshire: in due course, his wife with Charlotte and her son sought refuge at this man's. Mrs. Carpenter, as she became known, died soon afterward in London and Lord Downshire became the girl's guardian. While they were out riding one day in the Lake District in England, she was espied by young Walter.

The Scotts both had a good knowledge of each other's mother tongue. Scott himself had learned French while quite young and was an avid reader of French novels. He also knew German, and Italian which, it is said, he learned at the age of fifteen so that he could read Ariosto and Dante. Early in life Walter showed a predilection for fairy tales and historical narratives. A limp and tendency to sickness dating from his childhood prompted his parents to send him to his grandfather's farm on the Scottish-English border. There, from the lips of his grandmother he heard the tales of Scottish folklore. The telling and hearing of these stories and local ballads was a leading pastime in remote parts. In due course a fond aunt lent him some old books and he seems to have spent most of his adolescence devouring these stories of battles and other events.

His was a distinctly martial taste, which remained all his life and pervaded his works. He also had an enthusiastic love of exercise, perhaps due to his own physical handicap. He particularly loved walking, and wandered about among the historic places of his homeland.

In 1797 there were rumours that the French were about to make a landing in Scotland. With the assent of the Scottish authorities, Walter Scott got together a squadron of volunteers and, afire with enthusiasm, awaited the enemy with his horse *Lenore*. This name was the title of the ballad of Gottfried Burger (1747-1794) which Scott had recently translated from the German, at the same time as some ballads by Goethe together with the latter's *Goetz von Berlichingen*. Goethe became in due

time a keen admirer of the young translator.

In the years that followed the French Revolution, there existed in Edinburgh a large circle of literary men and women—people infatuated with the past and its titles—who promoted the cause of German romanticism. This was Walter Scott's first important public for the folklore he passed on in poetic form. He would listen to the local people's ballads, and he finally collected them into a book called *Minstrelsy of the Scottish Border* (1802-1803). One of his most likeable traits was his modesty. As a young magistrate (he held the job of county sheriff, which enabled him to live reasonably well) he did not really take very seriously the works on chivalry which he produced in verse.

One day he met old college friends who had gone into the printing business, the Ballantyne brothers, and he gained a wider public through them. But meanwhile his job as a magistrate took up more time than before.

He wrote *The Lay of the Last Minstrel*, which began a series of poetic works of which *The Lady of the Lake* (1810) became the most popular. Yet his parents and even his own children did not know he was acknowledged as a poet.

Some admirers in Edinburgh compared him with the great Scottish poet Robert Burns, but he replied that their two names should not be mentioned together. Then in 1811 he produced a poem which reached a wide public, *The Vision of Don Roderick*. This, in fact, was a mediocre work, but it sold widely when it became known that Scott was donating the profits to help Portuguese citizens who had suffered at the hands of Napoleon's Field Marshal Masséna. Despite the poem's faults of style, it seems to have responded to the British public's taste.

Eventually Scott came to realize that his continuation in the legal profession was incompatible with serious writing. After some time as sheriff he took the decision—as Balzac also did—to set up his own print works and become a publisher of his own novels.

The stories of Sir Walter Scott, like those of Balzac, were to make fortunes for their publishers. But, just as in the Frenchman's case, they failed to make their author rich. He ruined himself by being his own publisher, and not all the sentiments of his many lady-admirers could get him off the rocks again. In this respect he contrasted with Balzac who was partly "refloated" by Madame de Berny. Among his short stories that were extremely popular were *Waverley* (1814), *Guy Mannering* (1815), *The Antiquary* (1816), *The Tales of My Landlord, The Black Dwarf, The Bride of Lammermoor, The Legend of Montrose, Rob Roy* in 1818, *Ivanhoe* in 1820. These titles are his most famous and represent only a fraction of his vast output between 1814 and 1820. We need to mention also his *Border Antiquities*, his works on Swift in nineteen volumes and many other books, if we are to gain a more accurate picture of his fecund mind.

Scott might be compared with Anthony Trollope (1815-1882) who wrote novels of English provincial life, but Trollope had not the great diversity that Scott could boast of. This "overproduction" of Scott's is the more extraordinary when we recall that he spent most of the day in wig and gown performing his judicial functions, and most evenings with friends. The explanation is that he wrote at night, taking up sleeping time, which he could well have used, as he needed plenty of rest.

The result was a foregone conclusion. His fragile health broke down. From 1817 onward he became aware of the consequences and had an attack of apoplexy from which he recovered and straightaway returned to his former ways, urged on above all by the poor state of his finances.

His difficulties as a publisher forced him to sell his residence at Ashestril near Selkirk and he moved to Melrose. Soon he bought some land and a small farm which was later to be transformed into the present castle. His labourers, animals, children and dogs all moved into the new home, which overlooked the river Tweed, as it meandered through typically Scottish ferns and thickets. Following his move from a middle-class residence to this farm which was called Clarty Hole—a shift that reflected a sharp drop in wealth—historical treasures from the entire region began to make their way to the Scott home. For, in less that ten years, Clarty Hole became a castle as huge as the imagination of its owner.

Sir Walter called it Abbotsford, and his author's royalties were poured into the embellishment of this amazing place.

By 1804, Scott was a ruined man as a result of his printing venture, but by 1820 he was rich again, and King George IV made him a baronet. The actual purchase of Abbotsford land occured in 1811 and it cost him 4,000 guineas. By 1812 he was somewhat precariously installed in the farm and in 1818 he enlarged the structure by joining up the farmhouse with certain other buildings. Already he had plans for an armoury, dining room, studio, conservatory and three rooms.

The Waverley Novels were published in 1814 and by 1822, after a change of plans, he had destroyed the entire property to build the present castle. It is a fantastic structure, surrounded by acres of land, gardens, cultivated woods and walls. Abbotsford is a crenelated castle with aiming points, as enormous as any castle of the Rhine Valley or the Loire. Scott succeeded in dying among the beloved treasures and furniture he had wanted all his life. This was in sharp contrast to another writer who loved expensive objects, Honoré de Balzac (see page 45) who married the wealthy Countess Hanska but still died a pauper in a house he was still paying for.

Despite his expensive tastes in housing, Sir Walter Scott was never a dandy. His adult life began with a sensible marriage, and his life, as a whole, was a sensible one. He built his castle and passed it on to his descendants; yet Abbotsford was a folly, in the strict sense of the term, a castle from centuries ago built in the full bloom of the Romantic epoch. It is consequently both charming and an exaggeration.

It is even more mysterious than an ancient castle, because Scott wanted it that way. There is not one square foot of the place that escapes dedication to some hero or historical event. Everything at Abbotsford derives its worth from

309

Scott's love of history. Second hand dealers, antique shops and abbeys throughout Scotland contributed to decorating the place. He built an imitation in a spirit of truth to find his own truth. Everything is labelled, classified and properly organized. But the spirit that blows through the castle is that of a breathless, untamed imagination. We need to visit Abbotsford, if only to see how this little Edinburgh lawyer with a head full of dreams was able to express the dreams in architecture—in the manner of Citizen Kane!

A hundred years separate Walter Scott's castle from the one Orson Welles thought up for Rose in the famous movie; the newspaper magnate's folly continues its strange existence in the American Middle West. Both are examples of extravagant architecture borrowed from nostalgia for the age of chivalry.

Neither Lamartine nor Chateaubriand, who grafted Gothic embellishments onto their ancient castles at Saint-Point and Combourg, succeeded in giving their residences the unusual purity we find at Abbotsford.

Sir Walter spent ten years of his life, from 1822 to 1832, in the creation of his masterpiece. From the moment one enters the main courtyard, it is easy to see that Abbotsford is not just an ordinary castle. In the centre of the yard is an old fountain which in former ages spurted forth wine in abundance. Two stone dogs guard the main porch, and immediately on arrival inside, the visitor sees before him a romantic, even theatrical decor of weaponry and other items disposed about the gigantic granite chimney piece. On the chimney lie pottery objects and human skulls including that of Robert The Bruce, whose tomb was opened up in 1818. These are authentic medieval Scottish relics. The chimney piece is, in fact, a copy of a stall used by Abbot Mitri at Melrose Abbey. Also from Melrose are statues of Saint Paul, Saint Peter and Saint Andrew, the patron saint of Scotland, which are placed in little wall niches. The grill dating from 1679 came from Archbishop Sharps, the cannon balls were actually used in the seige of Roxburgh Castle. There are relics from Waterloo, French breastplates, rifles, a lock from Selkirk prison, Scottish branks, a stag's head found at Abbotsrule Moss, skulls and horns of various Scottish wild beasts now extinct.

Another striking "exhibit" is a so-called Border touting horn from another castle, along with a collection of axes and some keys from a former Edinburgh prison, fifteenth-century armour worn at the Battle of Bosworth Field, some French sixteenth-century jousting armour, two Highland sabres found on the battlefield of Culloden in 1745. This list is still far from complete; mention must also be made of the prehistoric animal skulls and the suits of armour feebly lighted by the heraldic-style windows. Sometimes the visitor feels he is backstage at a theatre and on other occasions really in an authentic Scottish castle. All that is missing is the ghost; perhaps Scott's own presence is too vividly felt here for phantoms to venture forth.

The author's library is no less extraordinary. It contains some 20,000 volumes many of which are marked at the back with the anagram on Gualterus Scotus : *Clausus tutus ero*. It is more like a national library than that of a private individual. As we wander along by the shelves, we can see the Tweed flowing by in a quiet almost desolate countryside. Occasionally a few horses from the farm move across this background.

Over a chimney is a portrait of Scott's first son, a lieutenant in the 18th Hussars; the feathered hat is unfortunately missing from the painting. Here also are some hooks in the form of golden bees from Napoleon's coat, found in his carriage after the Battle of Waterloo, a tray for his pens which was once at Fontainebleau, a cup used by Bonnie Prince Charlie, Rob Roy's moneybag and some miniatures of Sir Walter and Lady Scott which they exchanged before they got married. Under a glass cover can be seen souvenirs of various kinds, including his mother's amulet which she put round his neck as a boy to keep away the fairies. A goblet used by Robert Burns, some of Bonnie Prince Charlie's hair and a notebook of Flora MacDonald are among other keepsakes acquired by Scott.

Next to the big library is the drawing room,

also large. The Chinese-style dark green wall-paper is still in very good condition. It is rather like the paper in the room Madame Récamier had at Coppet Castle, and was hand-done in China at the start of the nineteenth century, being a gift to Sir Walter from his brother Hugh. The paper gives a gay air to the drawing room in this somewhat terrifying castle. This room also manages to escape the general medieval influence with its crystal glass lamp hanging by a golden "sun", the Coalport porcelain in its cases, and Portuguese ebony furniture which the owner received as a gift from George IV.

Scott's own study is a small library in itself, and looks over a half-height balcony. The balcony is merely for decoration, and the study recalls Scott's early days as a lawyer. The author's dreams of grandeur ended at the study door; he doubtless felt no need of them in order to write, but the moment he emerged from the room he could wander at ease among his armour in little rooms tucked under ribbed stucco arches bearing indigo paint. The walls contain hundreds of objects and weapons, and they look almost as if they were put there to amuse people as they go past; they include a hunting canteen owned by James VI, a Spanish double-barrelled flint rifle, a carbine that belonged to Speckbacher—the Tyrolian patriot who raised up the Tyrol against Bavaria and the French in 1789—Rob Roy's sword, Sir Walter's blunderbuss. And above a piece of furniture is a picture of the Scottish crown jewels next to one of Scott's dog Ginger and his cat Hinse of Insefelt. Scott's wide-ranging sentimentality was quite insular; in the huge dining room where Scott died we can see a portrait of "Beardie", his great-grandfather, who refused to cut his beard until the Stuarts returned. On the buffet is a silver urn given to Scott by Byron, and there is James VI's sword, given by the writer John Ballantyne, lying under a glass casing with a Highlands broadsword donated by the Celtic Society. All this demonstrates that the author of so many legendary stories used the castle as a means of making real the atmosphere he desired to create in his works.

After 1818 the publishers Ballantyne Brothers were succeeded by Constable and Cadell, who went bankrupt in 1826. Scott also lost money through this. He was celebrated and had a wide reading public, and naturally imagined he would never be in serious need again. But he had less control over his publisher's commercial affairs than over his own taste for grandeur and hospitality. He felt so insured against any risks that when a friend gave him the first warning about the publishers, he carried on with his whisky and cigar and asked to finish his after-lunch rest in peace. It so happened that a short while afterwards he began a diary whose contents became more dramatic as the weeks passed.

In the diary we can see a description of his wife's death. It says she died at 9 a.m. and expresses the fear that his heart would give out as a result of comparing their home before and after her death.

The only future he could see was an old man, alone and poor with no family. At this juncture, Scott's life, so blessed by Providence so far, took a heroic turn. He aimed to devote the rest of his life to hard work, so as to reimburse the debt arising from his publisher's business failure. In addition to a large number of magazine articles, he wrote *Woodstock* (1826), *The Life of Napoleon* (1827), *Chronicles of the Canongate*, *The Two Droves*, *The Fair Maid of Perth*, and the last series of *Tales of My Landlord*.

Such prodigious output was achieved at the cost of a certain neglect of style. In spite of his aristocratic views, Scott depicted the lower orders with a very human realism. Yet he was not appreciated by Chateaubriand who wrote: "The illustrious painter of Scotland seems to me to have created a false style, and in my opinion has perverted both the novel and history. The novelist has attempted to write historical novels and the historian romantic history." He might in fairness have added that Scott also built a historic home and it is doubtless that this gives the book *Ivanhoe* the authentic realism that has enabled it to resist the passage of time without suffering one bit. Chateaubriand criticises Scott's superficiality and romanticism, but it could be said in reply that the author of *Atala* was no less open to attack with his minstrel-style conversions at the farm he bought called La Vallée-aux-Loups.

Goethe's friendly understanding of Sir Walter's spirit compensates for Chateaubriand's severity. He wrote: "One can always find in Walter Scott a solid reliability and a great skill to lay out his stories. These characteristics stem from the immense knowledge of the real world that he attained, by observing and speculating on vital problems all his life."

As a result of his colossal output, Sir Walter paid back most of what he owed, but the effort ruined his health. Symptoms of paralysis appeared in 1829 but he refused to stop work, against the advice of doctors and his family. In 1830 he produced an introduction to a new collection of his poems, and some pieces on demonology and magic. Toward the end of the same year illness made him stop work. But by spring he was back at his desk again and *Count Robert of Paris* was published. The idea of paying back his debts became a fixation with him, but as a consequence of his illness, he lost his mental balance. He imagined he had actually reimbursed everything and was once again a "free man".

He could still move about but spoke only with difficulty. It was suggested to him that travelling might help, and the government made a ship available to him. Scott embarked on a Mediterranean cruise but from May 11, 1832, he lost serious interest in practically everything that went on around him. In Venice he refused to visit anything but the Bridge of Sighs.

Later he went on a European tour, to the Tyrol and to Munich where an unsuspecting shop assistant tried to sell him a picture of Abbotsford. He grunted: "I already know the place." Even in bitter weather he insisted on travelling day and night, touring the Rhine castles but saying absolutely nothing. He had an attack of apoplexy at Nijmegen and bloodletting was resorted to.

He asked to be taken back to London and on arrival was confined to bed at Saint James's Hotel. Friends called on him but he showed interest only when Abbotsford was mentioned. Newspapers published articles on his work daily and gave health bulletins. People hung about outside the hotel. Court emissaries were sent to inquire about him. A newspaper reported that his journeys on the Continent were cut short because of money and that, if Sir Walter knew this he would be unable to rest; in consequence the government sent a message that the Treasury was "at his disposal". But the great man no longer needed earthly riches.

Scott never spoke again, except once to ask that he be taken back to his beloved Abbotsford, his dream, and the cause of his ruin and decline.

On July 7 a steamer took him down the Thames and on to Newcastle whence he journeyed to Abbotsford by road. He lived there for another two months or so, occasionally having the Gospel of Saint John read out to him, or some excerpts from Crabbe.

Scott died on September 21, 1832. One of the bystanders later said: "It was a fine day and so calm. Through the window we could hear the light splashing of the Tweed."

273. This view of Abbotsford Castle shows the main courtyard. Thanks to the royalties he earned on his adventure stories, he was able to remodel it according to his fantasy.

274

274. *In this small arched room, Scott hung the relics of former battles which he found in antique shops.*

275

275. *The simplicity of Sir Walter Scott's study contrasts with the other rooms.*

276. *Scott assembled, in this majestic entrance, his collec-* ▷ *tions of hunting trophies, armour, weapons and even human skulls.*

276

277. *Anne of Geierstein inspired "The Lady of the Lake".*

279. *Walter Scott's property is seen from a window in Abbotsford Castle.*

278. *A painting of the period depicts Walter Scott with peasants. Despite his aristocratic leanings, his attachment to tradition was romantic rather than snobbish.*

281

281. *A dashing Scott in military dress hangs in the library.*

282

282. *Armaments collected by Scott.*

◁ 280. *The main hall is decorated in hand-painted Chinese-style paper. Above the mantle piece is a portrait of Walter Scott.*

Madame de Staël

at Coppet Castle

Coppet Castle lies on the lakeside a few miles from Geneva. Jacques Necker, Swiss-born finance minister to Louis XVI from 1777 to 1788, bought it for himself and his daughter Madame de Staël, originally with the idea of using it as a holiday residence. As it turned out, the castle served more as a refuge where the family lived out the disgraces stemming from the political changes in France between the Revolution and the Empire.

It was to be the golden cage where the 1789 Revolution leaders, and later Napoleon, shut up the members of Necker family, whose members thereafter spent their time dreaming of *salon* life, receptions and political activity in Paris. The Neckers were a very united clan: the father, mother and daughter admired each other to such an extent that they were often the laughing stock of their circle. Napoleon did not like them at all and wrote of them: "Madame de Staël's family is indeed extraordinary. Her father, her mother and herself—all three are continually on their knees admiring each other, breathing in reciprocal incense for the greater edification and mystification of the public."

Feeling was particularly strong between father and daughter; today, we should say it was an example of the "father-figure" complex. In the case of Germaine de Staël; it is probably this that explains the long periods of residence at Coppet, where Monsieur Necker finally

went to live after the sovereign fell in 1792.

For Madame de Staël, living at Coppet was like being buried alive.

She could not stand Geneva's *salons* and literary life. The French Revolution had forced her to take refuge in the castle, but her lover Narbonne, Louis XVI's war minister, had fled to London, at the same time as Germaine was about to produce a baby. Between the lover and the father, she chose the father. As to her husband, the Swedish ambassador, he returned alone to Stockholm.

For a lively woman attached to political adventure and the Parisian *salons* where the reputation of ministers and revolutionaries were made and unmade, Coppet was indeed a living death. In order to sense more keenly the boredom she felt in this residence, this land where nothing ever happened, we may recall something of the charmed life she led as a child, between the king's *salons* at Versailles and those of her mother at the Faubourg Saint-Germain. Necker appears to have been chosen by Louis XVI because of his serious nature, his foreign nationality and obscurity. He was outside of any clique; a capable, rich, unknown man who provided the kind of assurance the king needed. Later on, he made available to the king his immense personal fortune, although it gained him nothing. Madame Necker, once in Paris, proved capable, thrusting and methodical. She devoted her brains to the cause of her

321

283. *The beautiful Germaine Necker at thirty-one in 1797 became "The conscience of Europe". Her mother made her an international blue-stock-ing. She shone before contemporaries but, opposed to the idea of personal rule, she irritated Napoleon.*

husband's career and to the formation of a blue-stocking of international class—her daughter.

The education of Germaine was a kind of challenge; Madame Necker made use of her to demonstrate her skill, playing pygmalion with her only daughter. "Oh, it's nothing, really nothing, compared with what I wanted to do with her," she would say when people complimented her on her Germaine. The task in hand was to form this child into a woman able to reign over the hearts and minds of the men of her epoch, a woman as much at ease at Versailles as in the company of a foreign philosopher. Germaine was hardly five years old when Madame Necker included among her friends Buffon and Abbé Raynal. She obliged them to converse with the child.

Necker himself was all-powerful at Versailles. The king had borrowed from him two million francs to meet the state deficit, the first time a minister had lent money to his own king. He must also have been the first to waive his repayment claim when the nation ran into difficulty and he risked losing the cash with the fall of the régime. Necker's wealth made life easy for his wife: who would dare to contradict Madame Necker? Thus, because her mother desired it so, Germaine was able to converse with the best minds of the day.

The guests and she herself, after each reception, made it their duty to draw up a report on what was discussed. Madame Necker never allowed her daughter to walk alone in a park or play with children of her own age, yet she wanted to bring her up like Emile, the character in the book *Emile, ou de l'Education*. Instead of the joys of nature, she offered Germaine her *salon*. It is understandable that, later on, the rustic atmosphere of Coppet had little interest for Madame de Staël. All that appealed to her were political goings-on, which she could stir up or direct from a *salon*. The child had Buffon to amuse her instead of a doll, and she really never was a child at all. Before she was ten years of age her mother had taught her all the tricks a woman should know in order to make her way in Paris. If, for example, Voltaire would not come to her receptions, she found

some way or other to imply that he was among her friends. She in fact decided to have a statue made of him, so that she could ask him to receive the sculptor. Voltaire, flattered, accepted both the idea of the statue, and a regular correspondance with Madame Necker. This was enough to make people say that "Voltaire goes to the Neckers' receptions".

In this training school, Germaine learned how to acquire a public and hold it. When she reached nineteen years of age, "a suitable match" was sought for her—at one time her mother thought about England's William Pitt. The idea of connecting the two big financiers of the world appealed to Madame Necker, but Germaine refused because it would have meant living in London away from her father. De Staël, a Swedish gentleman, appeared before the family as a possible suitor for Germaine. He was clearly attracted by the money.

The Necker family was not very impressed and subjected him to a series of extraordinary tests and demands. He was required to become a count before he could marry Germaine. Then he had to be an ambassador, arrange for the king and Queen Marie-Antoinette to be witnesses at the wedding, and finally he had to obtain a Pacific island from Louis XVI. The amazing thing is that he passed all the tests and even got the Pacific island, although it took six years for him to do it.

The ambitious hero, now wedded to Germaine, fell in love with her. But he never succeeded in winning her love in return and, to console himself, absurdly acquired a mistress of seventy-one years of age. This was the actress Mademoiselle Clairon, who ruined him. Germaine, to prevent him landing in prison, paid the pension to which the actress laid claim. Monsieur and Madame de Staël had one child who died, and they soon agreed to live apart. Her later children were all by lovers, one might say the fruit of sentiment and politics, since Germaine always chose her lovers with a view to extending her political power.

In 1792, when the revolution made it impossible for the De Staëls to live in Paris, Germaine moved to Coppet. She left behind her a more brilliant *salon* than her mother's, and an undisputed reputation as the most vivid woman of her times. She also left behind two famous lovers : one who probably made her, Talleyrand, and the other whom she herself made, Narbonne. Viscount Narbonne-Lara, was a constitutional monarchist whom Germaine succeeded in getting appointed war minister by the king. Queen Marie-Antoinette commented in November 1791 : "Madame de Staël strives hard for Monsieur de Narbonne. I have never seen a keener or more tangled intrigue... Count Louis de Narbonne became war minister yesterday ; what glory for Madame de Staël and how nice for her to have the whole army for herself." But Germaine failed in one venture. She unsuccessfully tried to use Narbonne as intermediary—backed by the Girondins—and get Louis XVI to accept on February 24, 1792, a memorandum suggesting that his majesty abandon the aristocracy and put his trust in the bourgeoisie. She tried in vain to save royalty through the mediation of her lovers. Germaine had a penetrating and generous mind, but she shocked people by the methods she employed.

At twenty-six years of age, having experienced the power that money, wit and love can win, she was suddenly forced to withdraw to Switzerland, and arrived at Coppet in September 1792. No longer did she enjoy the chatter of Paris. The castle drawing rooms and huge library which Madame Necker decorated for her, the busts of the classical Greek and Roman authors overlooking it reflected no life at all. The castle was deserted, and nobody came to see her.

In France itself, Marie-Antoinette had just been charged with treason. On learning of this, Germaine decided at once to write a book in her defense. She fondly imagined French public opinion could be influenced from a Swiss castle. But as heads rolled in the Paris streets, who cared what Madame de Staël had to say ? This first political work from neutral territory, written in a mood of indignation, was to be followed by other, more elaborate efforts. Germaine, from her remote belvedere coldly analysed the Revolution and later the Empire, uncovering the abuses of the régimes. She was to become public

enemy number one as far as the leaders of the Terror were concerned, and then to evoke the hostility of Napoleon. She emerged as "the conscience of Europe" to the observers of the epoch, although today we can hardly comprehend the importance of such a personage. At Coppet, Madame de Staël made an attempt to reassemble her Paris *salon* and regroup her friends around her. But Talleyrand and Narbonne were in London and refused her invitation to join her in Switzerland—the former because he wanted to go to America, the other because he loved her less. Only a short while after recovering from the birth of her son, she left Coppet for London and tried to persuade them to change their minds. But after a few hours at Juniper Hall, she was obliged to return alone to Switzerland.

Disappointed at this setback, she acquired several plots of land north of New York. Germaine forgot about Narbonne because he had failed to come up to her expectations. Other fugitives from the Revolution began to appear at Coppet. She started sending people with Swiss papers to bring back her French friends ; among those she "saved" was the Duchesse of Broglie whose son was later to marry her daughter Albertine after she, too, came to stay at Coppet.

By 1794, although still in the Swiss castle, Germaine was not to be bored any longer. She loved "one of the leading minds of Europe," as she called Benjamin Constant, whom she met by chance on the roads while in a coach as he trotted alongside on horseback.

Constant was the former chamberlain of the Duke of Brunswick, but now he was nothing ; he was unhandsome but brilliant. They both realize in a flash that they could not be fully alive without each other. They agreed on all major points but they spent years tearing each other to pieces. The public was to be stimulated by their shafts of wit.

Madame Necker died about the same time as this strange encounter. As she requested, they buried her at Coppet, embalmed and submerged in eau-de-vie spirits. "That is not how I would like to avoid being forgotten," Germaine wrote to her friend Meister. Each evening, Monsieur Necker paid a visit to his wife, whose face was uncovered. The grave is hidden by a huge wall in the center of the castle grounds.

Gradually life began again at Coppet, faces came and went. Narbonne arrived in Switzerland but he had virtually no feeling left for Germaine, who in any case thought only of Benjamin Constant. The Neckers had a second Swiss residence called Mezey, which was in due course visited by a fine-looking Swede named Rilbing, fleeing from his own country because he had plotted against King Gustav III. He had pointed out the king to an assassin by touching his majesty (who was in disguise at the time) and pronouncing the words : "Good evening, beautiful mask." "No other story was so interesting to me as his," wrote Madame de Staël. It is possible she loved him.

Just then, Monsieur de Staël arrived in Switzerland for a temporary visit, and drove off the conspirator. Because Germaine showed too much interest in Rilbing, Benjamin Constant tried to commit suicide with poison at Mezey to prove his love for her. He was saved by friends who administered an antidote. Germaine gave herself to him, as he had expected.

In May 1795, Madame de Staël left Coppet with Constant for Paris, both "wonderfully crammed with republican ideas and hopes." Constant, like Talleyrand and Narbonne, was to be her political ally. Madame de Staël's *salon* at the Swedish embassy reopened. Barras, Sieyès, Tallien and Chénier, government officials and artists, were among those who appeared there, together with some who had already been seen inside before 1792. Germaine's idea was to establish *rapprochements* between all parties. She wrote *Réflexions sur la paix*, but merely succeeded in making herself unpopular. She had to leave France in the end.

The whole of 1796 was spent at Coppet, struggling with a new book "on the influence of the passions on the well-being of individuals and nations." Earlier works produced at the castle were *Zulma* (her life with Narbonne), *Histoire de Pauline, Essai sur les fictions*. Coppet was her literary retreat.

Germaine returned to Paris in June 1797 but in the Autumn left again. She could never get on with Napoleon. According to Napoleon's Code "woman is made for the repose of the warrior." That was not her opinion. Bonaparte did not care a bit for this blue-stocking. From their first encounters, she "interviewed" him in such a peculiar way in public that he conceived an immediate dislike for her." What type of woman do you like ?" she once asked him, to which he replied : "Those who produce children."

She accused him of having said, in reference to her, that he hated "ideologists". Through his brother, whom she frequently met, she conveyed to him that he was "a mere ideophobe." Napoleon, angered at this, cried : "What ever does she want ?" and offered to pay back the two million francs debt Louis XVI contracted with her father and family. "It is not a question of what I want, but what I think," she proudly replied, which hardly pleased the emperor. Later Madame de Staël sought his consideration and, again through his brother, was invited to one of the soirées of the régime. Napoleon himself spoke with her. The meeting was curious. The emperor approached her, stared at her *décolleté* and demanded : "Have you breast-fed, Madame ?" She was so stupefied, she remained mute. He hereupon added : "You see, she never says yes or no !"

Napoleon could not bear that this woman should intrigue at his expense. Since she was not his ally, he treated her as an enemy. Although at first he agreed to have Benjamin Constant in the government, this did not last long. In January 1800, he drove them both out of Paris, Constant having read a speech calling for a free parliament. They did not go to Coppet; the minister of the police, Fouchet, in a friendly gesture, confined them temporarily to the De Staël Saint-Ouen residence. Monsieur de Staël was very ill and even the emperor himself was indignant about the indifference Germaine showed toward her husband. To help him get well again, she took him to Coppet. They left together but it was a coffin that arrived at the castle instead of a husband, as he died on the way. His burial at Coppet was much less of an affair than the funeral of Madame Necker a few years earlier.

Germaine was back in Paris at once, but the emperor was not in agreement with the tenor of her latest books. She published *Delphine*, a story advocating free living for women, whereas the emperor at this time favoured marriage. He additionally noted that "people liked the emperor less when they emerged from her place". He ordered her to get back to Coppet within five days. This was in October 1803. She returned to Coppet by way of Weimar, because she planned to write a book on Germany, and for that she needed to talk with the "greatest minds" of that country. Although speaking not a word of the language, she wanted to meet Goethe; he was absent but she obliged him to return home. She also met Herder and Schiller in Berlin and had her children taught by one of the Schlegel brothers.

She was received by Queen Louise but suddenly had to rush to Coppet where Monsieur Necker lay dying. He passed away during her six-day journey, and did not see his daughter "Minette" again.

On reaching the castle, Germaine collapsed in the courtyard, falling from her coach. She was to remain at Coppet for six months, sorting out her father's papers and writing a book in memory of "his virtuous genius", entitled *Du caractère de Monsieur Necker et de sa vie privée*. For a change she went with her children to Italy in December 1804, returning with *Corinne*, an autobiographical novel in which she relived her love life with Pedro de Souza who appears in the book as Oswald. Material for the subsequent unhappy love of Corinne was provided by an adventure with twenty-four-year old Prosper de Barante, who fell in love with her. Italy was a short respite. She had to return to Switzerland, which the emperor had designated as her forced residence. But now Coppet became a veritable paradise for her, since all of Europe, which was wholly against Napoleon, came to Coppet to converse with this active opponent of the Napoleonic régime. Chateaubriand wrote to her: "If I had a nice castle like you have on the side of Lake Geneva, I would never leave it."

One visitor was Madame Récamier. Together the two ladies played the harp in the large library where Monsieur Necker had had his office. It is still there today as he left it with his papers and souvenirs; on the large table where he worked is the casket containing the state accounts of France. It is said that the revealing of them was the first shot fired against royalty. Madame de Staël's bedroom with its huge damask bed is also there, next door to Madame Récamier's room which has eighteenth-century wallpaper depicting birds, and Louis XVI furniture upholstered in water-green satin. From the large *salons* on the first floor, the lake can be seen. Judging by the number of armchairs brought from Paris, one can imagine what the Coppet receptions were like. Soon Madame de Staël, as Napoleon's enemy, found herself playing host to foreign kings of the coalition against him together with their suites.

The waterfall and the décor in the castle grounds counted less for Germaine than the talks she had with Frederick Schlegel, the German poet-scientist and a founder of the romantic school. His brother was the author of the famous *Course in Romantic Literature*. They discussed the talent of Schiller.

Madame de Staël had written: "I feared deeply that my father wanted to spend his life in his own country; he must forgive me, because I have not yet accumulated enough memories to live on them for the rest of my life." The whole of Europe was now to bring to Coppet enough material to provide the memories she lacked. The poised Madame Récamier, whom Germaine met in 1798 and loved passionately from the start, formed the centre of the Coppet "court". Because of her virtuous love life, Prince Augustus of Prussia fell madly in love with her; in an exchange of letters she promised to marry him. But a few days later when she tried to persuade her husband to release her, he dissuaded her. Then later, Auguste, Madame de Staël's own eldest son, fell in love with her, much to his mother's annoyance.

The entire world rotated round these

two extraordinary ladies : Germaine de Staël and Juliette Récamier. At Coppet were to be seen their friends from Italy, those from Germany (Frederick Schlegel, John Müller, Baron Voght), Russia (the mystical Madame de Krüdener who was later the Tsar Alexander's secret counsellor), Baron Balk, Benjamin Constant, Lullin de Châteauvieux, the Bailiff of Nyons, Bonstetten, Sismondi, Albertine Necker of Saussure and Mathieu de Montmorency.

The summer of 1807 brought a festive mood to the castle, according to Chateaubriand in his *Mémoires d'outre-tombe*. He wrote : "Everybody was upset, but it sometimes happens that the joys of youth can be redoubled when mingled with the effects of public catastrophes. One more eagerly embarks on pleasures that are felt to be near an end."

At Coppet conversation was regarded as the greatest of pleasures to be had, and in that castle, wrote Sainte-Beuve, it ruled supreme. The talk began at eleven o'clock as lunch was served and continued in the garden and during walks, through dinner at six o'clock, then far into the night. Another participant, the Bailiff of Bonstetten, said : "More wit could be heard at Coppet in one day than elsewhere in the world during a whole year."

Madame de Staël sparkled in conversation. Goethe wrote : "It was her pleasure and passion. But her joy, too, was to philosophize in a *salon*. Her manner of doing it was to hold forth brilliantly on problems that were impossible to argue about... She threw herself into the heat of the conversation and thoughtlessly plunged into the depths of that intimate region where sentiment and thought lie hidden... This amazing Frenchwoman conveyed her views with energy, eloquence, with an obstinacy that was often sophistic ; and hardly listened to her antagonist's objections, or at least did not weigh them with any care."

Her main interlocutor at Coppet was Benjamin Constant. Sismondi wrote : "You have not known the real Madame de Staël until you have seen her with Benjamin Constant." He alone had the right, owing to his equal wit, to bring into the game all her spirit and to make it bloom in the combat, to awaken her eloquence, to find the depths of her soul, and thoughts that were never revealed in all their brilliance except when set against him—just as he was never his real self except at Coppet.

Against the blackcloth of the castle walls were played out some painful and celebrated scenes. Benjamin Constant wanted to abandon Madame de Staël who would use the role of Hermione to cry out her suffering before the Coppet public. She loaded passionate reproaches onto him during performances of *Andromaque* in the ground-floor balcony. Constant was Pyrrhus, Madame Récamier was Andromaque, and Madame de Staël Hermione. Germaine played admirably well, but Constant was so bad that a member of the audience was heard to say in a brilliant French pun : "*Je ne sais pas si c'est le roi d'Epire, mais c'est certes le pire des rois.*" ("I don't know whether that is the King of Epirus, but he is certainly the worst of kings.")

At one point Constant was supposed to say : "I am marrying a Trojan. Yes, Madame, and I confess that I have promised you the pledge which I now vow to her..." But he got so mixed up and his voice was so unconvincing that Madame de Staël wailed : "I never loved you, cruel man, what ever have I done ?"

A cousin of Madame de Staël wrote : "It is unbelievable that her circumstances should be publicly exposed in this way." As to Juliette Récamier, playing Phèdre and adressing the Prince of Prussia whom she loved, she pronounced the following words with clear allusion to their relationship : "Go, Prince, and carry out your generous designs. I accept all the gifts that you wish to bestow on me."

The audience applauded with glee, enchanted by the parallel between the real life characters and those in the plays. In the midst of this whirlpool of events, Madame de Staël found time to write. She moved her desk from room to room, concerned as always with matters of love or politics. At Coppet, she was nostalgic for her *salon* in the Rue du Bac in Paris and, naïvely, in 1807 she sent her seventeen-year old son to Chambéry to meet the emperor on his way back from Italy, and to ask his permission to return to Paris to live. Napoleon rejected the appeal: "Madame de Staël would engage in intrigues," he said. "She doesn't take much notice of them, but I do: I take everything seriously. If I let her go back to Paris, she would talk slander and lose me all the people I have round me. Apart from that she can go anywhere she likes: Rome, Naples, Vienna, Berlin, Milan and even to London to create rebels. Only your mother is unhappy when she is given all Europe."

Shortly afterwards, Madame de Staël turned up in Vienna and was in touch with an English secret agent, Gentz. The emperor learned of this and ordered her to be placed under surveillance at Coppet. "Hitherto she has been regarded (by us) as a madwoman, but today she is beginning to join a clique that is acting against the public peace," he declared.

She was back in Switzerland in July 1808. On arrival she learned that Benjamin Constant had betrayed her and just married Charlotte de Hardenberg. She thought of leaving for America but decided in the end to stay in Europe a while for the appearance of her book *De l'Allemagne*. She was given permission to stay at Chaumont Castle in France, which she tagged "Coppet-sur-Loire". This was still only half a victory because she yearned to live in Paris. So once again she wrote to the Emperor. Exasperated, he ordered her to embark immediately at an Atlantic port. She went back to Coppet crestfallen. Luckily, *De l'Allemagne* was a huge success in Germany and England, although it came as a shock to the French. The book was a century ahead of its time, by putting forward the idea of a united Europe. It also introduced France to the German romantic movement which dominated the 1830 period.

Again, Coppet fell into a neglected state: "The isolation of Madame de Staël is on the increase," the Prefect of Geneva reported. "People look for a thousand excuses not to visit Coppet, not to have her—in a word to avoid her."

"My life is like a ball when the music has stopped," was her own comment.

Napoleon by now dominated Europe and Napoleon had exiled Madame de Staël. So it was flight for her. At this juncture, love in the form of the young John Rocca arrived to distract her from the rebuffs. He was a romantic young fellow who made his horse Sulton gallop fast to gain her attention. Though only twenty years of age, he was madly in love with her, and dreamed of the future. He was also a TB sufferer. "I shall love her so much she will end up by marrying me," he predicted. Germaine discovered that she was loved for herself and not for her fame. So she loved him in return, and on April 17, 1812, a child called Louis-Alphonse was born. They hid him with a nurse under a false name, after pledging before a pastor to get married as soon as circumstances permitted.

Madame de Staël felt herself a prisoner, even in the company of John Rocca. On May 23, 1912, she went for a drive ostensibly in the surrounding countryside, with Albertine. On the way she met with Rocca and Schlegel. The drive took in Salzburg and Vienna and she ended up in Moscow on July 1, having left her eldest son Auguste at Coppet to look after the property. Of Moscow, she said: "I saw the huge city radiating with all its golden turrets and its temples, five weeks before it became victim of the flames."

We can imagine how much this woman must have disliked Coppet for her to fly without hesitation to Moscow, sneaking through the net of Napoleon's agents in her own castle. Moreover, there was every chance she would fall among the emperor's *grognards* ("soldiers") in the Moscow area. She reached Saint Petersburg and was well received by the tsar. Seeking a useful role, she acted as anti-Napoleonic agent, and at her own suggestion left for Stockholm and Bernadotte, carrying from the tsar a proposed treaty of alliance against Napoleon in which the Swedish king would gain the French throne after their victory. For her son Albert she obtained a post as second lieutenant in the Swedish army, and another job for Auguste when he should reach Sweden. She had Schlegel appointed the prince's private secretary.

Having achieved this much, she went off to London where her book *De l'Allemagne* was enjoying an immense success. While in England she learned that her son Albert had been killed in a duel with a Russian officer. So she stayed there alone with Albertine and Rocca.

On May 8, 1814, two years after leaving Coppet, she found Paris open to her again. Napoleon had fallen but the enemy occupied Paris. She was sad; Constant had proved anti-French, Talleyrand disappointed her, the liberal Mathieu de Montmorency had joined the "ultra" right wing. Furthermore, Juliette Récamier had made her suffer unduly through her eternal coquetries and there was no rebirth of their former companionship.

Only two months after returning to Paris, she took the road to Coppet again, this time of her own free will. Once there she was welcomed with flowers and all Europe went back there as in former times as Stendhal was to write.

Yesterday, life at Coppet had exasperated Madame de Staël: today she sought there the tranquility needed for her to put life's events in their right order. She even wrote to Napoleon telling him to be careful not to get poisoned, since she had heard rumours of a plot on the Island of Elba.

She also had time to think of her daughter: "I shall force her into a love match." The daughter in the end married the Duke of Broglie, a man of liberal ideas whom she loved. Louis XVIII started them off with a fortune in the form of the two million francs Necker had lent to the state. In this way the marriage, celebrated February 19, 1816, crowned all the efforts of Madame de Staël.

Meanwhile Rocca was dying of consumption. On October 10, Germaine married him and they gave the little Louis-Alphonse a name. After which she made her will, giving over Coppet to Auguste and Albertine.

A short while later she was in Paris, never to see Coppet again. She had an attack of paralysis that degenerated into gangrene. Rocca and she died within a short time of each other. Chateaubriand recalls in his *Mémoires* the following scene: "One morning I went to her place.

Madame de Staël was half-seated, supported by pillows. I approached and, when my eyes had become a little accustomed to the dark, I could see the patient. A vivid fever animated her cheeks. Her fine look met mine in the shadows and she said: 'Good evening my dear Francis. I am suffering but that does not stop me loving you.' She held out her hand which I pressed and kissed. On raising my head again I perceived in the alcove something white and thin that rose up. It was Rocca, with a worn-out face, hollow cheeks, blurred eyes, an indefinable colour, dying. He did not open his mouth and bowed toward me, and went away again like a shadow. These two ghosts looking at me in silence, one standing and pale, the other seated and highly coloured with blood ready to descend again to freeze round the heart, made me shudder."

Germaine died before Rocca, who spent the few months left to him watching their child, all that remained of Germaine, playing behind a glass partition.

The grave of Monsieur and Madame Necker at Coppet was opened to allow the body of Madame de Staël to be laid to rest with them. All those who had spent so much time with her died soon after she did: Rocca, Auguste, Albertine de Broglie (Albertine's daughter), and a few years later, the child of Rocca and herself.

One day in 1832, Juliette Récamier took Chateaubriand to Coppet.

Madame de Récamier visited the grave of Germaine while Chateaubriand waited in the grounds, sitting on a bench. He later wrote: "At the foot of Madame de Staël's grave so many absent illustrious persons came back into memory. They seemed to want the shadow of their equal so they could fly to heaven with her, and act as cortège during the night. Then Madame de Récamier came out pale and in tears, herself like a shadow. If ever I have felt the vanity and truth of glory and of life, it was at the entrance to that silent copse, sombre and unknown, where sleeps she who had so much brilliance and renown. I saw what it is to be truly loved."

284

284. *Jacques Necker.*

285. *Suzanne Necker.*

285

286. *Germaine Necker at fourteen.*   286

287

287. *William Pitt.*

288. *E. M. de Staël-Holstein.*

288

289. *Coppet is seen here as it was when the De Staëls inhabited it.*

289

290

290. This engraving depicts Louis XVI summoning Necker to save the good order of France and its finances. The event, important for the Necker family, was but an episode in the French Revolution and it hindered neither its march forward nor the outcome.

291. Coppet Castle became the "golden cage" ▷ of Germaine de Staël in 1792. The fine library did not divert Germaine from thoughts of Talleyrand, her ex-lover exiled in London, or of her new friend Monsieur de Narbonne. After bearing de Narbonne's child at Coppet, she crossed France to join him. She preferred living to reading about life at this stage.

Next page:
292. Coppet Castle.

293. Madame de Staël's room at Coppet.

299. In this bedroom at Coppet, Madame Récamier dreamed of marriage to Prince Augustus of Prussia, but her husband would not release her.

294

294. Talleyrand.

295

295. Louis de Narbonne.

296

296. Rilbing.

297

297. Benjamin Constant.

298

298. John Rocca.

293

Tolstoi

at Yasnaya-Polyana

Forty miles from Moscow lies the property of Yasnaya-Polyana, the Radiant Plain, a vast estate whose unkempt grounds are one of its greatest charms. The residence where Leo Tolstoi spent most of his life is an eighteenth-century building with a slate roof and a classical frontage, quite Western in appearance. The birch-tree benches and the glass veranda with sculptured wooden base, resembling the izbas of North Russia and decorated with simple designs of horses, hens, country yokels and open hearts, were all that Tolstoi added to the house, which came down to him from the Volonsky family via his mother, the Princess Maria. He was born there, and spent his childhood and mature years in the house, writing *War and Peace* and *Anna Karenina*. But at an early stage Yasnaya-Polyana became a heavy burden on his mind. He hated owning anything, and yet was obliged to hold on to the property. He was beset by feelings of self-reproach until one day in October 1910, at the age of eighty-two, he left it in secret, leaving behind a note saying he renounced everything he had in this world and would never come back. But only a few miles away he had an attack of fever. He was looked after by a railroad crossing keeper, who returned him later to the residence, where he died surrounded by his family.

Throughout Tolstoi's life, Yasnaya-Polyana failed to play its natural role as an ancestral home respectfully preserved, or retained because of the calm it provided for the owner. Only childhood was golden for Tolstoi at Yasnaya-Polyana.

His mother brought him up in accordance with Jean-Jacques Rousseau's child guide-book *Emile* ("Man is naturally good"), while his father hunted wolves and read Buffon and Cuvier in the evening. Leo Tolstoi, outside the hours he devoted to study, spent his time playing in the fields. He was the youngest boy; his mother died while giving birth to his sister when he was hardly eighteen months old.

It was an aunt, Tatiana Alexandrovna Iergolskaya, who brought up the Tolstoi children thereafter. In due course, in 1841, the four brothers were taken over by another aunt at Kazan called Pauline, who taught them good manners and gave each a servant of his own age, so that when they became adults they would have as servants people who were devoted to them as masters. At this time Tolstoi dressed as a dandy, spoke in French, and his free-style education was followed by the upbringing of a leading aristocrat.

He entered Kazan University with flying colours. The three years that Tolstoi spent in Kazan from 1844 to 1847 were the most vital in his intellectual formation. The academic side of university life repelled him and he preferred its social activities, Kazan being third in importance (after Saint Petersburg and Moscow) among tsarist Russia's poles of attraction. When he was not dancing, gambling or conver-

337

300. *Yasnaya-Polyana which Tolstoi inherited was used by him as a centre for social experiments. First he freed his mujiks, and later went one better and handed over land and author's royalties to his labourers. His wife, who did not share these advanced ideas, fought against him to keep their estate. She won.*

sing, Tolstoi spent his time reading Rousseau, whose philosophy was to prove a decisive influence on his own ideas. Brought up as a child on the principles of *Emile*, speaking French like all Russian aristocrats, reading and thinking about *Le Contrat social* at a time when social matters began to assume key importance in Russia, Tolstoi started adult life with a cultural foundation more French than Russian. Some commentators have seen this as a historical anachronism; others on the contrary find in it the murmurings of later dramatic social change, and consider Tolstoi was well ahead of his times. In 1847, having failed to pass an important exam, he decided to continue his own education. He began to take a special interest in the serfs in his charge. He imposed on himself an extensive study course in mathematics, natural science and literature, and planned also to write a thesis and reflect on the meaning of existence. He seemed then to have recognized certain events in his life as revelations from heaven. His educational failure led to his immediate return to the residence and a deep rethinking about the future. He grew closer to the peasantry and his sister tells us that he had made for himself a shapeless mujik's blouse which he wore day and night, and that he attempted to improve the lot of his peasants.

He organized a school at Yasnaya-Polyana for the mujiks' children, but the various social schemes he embarked on were a failure, as was his lecturing. To the mujiks these were just artful tricks of the master. He wrote: "My God, my God, is it possible that by desiring this mission and duty, I have been merely a dreamer? I have not found happiness here and I desire happiness, want it passionately. Before even indulging in pleasure, I abdicated all that they could give me. To what good? Why? Who has gained? Are my mujiks the wealthier for all that, more educated, brought up better?"

He departed from Yasnaya-Polyana and went to Moscow, where he lived the life of a dissolute student as it was known in those days—a round of the bawdy house, drinking and gambling. His officier brother on return from the Caucasus induced him to take up a military career in the Crimea, where he became famous for his realistic reporting. The experience provided him with material for *War and Peace*, but the soldiers bored Tolstoi, who finally resigned and left for a European tour of England, France and Italy. Two people whom he met on his journeys were "revelations" who caused him to regard Yasnaya-Polyana with a fresh eye. He first met Proudhon in Belgium early in 1861 and adopted his slogan "Property is theft" as the basis for his future beliefs. In Switzerland he met a young street musician, scoffed at by idlers, whom he took back to his Schweizerhof hotel, and asked him to eat with him. The injustice of the day irritated his sense of social rightness. Back in Russia he began to detest the property-owning classes and the decadent aristocracy. As it happened Alexander III had just emancipated the serfs and Tolstoi arrived home in the midst of a socializing trend. The property suddenly became for him a social research centre, where he decided to share out his land with the mujiks and work with them. With the emancipation of the serfs—an idea he did not think of first—Yasnaya-Polyana was again his absorbing interest. He made up his mind to spend his whole life there and get married so that a wife could share the responsibility of the property with him, and thus leave him time to write. He left for Moscow and was back in September 1862 with an eighteen-year-old wife, a doctor's daughter, Sofia Behrs.

Only three months later she wrote: "He disgusts me with his people. I must impose a choice; either it is me, that is to say the family which I represent, or it must be the people Leo loves so much. Is that egoism? So be it. It is for him that I live and I expect the same from him, otherwise I shall suffocate here. Today I have escaped because everything and everyone is repugnant to me. Leo does not revolt me but I suddenly felt that we were on two sides, that his people cannot hold my interest completely as they do his, and that I am not the entire concern of my husband, whilst at the same time he is my sole care."

As to Tolstoi, he wrote in his *Confessions*:

"I got married. The new circumstances of a happy family life diverted me entirely from all research on the general meaning of life. My whole interest at that time was concentrated on the means of increasing my income. My aspirations of perfection gave way markedly to my desire to have for myself and my family a very comfortable life."

Was it three months or fifteen years after their marriage that the trouble started ? This gap seems to indicate that Tolstoi was for many years unaware of the suffering he caused his wife. Whatever the truth of the matter, life with a large family at Yasnaya-Polyana virtually absorbed the whole existence of the reformer and writer. In one sense it fostered some works, since he had to write "to improve his material position," but at the same time family life militated against thought, meditation and the gnawing desire he had always felt to "perfect" himself. A degree of "sacred egoism" is called for by family responsibilities, because of material needs, and family comfort, so at variance with reflection on "the meaning of life in general." Tolstoi even disclaimed the worth of literary output, regarding it as just a job that would enable him to provide for his dependants. In this can be seen the basic drama of Yasnaya-Polyana and the Tolstoi family. The critic Charles du Bos has written : "There exists between family life and the destiny of the searching spirit, a fundamental contradiction contained in the very nature of things. For the searching spirit, the meaning of life is perpetually under review and in consequence forever questioned, whereas for the family, on the contrary, the point of life is a matter that has already been settled, because it is itself the meaning of life..."

The searching spirit is, however, not always a creative spirit. Tolstoi's true vocation was to ask himself about life, a vocation incompatible with family life which forced him to create. Posterity owes the epic works of Tolstoi to this dramatic conflict, but this incompatibility was to penetrate the lives of those in the real-life drama until it finally broke out in tragedy.

This strange hearth and home was like the scene of a battle between two ferociously opposed clans : Tolstoi who dreamed of abandoning all for his mujiks, and Sofia who fought to preserve the ancestral heritage, arguing point by point each day over the decisions her husband reached, defending the land as she protected his literature—and for the same essential reasons. He would spend long periods with mujiks, listening carefully to their humble views ; yet he was waited on by servants in white gloves at his Moscow house. He would also don a disguise to mix with peasants and beggars on a pilgrimage to Optina Monastery. With him, it was as if the solution between actually living and thinking about life lay in becoming someone wretched—which he was certainly not. Possibly the truth he thought he arrived at over these problems was merely one aspect of another subject that haunted him : death itself. He had a rope hidden away, ready to hang himself from a beam in his room where he retired every evening. Such ideas are not play-acting.

One evening in December of 1885, he surprised his wife as she was writing by declaring : "I want to divorce. I propose to go to Paris or America." She asked : "Whatever happened ?" "Nothing," he said, "but when the carriage is overloaded, the horse cannot pull it." Hard words and reproaches followed, and Sofia Tolstoi ordered her trunk to be brought. The children cried and the master finally withdrew his threat to leave, and beseeched his wife to stay. But Sofia Andreyevna was struck literally dumb and lost her voice for three months. Yes, it was a strange family at Yasnaya-Polyana.

In 1891 Tolstoi decided to share out his wordly goods while he was still alive, partly to provide for his children, but also, more importantly, to enable him to pursue his social programme. He gave up his entire author's rights to the people but Sofia refused to allow this and managed to obtain rights on works published prior to 1881. After all, she had herself copied out every evening over a period of months the manuscripts of *War and Peace* and *Anna Karenina*. Life at Yasnaya-Polyana was a succession of storms followed by periods of calm for Leo and Sofia. In between the disputes Tolstoi experienced the same mystical "revelations" he knew as a child and as a youth, which only strengthened his determination in the social field. These feelings nearly always occurred when he was away from the house, in an ordinary hotel room or in a monastery, but they usually came to fruition upon his return. It is thought likely, moreover, that Tolstoi unconsciously sought these experiences, which usually took place during an intellectual or religious retreat. So it was, for example, at the outset of his marriage, in August 1869 shortly after completion of *War and Peace*, that he left Yasnaya-Polyana alone with a servant under the pretext of going to look at some property in Penza province. On his way, he stayed the night in a inn at the small town of Arzamas, and during the dark hours was possessed of overwhelming anguish in which he struggled with the notion of death. The experiences of that night were to serve as the theme for *Master and Man* and the extraordinary *Death of Ivan Ilyich*. On the day after that night at Arzamas, Tolstoi decided not to buy the property in question and had only one idea in his head: to return to Yasnaya-Polyana having discovered that for him there lay nothing beyond death, only complete emptiness. All that mattered was what a man achieved in life. The Good for him thereafter assumed the position that had formerly been occupied by God. Later, in 1875, having in three years lost three children and two aunts, he again felt the anguish of death. At Yasnaya-Polyana itself he seemed to play with death, and it was a mujik that gave him back his sense of proportion by telling him a peasant tale about a servant called Mityuka who reached a good position and then exploited the other mujiks, living only for his belly—whereas Plato lived for his soul. Tolstoi subsequently endeavoured to identify himself with the people by adopting their beliefs and their religious superstitions.

So it was that he left Yasnaya-Polyana on foot in a peasant blouse with the local teacher bound for Optina Monastery, where he ate his soup with the mujiks. At last "Count Tolstoi" and the "Great Tolstoi" could actually be among the beggars of this world; but unfortunately he was recognized the following day and two monks took him to a hotel.

He was eventually excommunicated by the Synod in 1901 for his ideas. He used to work a lot in the fields with the peasants. When Turgenev came to see him one day and found him working a plough, he believed he was lost to literature for ever.

From his deathbed in Paris Turgenev, although he had broken with Tolstoi a long time previously, asked him again not to abandon literature for the mujiks. But the tension at Yasnaya-Polyana never ceased to hold sway from the start of his marriage, and this is confirmed by Sofia's own diary.

On July 14, 1910, after a sleepless night, Tolstoi wrote to his wife: "The fatal cause, for which neither of us is responsible, lies in the diametrically opposed fashion in which we conceive the sense and purpose of life. We disagree on everything, our way of life, our attitude toward mankind and the means of existence. I consider my ownership of Yasnaya-Polyana to be a sin, and yourself as a *sine qua non* condition. In order to avoid leaving you I have submitted to requirements that have proved quite painful to me. You have thought to see in this a concession to your ideas, but in fact the misunderstanding has only continued to grow between us..."

At this, Sofia replied, on September 12, 1910: "I ask you to try and understand that what you regard as my requirements—in fact they are wishes—have never had any other motive but my love for you... There are as you know hundreds of women who demand much of their husbands. They say: 'Let's go to Paris to buy some clothes or play roulette...' God has preserved me from all those temptations and demands... For the first time I wish with all my wounded soul that the past could return, but it is now perhaps impossible." She was right. A return to the past proved impossible. Tolstoi ended the matter definitively by leaving the house for good. Yasnaya-Polyana was for him a synonym of sin, which he spent all his life trying to cast off.

301. The Tolstoi family gath-
ers at the dinner table. Sofia
sits at the head of the table
with Tolstoi on her right.
Dostoevski wrote of him: "Despite his immense artistic gifts,
he was one of those Russian
souls who see clearly only what
is just under their noses...
They are apparently unable to
turn their heads either left or
right to see what is going on
alongside: they have to turn
their whole bust and body.
Then they start to declare the
opposite of what they were
saying previously, but they
are always completely sincere."
Chekhov wrote: "Tolstoi moral
views do not stimulate me; in
my heart I am not favourable
toward them. I have peas-
ant's blood in my veins and
you cannot make me believe in
the virtues of the peasant."

302. Tolstoi on his property
dressed as a mujik. Heir to
his father's huge estate, he
was struck by a sense of social
injustice at an early date. A
meeting with Proudhon and his
marriage to the daughter of a
highly-placed doctor in the imperial court led him to champion
the freedom of the Russian
people. In his eighties, he
fled on horseback from an
existence which he thought was
compromising his ideals as a
result of his wife's bourgeois
ways of life. He was found
dying a few miles away at
Astapovo railway-station, and
taken home to die. He went
to his death as a great man,
doubtless against his wishes.

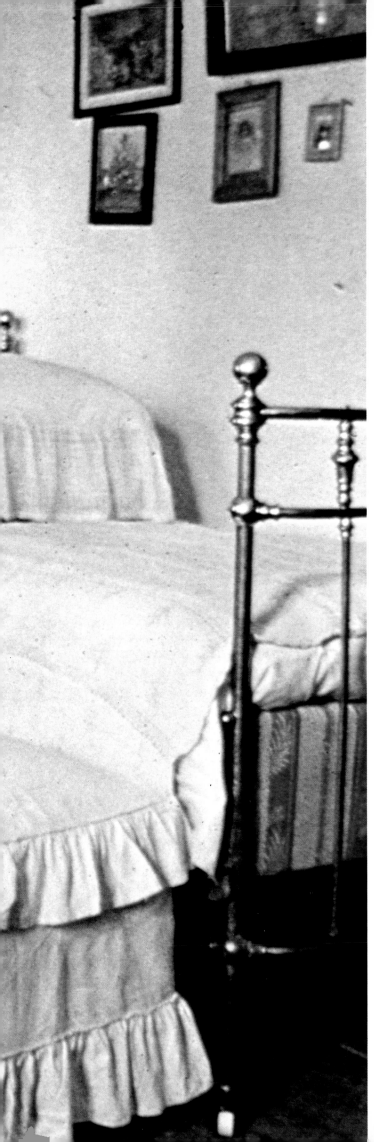

304

304. *Yasnaya-Polyana became a burden to the great writer, and a cause of endless marital disputes.*

305

305. *Toward the end of his life Tolstoi wrote: "The false role played in our society by science and the arts is due to so-called civilized people being led by scientists and artists with a privileged existence like that of priests."*

303

◁ 303. *Tolstoi's room at Yasnaya-Polyana is preserved as a museum.*

Voltaire

at Ferney

"Paradise is where I am," Voltaire once declared. When he bought Ferney it was with the idea of creating an Eldorado, educating and enriching the local peasantry, cleaning up the clergy and sweeping injustice from the area. He was sixty-five, an age at which one is allowed to say virtually anything, when he bought this residence near the Swiss border a few miles from Geneva. On this wonderful site, he razed a dramatic Gothic castle to the ground and built another with an impressive classical façade. Without pomp or mannerism, this was to be the home of a local gentleman who took his role seriously, a place to exploit a great idea : to reform the world according to his own views, manage it, control it, develop it—and slip over into Swiss territory if the royal or Church authorities came after him. "Better to hear the echoes of a storm," he had once sagely remarked.

Here it was that he could realize his dream ; he enriched the populace, defended its interests and used it against the clergy. After a few years, it must be admitted, there were no longer any poor peasants in Ferney. Voltaire advanced them the money they needed to plant their land. He reorganized their property, found husbands for the girls, and acted for his peasants in Paris. The mail-bag he received at Ferney was as big as that of a cabinet minister. Ceaselessly he harassed the authorities to win pettifogging arguments. He triumphed by exasperating the authorities with his insistent demands ; he won also because he could make people smile. He had Monsieur de Choiseul and Madame de Pompadour in the palm of his hand, which was very useful. Often, after a word from one of these, a local judge would rule in Voltaire's favour. But his argument over the tithe the peasants had to pay to the clergy, which Voltaire wanted abolished, set the Master of Ferney squarely in conflict with the Bishop of Nancy. Voltaire lost, and in the end had to pay the tithe from his own money.

Voltaire created a local silk-stocking industry. To keep it going, he sent them as presents to various people such as the Duchess of Choiseul so that she would show them off and get the court to buy some. He also sent some to Catherine of Russia. Another project was a silk farm which he looked after himself. A third was a pottery factory, and the very beautiful ceramic stoves in his room and the drawing room at Ferney came from there. The workers gave them to him as a present ; one has his heraldic arms on it—musical instruments and theatrical masks—and is surmounted by a bust of him. Another is in a naïve baroque style, of imitation blue marble with gold features. A third is a memorial designed by Villette after Voltaire's death, and for a short while it contained his heart.

The patriarch of Ferney was stimulated by the competitive spirit ; he gave a boost to the

345

306. Voltaire at Ferney. The Father of the French Revolution wrote: "Nothing is lost when the people are permitted to see that they have a mind. But all is lost when they are treated like a herd of cattle, because sooner or later they will poke you with their horns."

local watch industry and bought a great many watches which he sent to monarchs. They cost eighteen *louis* at Ferney and forty in Paris. In point of fact it was not the local industries that made him prosperous : an armaments factory in which he was a share-holder, gave him his huge fortune.

He was involved in business with the Frères Pâris; for example we know he was paid 600,000 francs by a certain Monsieur Pâris-Duverney at the end of the war of Polish succession. Voltaire also dealt with d'Alembert, a philosopher who had worked out a scheme for a lottery. Furthermore, Voltaire lent money to the nobility without security against a life annuity at ten per cent. With all this money he could really do great things. The financial profit from the supply of weapons was used by him to fight injustice. He liked to be the arbiter and distributor of fortunes and he acted almost as if he was Destiny itself with head-quarters at Ferney. Naturally his financial successes became quickly notorious and a queue formed at his door. By 1760 veritable pilgrimages were made to Voltaire's house. At about this time he adopted a girl who was a descendant of Corneille on her father's side. This idea enchanted Voltaire who was deeply interested in Corneille. He both praised and criticized his work : "I have spoken the truth about Louis XIV and will not keep quiet on Corneille," he declared.

At this time, also, his relations with Rousseau became very bitter, and because of Rousseau they were to grow even worse. In 1761 when *La Nouvelle Héloïse* appeared, Rousseau wrote to a friend concerning Voltaire : "Why does the name of this buffoon soil your letters ? This wretched man has ruined my country. I would hate myself more if I hated him less." He told Voltaire frankly : "I loathe you."

Voltaire confided to his friend Thuriot : "I have had a long letter from J.-J. Rousseau, who has become completely mad. It is a pity." Yet he had read *La Nouvelle Héloïse* and found it "an admirable piece about suicide which makes one want to die." Their positions were rigid; Rousseau who was from Geneva could never forgive Voltaire for being better loved by the Geneva people than he was himself. Their characters were not made for mutual understanding. Rousseau was dominated by feelings and imagination, whereas Voltaire lived for rationalism and humour. The former was a poor much-criticized tortured soul; Voltaire was gay, rich and worldly and had free access to the courts of Europe. In Voltaire's life Rousseau was of no greater consequence than the donkey in his grounds, which he named after his enemy : Fréron. "I need the feeling of anger sometimes, and his face evokes it when necessary," Voltaire said.

It was in this atmosphere that the Calas affair broke out. It gripped Voltaire for years, and stopped him sleeping. He no longer laughed and at the close of his life a young woman visiting him was astonished to find pinned up over his bed an engraving that depicted the Calas affair, and a portrait of Madame du Châtelet. The business took on as much prominence in his life as that assumed by the only woman he loved.

The event was really more "the Voltaire affair". Today we are more interested in him as a person and social reformer than in his work. In this business, where Protestant and Catholic bigotry led to injustice, France needed someone who was fully alive to his century, and could courageously bring to light the consequences of medieval superstitions, which continued to hold free rein in the provinces and often in Paris itself.

The Calas family was Protestant and lived at Toulouse. One of the sons was Catholic and the other on the point of becoming one, though he hesitated. By changing his religion he would no longer be able to practise a liberal profession as he wished to, and he would have had to become a tradesman. His father considered he lacked the qualities required. One day he was found hanging from a beam in his own house, while the rest of the family was on the floor above. As Voltaire was able to prove at a re-trial of the case, it was suicide. But the Catholic community insinuated that the parents had hanged him so that he would not change his religion. Some obscene poetry was found in the dead boy's pocket but it was thrown away without attention being paid to it. It turned out that, disappointed and even in despair, he had spent much of his time in taverns with girls. The Catholics gave him a sumptuous funeral and treated him as a martyr. The boy's father was beaten to death, crying out his innocence to the end.

Voltaire was worried about the entire incident and made certain inquiries at the Toulouse parliament. At his own expense and over a period of four months, he set spies on the brother, who had claimed he was present when his father hanged the boy. The brother, by the way, had come into some money as a result of becoming a Catholic. Voltaire by means of his Paris contacts, set about working up public opinion over the incident. He wrote: "What do we ask? Nothing but that justice is not as dumb as it is blind."

In 1763 he wrote *Traité de Tolérance*, which spurred progress of the case. Choiseul had become a supporter of his cause and the widow Calas was taken to Paris. Voltaire made her demonstrate her sorrow, to rouse up the people against the injustice. When the time was ripe, Choiseul raised the whole case again and the verdict was annulled. On March 9, 1765, Calas was rehabilitated and the queen herself received his widow and her daughters at Versailles.

From that moment onward Voltaire ceaselessly took over all illegal and unjust convictions of a religious nature. He carried out a campaign over persecutions that raged against lack of piety. This was an epoch when "infamy" must be crushed. He would sign off his letters *Ecrelinf (Ecrasez l'infâme)* "Crush the beast"). He wrote to one of his correspondents these words which prefigure the ideas of the French Revolution: "No, sir, not everything is lost when the people are made to see that they possess a spirit. But on the other hand all is lost when they are treated like a herd of bulls, because sooner or later they poke you with their horns." The anticlerical movement got into motion with the philosophers.

Deliberately out of fashion even in his dress, Voltaire wore a long puce-coloured regency coat with gold braiding and a bob-wig. He liked to behave oddly and had a field of his own where he turned over the soil, sowed and harvested; every day he went there, and was once found stuck in the mud with his crutches, becoming furious when people tried to extract him. On another occasion he threw himself to the ground on his knees in front of Mademoiselle Clairon, then visiting Ferney, and had to be helped up, but was able to joke that he had grown too old because he did not really believe this. When Boswell asked him if he could speak English, Voltaire replied: "No, because to speak English you have to put your tongue between your teeth and I no longer have any teeth." Five minutes later he startled his friend by speaking in an English that was "full of strange phrases". The two men enjoyed a drawing room tussle on the subject of Shakespeare. Boswell said: "What do you think of Shakespeare?" Voltaire: "Often two good verses, never six. A madman, by God, a madman from the fairground." Boswell: "I will tell you why we admire Shakespeare." Voltaire: "Because you have no taste." Boswell: "All Europe is against you and you are wrong."

On another subject, they were in agreement. Boswell: "Johnson says that Frederick II writes like your stableman." Voltaire: "Well then, he is a sensible man."

As a rule Voltaire did not appear at table in the evening. He would work in the morning and liked to receive people in the afternoon in his drawing room. Was there no shadow over this apparently quite pleasant existence? It seems there was. J.-J. Rousseau continued to attack him but Voltaire was unaffected. He was a good deal more famous than Rousseau, and had no idea that the French public would in due time make of them twin godfathers of the French Revolution, that one day they would be neighbours in the vaults of the Panthéon, and their skeletons would be seized from their tomb on the same night of 1814 and thrown together on wasteland at Bercy. In the future, shops would sell small busts of them together;

they became inseparable from each other in the French mind.

But for the moment, Voltaire just shrugged his shoulders. Rousseau was persecuted and Voltaire invited him to Ferney, but Rousseau haughtily declared : "No advance ; that would be cowardly." Voltaire's comment was : "If Diogene's dog and Erostrates's bitch had produced a puppy, it would be Jean-Jacques..." At Geneva he said : "He is the author of an opera and two comedies that drew derisive whistles." He made no mention of *La Nouvelle Héloïse* or of *Emile*.

When his friendship with Frederick II palled, he sought a king or a queen to serve. In 1759 he paid court to the Tsarina Elizabeth, and she sent him back her portrait set in diamonds. When Catherine succeeded her he approached the new empress, who thought to make good use of Voltaire as a mouthpiece to continue good legends about her and counteract bad rumours such as the one that she had her husband assassinated. By cultivating Voltaire she was sure to get European opinion on her side. She, too, sent him her portrait and wrote nicely to him.

Whereas Louis XVI went hunting and cared not a jot for the public views on his intellectual capacities, Catherine, as a young self-taught dictator, neglected nothing. She turned this talkative philosopher into her spokesman. He wrote : "I have a monarch 2,000 leagues away in my party, which consoles me for the cries of the naughty." He familiarly called her "my Cateau". In 1765 she sent an envoy to Ferney to ask him to recruit some Swiss women able to teach French to Russian children. Geneva refused to let any go, in the name of morality because one could not allow young women to be in the company of an empress so evil that she had her own husband killed. Voltaire was deeply upset about this and immediatly sent "Cateau" his latest work *Les Lois de Minos*, to make her forget this affront.

During all this time, Voltaire continued his work of righting legal wrongs ; his efforts reflected the mood of the age, and he made it his speciality. Between plays he wrote in two

weeks, there were always re-trials to take up his time. Voltaire virtually ran French justice from Ferney and he was consequently held in fear by many.

In 1762, for example, he took on the Sirven case concerning a simple-minded girl taken in by a convent, who was given back to her parents in a state of madness and committed suicide ; the religious authorities charged her parents with killing the child. Voltaire had a re-trial held and won the case. He also obtained the freedom of a convict and tried to get others released. Choiseul became anxious : "He has emptied the prisons of all the Protestants he can find, but that does not prevent him making the cruellest of jokes about Calvin and his ministers."

Then there was the Abbeville case, in which some students mutilated a cross on a bridge, and one of them was decapitated. Voltaire took on the case, had the innocent student declared not guilty and his family rehabilitated.

The case of Covelle the fornicator was quite different. A Geneva man was ordered by the Church to kneel down publicly because he allegedly was the father of a certain woman's child. He was willing to acknowledge the fornication but not to recognize the child. He asked for eight days to think over his reply. Would he or would he not agree to kneel down ? Voltaire found the whole case much too comical and jumped at the chance of intervening. Here was another opportunity to heap ridicule on the clergy and the Geneva bar. So Covelle took refuge at Ferney. But he proved so boring and so priggish that Voltaire got rid of him by giving him an annuity. Meanwhile he had obtained a ruling that kneeling down should no longer be among the legal punishments. To him this was worth a few crowns for the man responsible.

As one might well imagine after so many legal affairs, Ferney became a vast Voltairian "Court", and a hide-out for rascals supported by the local monarch. Richelieu himself sent Voltaire a "present" of Gallien, a blackguard who ran off with Voltaire's jewels, money and manuscripts. But the proprietor made no effort to catch him.

In 1768, Ferney saw the beginning of the great Voltairian farces. He announced one morning that he was going to make his Easter confession. With the help of a passing monk he accomplished this. But then one Sunday, he entered Ferney Church with some hunters during the service, and it is said, adressed the congregation in the place of the priest.

His old enemy, the Bishop of Annecy, descended upon him with all the weight of his authority. Voltaire extricated himself, pretending to be dying at Ferney and demanded urgent absolution. The parish priest refused to come, and after several day' argument Voltaire had him seized by the local bailiff. The priest arrived between two men of the law and was told: "I adore God in my room and I do harm to no one." The priest asked to see a certificate of confession without which he refused to give communion. Voltaire ranted and ordered: "Give me absolution at once." He got it and then dressed and went down into the garden. Stimulated, he straightaway wrote the humorous story *L'Homme aux Quarante Ecus*.

Unfortunately Voltaire at this stage lost the backing of Choiseul, who was himself disgraced. He had to obtain the ear of the minister who succeeded him in order to continue his efforts. He tried nevertheless to show his friendship for Choiseul, who did not want him to lick the boots of the new minister. They quarelled. Choiseul, in revenge, erected on a Paris roof in 1772 a metal silhouette of Voltaire which turned around in the wind.

Voltaire's *Irène* was now about to be shown and he was very keen to be at the first performance. Success was certain; his friends had sounded out Paris opinion and found it highly favourable to Voltaire. So he left Ferney on February 4, 1778. On arrival in Paris he told the customs officials: "My goodness, I don't think there is any contraband here other than me." To the Parisians he said: "I am eighty years of age and am guilty of a hundred follies." *Irène* was an extraordinary success. The court was reserved over it but a bust of the author, erected on the stage, was crowned by the actors. Voltaire himself was crowned as he sat in his theatre box. People even kissed his carriage horses, and Voltaire fainted with happiness. The day before he had almost fainted when he thought someone had "messed about with the text." The excitement of it all exhausted him, and his doctor Tronchin remarked: "He would have lived ten years longer had he stayed at Ferney". The great man promised he would go to Ferney soon for two months, but meanwhile he was called on by both wise and foolish celebrities. The wise ones included Glück, Franklin and Marshal Richelieu. One of the foolish was the Chevalière d'Eon; the big question being: would she turn up in pants or skirts? The lackeys were on the look-out as she arrived, hiding a smile in her sleeve, and then slipped away quickly. One wonders what these two actors could have said to each other: the one mystifying the world by writing, the other with doubts about his (or her) sex and switching from a pair of soldier-like pants to a gold threaded dress of the kind ordered by the queen herself.

Voltaire started to spit out blood but only worried enough to remark: "Well, I never! I'm spitting blood." It was a good opportunity to ask for extreme unction again. So his old friend Father Gautier was called in, and he told him: "Be careful, Father, that it's blood I spit, and watch you don't mix up my blood with God's blood..."

To Frederick II he wrote: "I am just as likely to spit up one thing as another." At the time he hardly imagined that he might die. When the idea did cross his mind, he started picturing the kind of grave he would have at Ferney; this, he said, would be a strange kind of tomb half inside and half outside the church so that people would say: "Voltaire is neither in nor out."

He went often to the theatre but began to feel very weak and, with the ever-rising stream of visitors, he agreed to take a tonic after his friend Richelieu advised him to. He drank the whole bottle-full and was immediately griping with pain. He accused Richelieu of killing him and collapsed.

Voltaire was one of those great men whose final words are awaited by an expectant audience. But, in fact, he became delirious and recognized nobody toward the end.

His death occured on May 30, 1778. His bladder and kidneys were later found perforated and burned out, and his brain was seen to be too big for the cranium. He was embalmed in accordance with his wish. The surgeon Mithouard took his payment in the form of the brain, which he placed in a bottle of alcohol. As to Voltaire's friend Villette, he kept his heart in a gold-silver casket.

Then began the arguments over Voltaire's body. There was no correctly signed "confession ticket", and no religious burial. He was kept out of the cemetery and was to be taken to the common burial ground. But his friends had foreseen these problems and spirited away the body during the night, as had been the case with Louis XV. Voltaire was snatched, dressed up, bound head and foot, and tied to the seat of his carriage. They took the body to the dissident Abbey of Sellières. It was planned to shroud the body secretly in the crypt and the bishop played dumb with the Paris authorities. His explanations were accepted, and when the news of Voltaire's death was officially announced the Encyclopedists and Frederick II had masses said for the repose of his soul. The philosophers were able to give the clergy a lesson, and for Frederick II it was a chance to give a lesson to France.

When the French Revolution broke out the Parisians demanded Voltaire's body and wanted it interred in Paris, either at the Champs-Elysées or under the statue of Henri IV. Men were sent to get the body at Sellières but it failed to arrive whole in the capital, because on the way a foot was stolen together with some pieces of his hands and two teeth. One of the teeth eventually reached a journalist called Lemaître who had it hanging round his neck with the inscription: "The priests have caused so much ill on earth that I have kept this tooth of Voltaire's in token against them."

The convoy of Voltaire arrived in Paris on July 11, 1791. By a curious coincidence it reached the capital exactly at the same moment as that of Louis XVI who was brought back from Varennes. The processions of the two almost met: in one procession the people were returning with the body of a writer whom Louis XVI had relegated to the common burial ground (Louis IV had however saved Molière from that end); in the other procession was Louis XVI, a king who was no longer wanted. Voltaire was lauded by the people and, as he passed by, flowers were strewn in the Rue des Fossés-Saint-Germain. Banners were put over his coffin with the words: "To the glory of his pen and the longevity of his intelligence. At seventeen years of age he wrote Œdipe and at eighty Irène." The body was later buried at Sainte-Geneviève and subsequently laid to rest in the Panthéon.

The "patriarch's" wonderful library remained at Ferney which became a monument "of taste". Voltaire had personally chosen each book in the library and a record was kept of most of them. Certain pages in some well-known books had been rewritten by him and the new version glued inside. He reduced Rabelais to one tenth of its original size. One admirer had the idea of buying the entire library—Catherine the Great. As soon as she heard about his death, she sent Madame Denis, Voltaire's niece, an envoy. A sum was offered equivalent to half the profit Madame Denis obtained from the castle, land and factories. Catherine did not scruple to have Voltaire's secretary sent to Russia with the books. He went to Saint Petersburg and laid out the books in her palace in the exact order as at Ferney when Voltaire was alive.

Next pages:
308. Voltaire had this church built on the Ferney property. Its crypt was partly inside partly outside "so people will say Voltaire is neither in nor out", as he explained.

309. Ferney Castle is near Geneva on French territory. Its owner declared: "Paradise is where I am."

307. The quarrel between Voltaire ▷ and Rousseau is depicted in a contemporary engraving. Jean-Jacques wrote to Voltaire: "I loathe you". Voltaire declared: "He's mad."

310. This portrait shows Voltaire at Ferney at an age when he was allowed to say anything: "I am eighty and commit one hundred follies!"

311. Posterity was to place ▷ Voltaire and Rousseau facing each other in niches at Ferney's entrance. Although they were enemies unto death, sculptors and the nineteenth century twinned them for eternity.

Next pages:
312. An eighteenth-century stove bearing Voltaire's coat of arms, in the castle salon, was given to him by workers at his Ferney pottery plant.

313. Against tyranny of ideas and régimes, champion of tolerance, Voltaire was scorned by Louis XV and became philosopher and "jester" to the Prussian king. Later he found in Catherine II of Russia a sovereign whom he could serve, although he never met her. In his bedroom at Ferney, he kept a portrait of her which she sent him.

314. *A short distance from Geneva, Voltaire would write what he thought of the authorities, law and religions at Ferney, on French territory. A tree-lined avenue led to the Swiss frontier a few miles away. The geographical position of his residence suited his free spirit.*

Picture credits

Most photographs are the work of CLAUDE ARTHAUD, assisted by the RICHARD ET BLIN Studio, assistant photographer JACQUES VAINSTAIN, with the exception of the following pictures :

ANDERSEN HUS, Odense : 5, 8 ;
ANDERSON, Rome : 182, 228 *(Uffizi, Florence)* ;
O. D'ANDLAU, Coppet Castle : 286 ;
ARCHIVES PHOTOGRAPHIQUES, Paris : 74 ;
ÉDITIONS ARTHAUD : Archives : 58 *(Bibl. nat., Paris)*, 137 *(Bibl. polonaise, Paris)* ; Photographers : H. Adant : 28 *(musée des Arts Décoratifs, Paris)*, 142, 150 and 260 *(Bibl. nat., Paris)* ; M. Audrain : 240 ; B. Aury : 78, 141 ; P. Dubure : 284 *(musée du Louvre)* ; J. Hyde : 32 and 261 *(Bibl. nat., Paris)* ; H. Paillasson : 16, 247, 310 *(coll. château de Ferney)*, 312, 314 ;
BAYERISCHE STAATSGEMÄLDESAMMLUNGEN MUSEUM, Munich : 248 ;
BIBLIOTHÈQUE NATIONALE, Paris : 49 ;
BILDARCHIV FOTO, Marburg : 158, 165 ;
BLIN, Paris : 215 ;
BULLOZ, Paris : 110 *(coll. Jamot)*, 121 *(musée Carnavalet, Paris)*, 186, 187, 222, 223 and 224 *(musée du Louvre)*, 225 *(private coll.)*, 241, 242, 243 *(Bibl. nat., Paris)*, 250 *(Munich Museum)*, 252 and 253 *(musée du Louvre)*, 258 *(musée Carnavalet, Paris)*, 285 *(coll. Le Marois)*, 288 *(coll. château de Coppet)*, 294 *(musée Carnavalet, Paris)*, 307 *(Bibl. nat., Paris)* ;
ÉDITIONS P. CAILLER, Lausanne : 57 ;
CARON, Amiens : 51 *(Bibl. municipale, Amiens)* ;
COLLECTION R. DAZY, Paris : 12, 17, 18, 19, 21, 45, 56, 65, 67, 68, 69, 71, 133, 154, 157, 164, 173, 300, 301, 302, 305 ;

COLLECTION G. SIROT, Paris : 148 ;
CONNAISSANCE DES ARTS : 44 *(R. Bonnefoy, coll. J. Peignot)*, 249 and 254 *(J. Guillot)*, 251 and 255 *(J. Guillot, colours)* ;
ÉDITIONS COURRIER DE LA CÔTE, S.A., Nyon : 289 ;
DEUTSCHE-FOTOTHEK, Dresde : 31 *(Stadtgeschichtliches Museum, Leipzig)* ;
DOISNEAU-RAPHO, Paris : 217 ;
GIRAUDON, Paris : 29 *(Angermuseum, Erfurt)*, 52 and 53 *(Bibl. nat., Paris)*, 265 and 283 *(musée du Louvre)* ;
GOETHE MUSEUM, Frankfurt : 153 ;
HARLINGUE-VIOLLET, Paris : 122, 123, 124, 126, 135, 136 ;
F. HÉBERT-STEVENS, Paris : 55 (collection) ;
ÉDITIONS LAROUSSE, Paris : 22 ;
E. LESSING, MAGNUM-PHOTO, Paris : cover, 60, 61, 62, 63, 64 (colour), 134, 139 (colour), 190 (colour), 192 and 193 ;
MAS, Barcelona : 105, 109 *(Institute Valencia de D. Juan, Madrid)*, 112 *(coll. Sedó, Barcelona)* ;
MAUROIS (coll. Simone André) : 144 ;
METROPOLITAN MUSEUM OF ART, New York : 175 *(coll. H. O. Have Mayer)* ;
MONDADORI PUBLICATIONS, Milan : 13 *(M. de Biasi, colour)*, 14, 15, 24 and 25 (M. de Biasi, colour), 26, 27 (M. de Biasi, colour), 30 *(Backhaus, Eisenach)*, 303 and 304 (A. Panicucci, colour) ;
MOZARTMUSEUM, Salzburg : 191 ;
MUSÉE D'ART ET D'HISTOIRE, Geneva : 298 ;
MUSÉE LAMARTINE, Mâcon : 208 ;
MUSÉE DE LA VILLE DE STRASBOURG : 189 ;
MUSEO DEL PRADO, Madrid : 180, 181, 183 ;
MUSEO DE SANTA CRUZ, Toledo : 188 ;

361

Contents

IMPRIMÉ EN FRANCE

THIS VOLUME, THE THIRTY-FIRST OF THE COLLECTION
« LES IMAGINAIRES »
WAS PRODUCED UNDER THE SUPERVISION OF CLAUDE ARTHAUD.
MONOCHROME PHOTOGRAVURE AND FOUR-COLOR OFFSET
PRINTED BY LES IMPRIMERIES DE BOBIGNY.
TEXT PRINTED BY L'IMPRIMERIE FLOCH, MAYENNE.
« MATHÉLIO » GRAVURE AND COATED PAPERS
FROM LES PAPETERIES PRIOUX.
FOUR-COLOR OFFSET PHOTOGRAVURE
BY LES ÉTABLISSEMENTS SCHWITTER, ZURICH.
BINDING BY LES ÉTABLISSEMENTS ENGEL, MALAKOFF.
CLOTH FROM TEXLIBRIS, PARIS.
PRINTED IN FRANCE.
25-6-1968 — N⁰ 7939.